Natural Chicago

Also by Bill and Phyllis Thomas

Indiana: Off the Beaten Path
Natural New York
Natural Washington
Lakeside Recreation Areas

Also by Bill Thomas

Talking with the Animals
The Island
American Rivers: A Natural History
The Swamp
The Complete World of Kites
Eastern Trips and Trails
Mid-America Trips and Trails
Tripping in America: Off the Beaten Track

Natural

Bill and Phyllis Thomas

Holt, Rinehart and Winston · New York

Chicago

For Sky—
who touched our lives briefly, but unforgettably.

Overleaf: *Bill Thomas*

Copyright © 1985 by Bill and Phyllis Thomas
All rights reserved, including the right to reproduce
this book or portions thereof in any form.
Published simultaneously in Canada by Holt, Rinehart
and Winston of Canada, Limited.
First published in February 1986 by Holt, Rinehart and Winston,
383 Madison Avenue, New York, New York 10017.

Library of Congress Cataloging in Publication Data
Thomas, Bill, 1934–
Natural Chicago.
Includes index.
1. Natural areas—Illinois—Chicago—Guide-books.
2. Natural areas—Illinois—Chicago Region—Guide-books.
3. Parks—Illinois—Chicago—Guide-books.
4. Parks—Illinois—Chicago Region—Guide-books.
5. Gardens—Illinois—Chicago—Guide-books.
6. Gardens—Illinois—Chicago Region—Guide-books.
7. Natural history museums—Illinois—Chicago—Guide-books.
8. Natural history museums—Illinois—Chicago Region—Guide-books.
9. Chicago (Ill.)—Description—1981–   —Guide-books.
10. Chicago Region (Ill.)—Description and travel—Guide-books.
I. Thomas, Phyllis, 1935–   II. Title.
QH76.5.I5T48   1985   917.73'20443   84-19198
ISBN: 0-03-059681-5

First Edition

Design by Jacqueline Schuman
Maps by David Lindroth
Printed in the United States of America
10 9 8 7 6 5 4 3 2 1

ISBN 0-03-059681-5

Contents

ACKNOWLEDGMENTS xi
INTRODUCTION xiii

1. Natural Attractions in Chicago

Chicago Academy of Sciences 4
Douglas Park 4
Field Museum of Natural History 5
Garfield Park 6
Grant Park 7
Indian Boundary Park 8
Jackson Park 9
Lincoln Park 11
Marquette Park 13
Shedd Aquarium 14

2. Natural Attractions in Illinois

Argonne National Laboratory 20
Belmont Prairie 20
Berkeley Prairie 20
Blackwell Recreational Preserve 21
Bluff Spring Fen 24
Braidwood Dunes and Savanna 24
Brookfield Zoo 25
Calumet Forest Preserve Division 27
Cantigny 30
Cary Prairie 31
Chain O'Lakes State Park 31
Chicago Botanic Garden 33
Chicago Zoological Park 34
Churchill Woods Forest Preserve 35
Crabtree Nature Center 36
Deer Grove Forest Preserve 38
Des Plaines Forest Preserve Division 38
Des Plaines Game Farm 41
Des Plaines River Trail 41
Des Plaines State Conservation Area 42
Dole Wildlife Sanctuary 44

Contents

The Ecology Center   45
Elgin Botanical Garden   45
Elsen's Hill Winter Sports Area   45
Fabyan Forest Preserve   45
Fermilab Prairie   46
Ferson's Creek Marsh   49
Forest Preserve Districts of Northeastern Illinois   49
Fullersburg Woods Nature Preserve   50
Gensburg–Markham Prairie   51
Glacial Park–Nippersink Trail   53
Goodenow Grove Forest Preserve   54
Goose Lake Prairie State Park   56
Great Western Trail   57
Greene Valley Forest Preserve   59
Grosse Point Lighthouse Park   60
The Grove   61
Harrison–Benwell Conservation Site   63
Hickory Grove   64
Illinois and Michigan Canal State Trail   65
Illinois Beach State Park   67
Illinois Prairie Path   70
Indian Boundary Forest Preserve Division   71
Izaak Walton Preserve   74
Kankakee River State Park   75
Keepataw Forest Preserve   77
Ladd Arboretum   78
Lighthouse Nature Center   80
Lockport Prairie   80
Maple Grove Forest Preserve   81
McHenry Dam State Park   82
McKinley Woods Forest Preserve   82
Messenger Woods Forest Preserve   83
Moraine Hills State Park   84
Morton Arboretum   87
Morton Grove Prairie   89
The Nature Conservancy, Illinois Field Office   90
Ned Brown Forest Preserve   91
Nelson Lake Marsh   93
Norris Woods   94
North Branch Forest Preserve Division   96
Northwest Forest Preserve Division   98
Oakes Forest Preserve   98
Palos and Sag Valley Forest Preserve Divisions   98
Peacock Prairie   103
Pilcher Park   103
Plum Creek Nature Center   104
Pottawatomie Park   105
Powers State Conservation Area   105

Prairie Path   106
Pratt's Wayne Woods   106
Queen Anne Prairie–Eckert Cemetery   107
Raccoon Grove Forest Preserve   108
Reed–Turner Woodland   109
Ryerson Conservation Area   110
Salt Creek Forest Preserve Division   111
Shaw Woodlands and Prairies   113
Shoe Factory Road Nature Preserve   114
Silver Springs State Park   114
Skokie Forest Preserve Division   116
Spring Lake Nature Preserve   118
Thorn Creek Forest Preserve Division   118
Thorn Creek Nature Preserve   121
Timber Ridge Forest Preserve   123
Tinley Creek Forest Preserve Division   124
Trout Park   126
Van Patten Woods Forest Preserve   128
Veterans Acres Park   128
Volo Bog State Natural Area   129
Wadsworth Prairie   130
Waterfall Glen Forest Preserve   131
West Chicago Prairie   132
West DuPage Woods Forest Preserve   133
Willowbrook Wildlife Haven   134
Winfield Mounds   135
Wolf Lake   135
Woodworth Prairie Preserve   136

3. Natural Attractions in Wisconsin

Bong State Recreation Area   140
Hawthorn Hollow   141
The Nature Conservancy, Wisconsin Field Office   142
Petrifying Springs County Park   142

4. Natural Attractions in Indiana

Cowles Bog   148
Deep River County Park   149
German Methodist Cemetery Prairie   151
Grand Kankakee Marsh County Park   152
Hoosier Prairie   154
Indiana Dunes National Lakeshore   155
Indiana Dunes State Park   158
International Friendship Gardens   160

Jasper–Pulaski State Fish and Wildlife Area   161
Langeluttig Swamp   164
LaSalle State Fish and Wildlife Area   165
Lemon Lake County Park   167
Marquette Park   168
Miller Woods   168
Moraine Nature Preserve   169
The Nature Conservancy, Indiana Field Office   170
Pinhook Bog   171
Stoney Run County Park   171

5. Natural Attractions in Michigan

Grand Mere Nature Study Area   176
The Nature Conservancy, Michigan Field Office   176
Robinson Preserve   176
Warren Dunes State Park   177
Warren Woods   179

INDEX   181

Acknowledgments

The authors are indebted to many people who generously contributed time and effort to provide information for this book. There is not enough space for us to be able to list each and every one of them, but to those named below we owe a special thanks.

In Chicago: Wayne Schennum, Illinois Field Office, The Nature Conservancy; Ira M. Berke, Frank Horath, Willa Walmsley, and Ben Bentley, Chicago Park District; Linda Devcik, Charlotte Shure, and Lloyd Van Meter, Chicago Convention and Tourism Bureau, Inc.

In Illinois (outside Chicago): Joe Kasperak and Charles Westcott, Cook County Forest Preserve District; Stephen Aultz, Will County Forest Preserve District; John Shiel, McHenry County Conservation District; Gail Wagner Letta, DuPage County Forest Preserve District; Judith A. Mason and Dan Broulliard, Lake County Forest Preserve District; Virgil Alsip, Kane County Forest Preserve District; Gladys M. Campbell, Natural Land Institute; Marlin L. Bowles, Illinois Nature Preserves Commission; Glenn W. Wegener, Karen A. Witter, and Gary C. Thomas, Illinois Department of Conservation; Robert M. Grosso, Illinois Beach State Park; John B. Schweder, Moraine Hills State Park; Alexia Trzyna, Volo Bog State Natural Area; Marianne Nelson, Elgin Chamber of Commerce; Terry Clarke, Crystal Lake Park District; Stephan Swanson, Glenview Park District; Mrs. Gill Morland, Cary Prairie Management Committee; James Waschbush, Cary Junior High School; Ferne Bork, Evanston Environmental Association; Charles Hughes, Woodworth Prairie Preserve; G.R. Nelson, Illinois Prairie Path; Barbara R. Turner, Reed-Turner Woodland; Fred W. Ullrich, Jr., Fermi National Accelerator Laboratory.

In Indiana: Les Zimmer, Indiana Field Office, The Nature Conservancy; Marie Marek, Indiana Dunes National Lakeshore; Robert Nickovich, Phyllis R. McNeill, and Larry Rose, Lake County Parks & Recreation Department; Charlotte J. Read, Save the Dunes Council; and Barbara Gast, Greater Valparaiso Chamber of Commerce.

In Michigan: David C. Mahan, Michigan Field Office, The Nature Conservancy; and the staff of Warren Dunes State Park.

In Wisconsin: Russell Van Herik, Wisconsin Field Office, The Nature Conservancy; John A. Nelson, Robert F. Winnie, and

Cliff Germain, Wisconsin Department of Natural Resources; Ruth Teuscher, Hawthorn Hollow.

Thanks, also, to Bill W. Dean, Midwest Region Office, National Park Service, Omaha, Nebraska.

Introduction

When the first settlers migrated across America, they found the flatlands and open prairies bordering the southern and western portions of Lake Michigan a delightful change from the dense forests they had hacked trails through to the east. Here were lush tallgrass grazing lands for their animals, fertile soils for raising crops, and just enough woodland to supply logs for building cabins and fueling fireplaces during the long cold winters.

Lake Michigan could accommodate oceangoing vessels that would carry locally produced goods and products to the rest of the world, making this a prime area for developing industry in subsequent years. With the advent of a vast network of railroads, the entire Midwest had easy access to Chicago, reinforcing the city's role as a leading trade center.

For so many years prime consideration was given to the expansion of industry and housing that it's indeed surprising that any natural qualities in and around the city were preserved at all. The Lake Michigan waterfront today is cleaner than it was at the turn of the century, and some of the streams made filthy by the abuses of too many uncaring people and a "progressive" industrial society have begun to show signs of supporting some life again.

There are natural areas strongly reminiscent of a bygone era when the countryside was wild and untamed, places like McGinnis Slough and Pinhook Bog, Goose Lake Prairie and Hawthorn Hollow, Indiana Dunes and the Grand Kankakee Marsh, Miller Woods in Indiana and Warren Woods in Michigan, the Skokie Lagoons and Langeluttig Swamp. The Chicago area abounds in places closely related to the natural environment, places of escape from the hectic pace and bustle of modern urban life. You can hike such fine trails as the Great Western Trail, the Prairie Path, or the Illinois and Michigan Canal Trail. Or you can sample a wild lakeshore environment at such parks as Warren Dunes in Michigan, Illinois Beach, or the Indiana Dunes National Lakeshore.

The Forest Preserve systems of Cook and neighboring counties represent one of the most remarkable stories of far-sighted preservation and conservation in the Midwest. Much of the impetus for this movement can be attributed to one man, Daniel H. Burnham, Sr., who in 1909 drew up a plan that called for a large part of the existing natural forests of Cook County to be set aside and preserved.

Action was delayed for sixteen years, until in 1925 the Chicago Regional Planning Association was established and began to implement Burnham's plan. By this time it was almost too late, for only about 40,000 acres of woodlands remained. The rest of the designated land had been developed, cut over, or otherwise exploited in the intervening years. In 1929, after intensive study, the association presented a plan for the Forest Preserve System of Cook County, and the project was underway. Other counties, such as DuPage, Will, Kane, and Lake, followed suit, leading to one of the most impressive and well-managed municipal preservation systems in the nation.

Two factors have exerted greater influence upon the scope of Chicago's natural areas than any other. One was the Ice Age of prehistoric times, when great glaciers reshaped the land and left behind a vast body of water known as Lake Chicago. Over the centuries, the waters gradually receded and formed the Lake Michigan we see today. Documented reminders of this ancient lakebed are visible in many places around the area, legacies of our prehistoric past.

Also of great importance was the prairie that once covered most of this land. The prairie is perhaps the most overlooked of our natural landscapes. During the early days of this nation, most grasslands were considered of little value unless they could be plowed or grazed, or both. As a result, only a few patches survived to modern times.

After World War II, however, people began to view the great prairie as something of value. The lovely tall grasses, the perennial wildflower gardens, and unique-looking plants such as prairie dock possessed a subtle, mystical beauty all their own. To lose them forever was akin to losing a part of paradise.

Consequently, The Nature Conservancy, a national preservation group, and other organizations, such as the Prairie Club of Chicago, joined with various government agencies to seek out and save the remnants of the prairielands that remained.

Most newcomers to greater Chicago are astounded to learn there are patches of virgin prairie just minutes from the heart of the city and primeval forests within an hour's drive of the Chicago Loop. True, many of the wild creatures have long since disappeared or greatly dwindled in number since the turn of this century, and the wild places are small in size, but they have been preserved as closely as possible in their original state.

Chicago is a place of botanical, biological, and geological diversity. Its charm is a subtle charm. It doesn't possess the awe-inspiring majesty of the Rockies, or the ethereal beauty of the Okefenokee Swamp, or the overwhelming grandeur of California's Big Sur. But it does offer a gentle loveliness that is an integral part of our planet's natural environment, and a glimpse of a time forever gone, when man could stand in this corner of the earth and view, in the words of William Cullen Bryant, "the gardens of the desert, the unshorn fields, boundless and beautiful, for which the speech of England has no name—the Prairies."

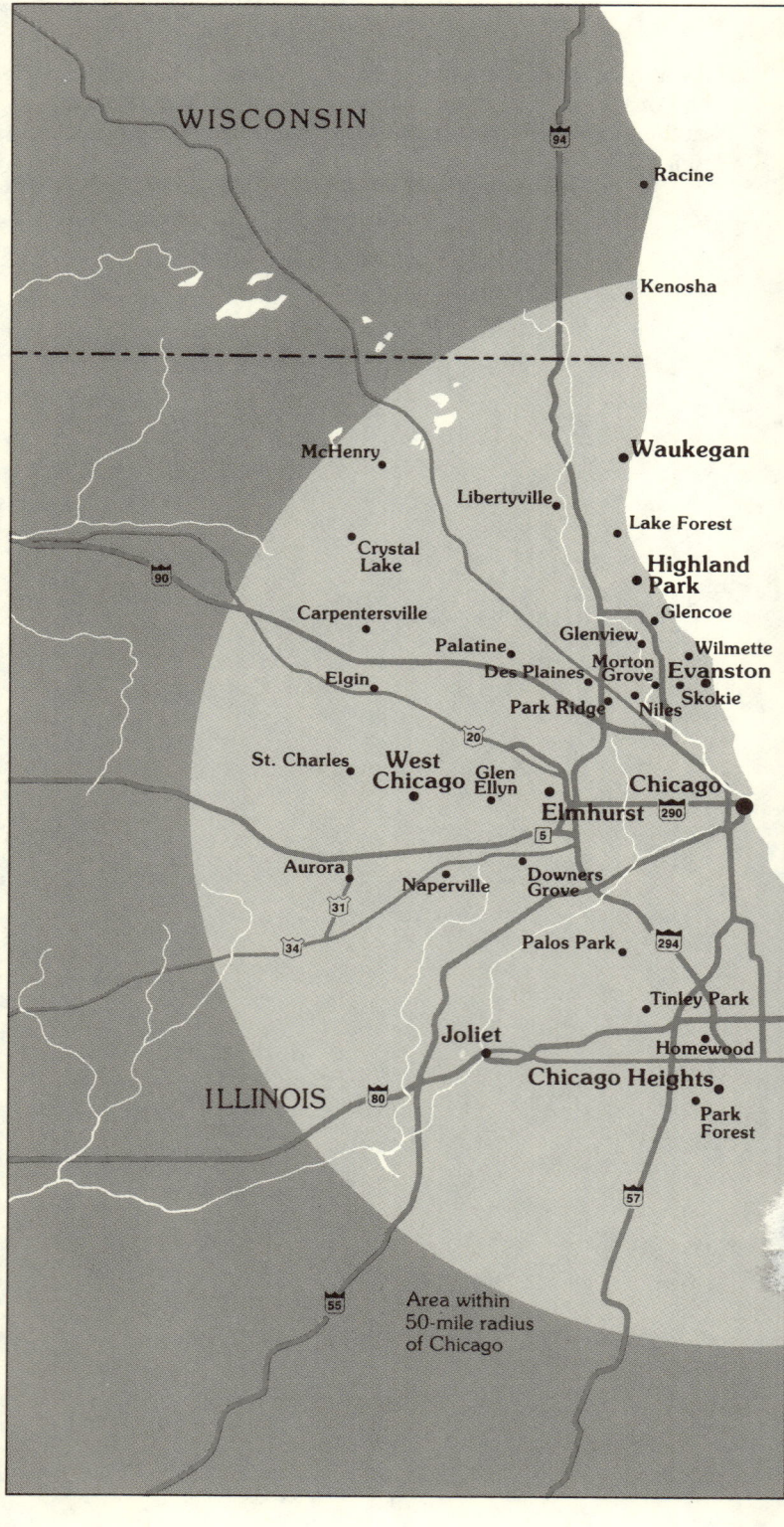

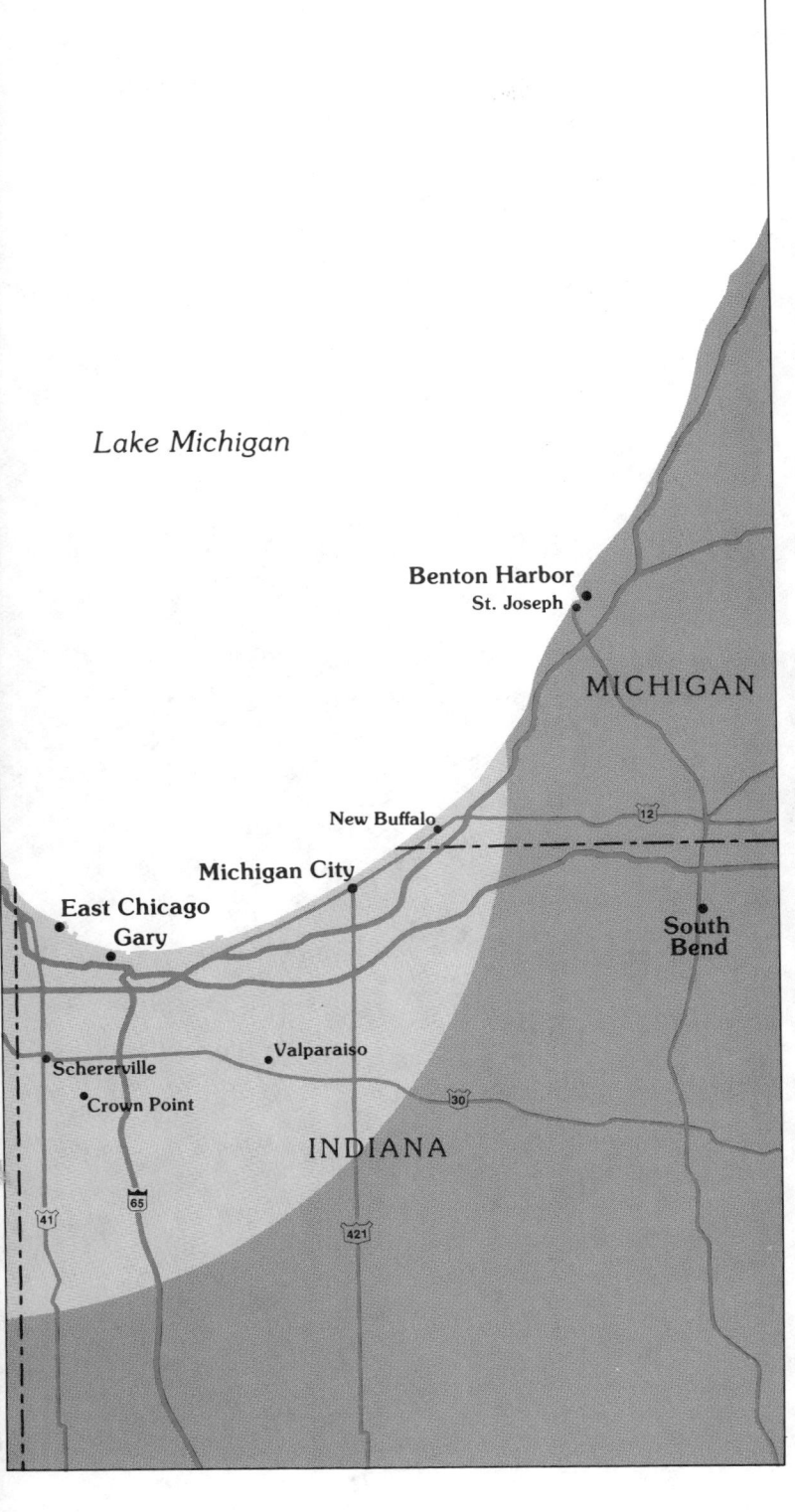

Part 1

Bill Thomas

Natural Attractions in
Chicago

CHICAGO

1. Chicago Academy of Sciences **C—3**
2. Douglas Park **B—5**
3. Field Museum of Natural History **C/D—5**
4. Garfield Park **A—4**
5. Grant Park **C/D—4/5**
6. Indian Boundary Park **B—1**
7. Jackson Park **D—7**
8. Lincoln Park **C—2/3**
9. Marquette Park **A/B—6**
10. Shedd Aquarium **D—5**

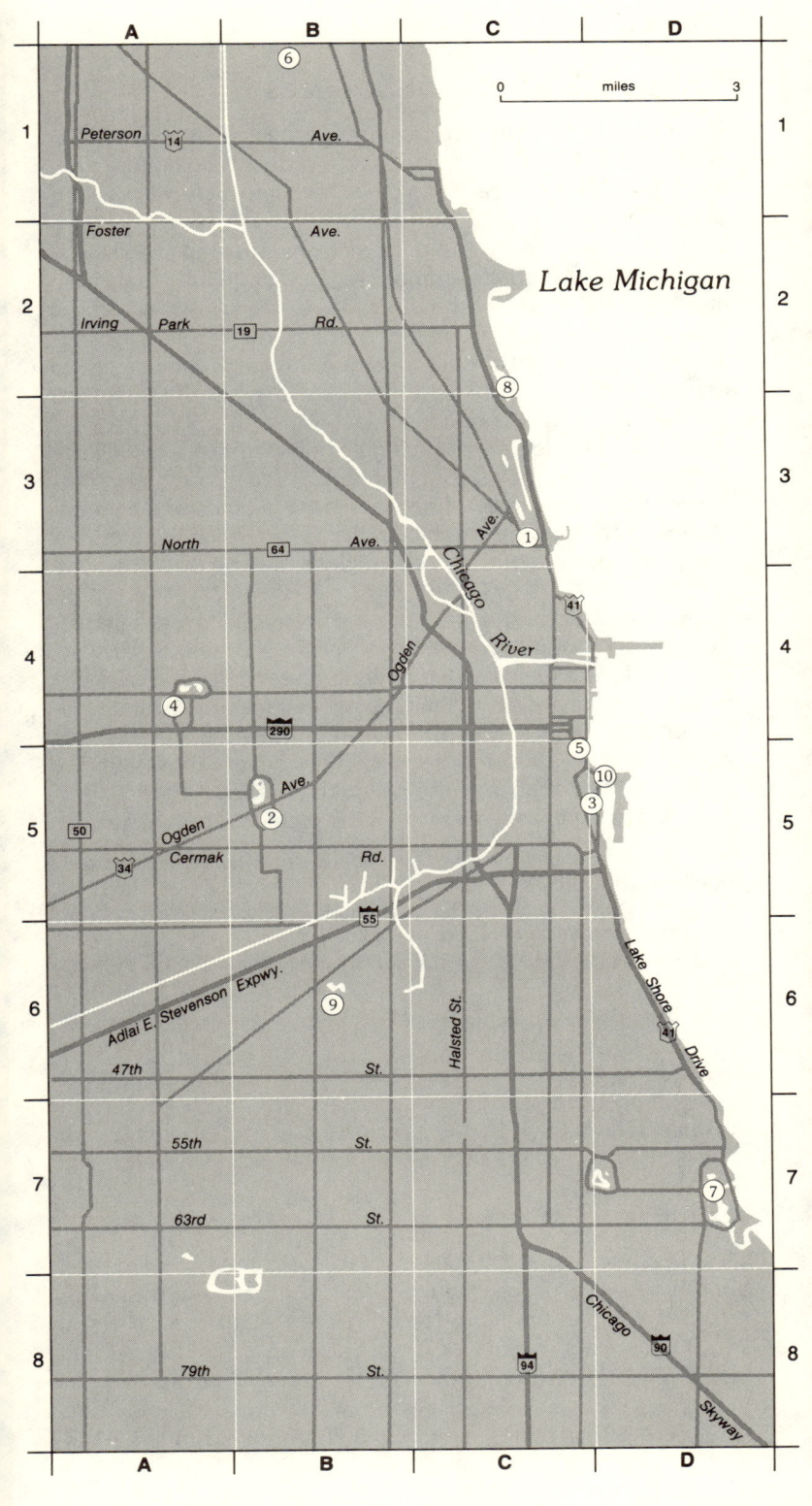

Chicago Academy of Sciences

The Chicago Academy of Sciences is the oldest science museum in the Midwest. Begun in 1857 to depict the natural habitat of the Chicago area, it has developed into a global museum of ecology.

The colorful dioramas, innovative techniques, and lifelike displays of insects, birds, mammals, reptiles, amphibians, and fish give a vivid glimpse of what life is like in the natural world not only at present, but through the ages. Floors, walls, and ceilings are all used, along with special mirror and black light effects, to create for the visitor the illusion that he is a part of the natural environment he is viewing.

A walk-in ecology and geology exhibit on the second floor begins with a journey through an ancient coal forest, and proceeds through a variety of habitats to the interior of a canyon. On the third floor are exhibits of the life zones of the world, a compact view of more than 100 regions of earth complete with sound effects.

Distinguished lecture programs are occasionally presented. In the past, such eminent scientists as Drs. Jane Goodall, Dian Fossey, and Birute Galdikas (pioneering researchers on the chimpanzee, gorilla, and orangutan) have been featured. During fall, winter, and spring, free nature films are shown every Saturday afternoon, and travel lectures are offered every other Sunday afternoon. The academy also conducts a dozen field trips each year to natural history sites within the greater Chicago area.

How to Get There: Located in Lincoln Park on Chicago's near north side. From downtown, go west on Madison St. to LaSalle St. Turn right on LaSalle St. to junction with Clark St. and turn left to museum. Parking is on the street or at rear of museum.

Open daily, 10:00 A.M.–5:00 P.M., year-round; closed on Christmas. Free.

For Additional Information:
Chicago Academy of Sciences
2001 N. Clark St.
Chicago, IL 60614
(312) 549-0606

Douglas Park

A sweeping expanse of greenery that covers 174 acres just west of downtown Chicago, Douglas Park includes pleasant lawns, mature trees, a charming formal garden that contains about 18,000 annuals, masses of shrubs, and a narrow lagoon that twists and turns through the northern section of the park. Its range of recreational facilities—a swimming pool, ballfields, children's playgrounds, a bicycle path, an oval running track, and basketball, volleyball, and tennis courts—is characteristic of most large inland city parks in Chicago.

Although this lovely and serene park has aged gracefully since its founding in 1870, it is most memorable because of the water lilies that adorn its waters in late spring and summer. A pool sprinkled with a mix of both day-blooming and night-blooming lilies is the showplace of the park's formal garden. Still more lilies float on the surface of the Douglas lagoon.

How to Get There: From downtown Chicago, go west on Randolph St. to Ogden Ave. Turn left (southwest) and proceed on Ogden to park. Ogden bisects the park in an east-west direction, and park roads lead from it. The park is bounded by California Blvd. on the east, Albany Ave. on the west, Roosevelt Rd. on the north, and 19th St. on the south. Some parking on site.

Open daily, year-round; sunrise to 10:00 P.M. in summer, daylight hours rest of year. Free.

For Additional Information:
Department of Public Information
Administration Building
Chicago Park District
425 E. McFetridge Dr.
Chicago, IL 60605
(312) 294-2492

Field Museum of Natural History

This remarkable museum near the Lake Michigan waterfront explores the entire panorama of our planet's natural history from the moment of its birth. The promise of future discoveries is as much an integral part of the Field Museum exhibits as the revelations of the past. Ongoing research and museum-sponsored expeditions to all corners of the world add new attractions each year, so that the museum you see on one visit may not be the same one you will see upon your return.

Founded in 1893, the museum is housed in an imposing marble building. Some 13 million artifacts and specimens are displayed in more than ten acres of exhibit space. Most of the museum's offerings are associated with one of four fields: anthropology, botany, geology, and zoology. Perhaps the best place to begin a visit here is in the Anniversary Exhibit on the main floor, where some stunning examples of these four sciences give visitors the chance to decide what to see in depth.

Children, with their affinity for monsters, are especially enthralled by the Hall of Dinosaurs and a fine collection of Egyptian mummies. One of the world's largest meteorite collections includes not only the Benld (Illinois) meteorite but also the car seat it smashed into. In the botany section are 430 handmade plant models—rare and unusual plants, useful plants, fossil plants. Ranging from simple algae to complex flowering species, they make up the most comprehensive collection in the world.

Man in His Environment, one of the newer and most popular exhibits, is a contemporary, multimedia display that focuses on energy and explores man's impact on various natural systems. In The Place for Wonder, visitors are encouraged to feel, try on, handle, sort, and compare all objects on hand; museum volunteers are available to answer questions.

An ongoing series of innovative programs breathes life into natural history concepts. Films, lectures, self-guided and guided tours are offered almost every day. Weekend Discovery programs are conducted year-round. Each spring and fall, biologists lead one-day field trips to local areas of ecological significance. Periodic special events may feature African dancers, Latin American musicians, or a Native American woodcarver. Facilities available to the public include some fine book and gift shops, a research library, a cafeteria that serves breakfast and lunch, and a canteen where visitors may use the vending machines or eat lunches they've brought with them.

How to Get There: Located at the corner of Roosevelt Rd. and South Lake Shore Dr., near the south end of Grant Park in Chicago. From downtown, go east on any through street to Lake Shore Dr., which parallels Lake Michigan, and turn right. Proceed on Lake Shore Dr. to Roosevelt Rd. (12th St.), which borders the north side of the museum. Limited free parking is available in a lot at the north (main) entrance to the museum; a Chicago Park District lot at the southeast corner of the building charges a nominal fee.

Museum opens daily, year-round, at 9:00 A.M. Closing hours vary from 4:00 P.M. in winter to 6:00 P.M. in summer, Sat.–Thurs.; open until 9:00 P.M. on Fri. Some displays have shorter hours. Free admission on Fridays, nominal admission fee other days. An information booth is located in the central hall of the main floor.

For Additional Information:
Field Museum of Natural History
Roosevelt Rd. at Lake Shore Dr.
Chicago, IL 60605
(312) 922-9410

Garfield Park

Although Garfield Park covers nearly 185 acres of vast green lawns with stately trees and a charming lagoon, it is best known for its 4^1/$_2$-acre conservatory. It has been justifiably called the most beautiful publicly owned botanical garden in the world. Housed beneath an all-weather enclosure at the north end of the park, the conservatory contains more than 5,000 varieties of trees, flowers, and plants.

Once described by the noted American sculptor Lorado Taft as "the most beautiful room in America," the Fernery is lush with a seemingly endless variety of ferns.

In the Cactus House, you'll see two rare species, the senita and the organ pipe cactus, that occur naturally in this country only in the Organ Pipe Cactus National Monument in Arizona. The warm, humid air of the Airoid House, where the temperature never falls below seventy degrees, permits a bevy of highly colored exotics to thrive.

Other parts of the conservatory include the Palm House; the Economic House, containing only plants that are commercially useful; and the Show House, where four major seasonal flower shows are held annually.

When the outdoors blooming season arrives, you'll want to visit a formal garden that covers more than four acres in the southern part of Garfield Park. The geometric patterns of its 56 flower beds are created by more than 25,000 plants.

One of the city park system's newest gardens, located just south of the conservatory, is designed for the blind. Here, visitors are encouraged to feel and smell approximately 1,500 plants selected to appeal to the senses of touch and scent as well as sight and labeled in both Braille and print.

Among the wide range of facilities available are a swimming pool, ballfields, horseshoe pits, a bicycle path, and volleyball, basketball, and tennis courts. Cross-country skiers glide across park lawns in winter.

How to Get There: Located in west central Chicago. From the intersection of Lake Shore Dr. (US 41) and Randolph Dr. near the lakeshore in downtown Chicago, head west on Randolph to Union Park, a small city-owned facility. Randolph dips south within Union Park boundaries and becomes Washington Blvd. Continue west on Washington Blvd. into Garfield Park. Parking on site near conservatory.

Park open daily, year-round, from sunrise to 10:00 P.M. Conservatory open daily, year-round, 9:00 A.M.–5:00 P.M.; open daily, Sat.–Thurs., 10:00 A.M.–6:00 P.M. and Fri. 9:00 A.M.–9:00 P.M. during special shows. All free.

For Additional Information:

Department of Public Information
Administration Building
Chicago Park District
425 E. McFetridge Dr.
Chicago, IL 60605
(312) 294-2492

Garfield Park Conservatory
300 N. Central Park Blvd.
Chicago, IL 60624
(312) 533-1281

Grant Park

Serving as a 305-acre buffer between Chicago's skyscrapers and the open waters of Lake Michigan, Grant Park adds a bright touch to the downtown scene. Its impeccably manicured lawns, tree-shaded walkways, and lovely gardens, caressed by cool breezes from the lake, are merely backdrops for one of the city's most beloved landmarks—magnificent Buckingham Fountain. A sculptural and architectural masterpiece, the fountain is worth seeing at any time but is dazzling when it is in operation, particularly at night when a colored light display plays on the water.

The fountain is complemented by four pools, two to the north and two to the south. During summer months, the lawns adjoining the fountain area are bright with the blooms of roses. Approximately 8,000 plants thrive here in a public test garden where new varieties are evaluated for this region before they are introduced to the market.

In the northern reaches of Grant Park is the Court of Presidents, a very formal garden containing some 20,000 summer bedding plants. Visitors soon discover that this garden provides one of the finest views to be had of the Chicago skyline.

During spring and fall migration, the park's plantings of hawthorns, lilacs, and crab apple trees provide good habitat for land birds, especially sparrows, warblers, and thrushes. This part of the lakefront, protected by breakwaters, attracts Bonaparte's gulls, ring-billed gulls, grebes, diving ducks, mergansers, and herring gulls. In March and October, rafts of scaups and goldeneyes can be seen.

The harbor along the Lake Michigan shoreline is home for myriad yachts and sailboats. Parallel to the water's edge runs a bicycle path that offers sweeping views of the lake. Ballfields and tennis courts are located inland.

How to Get There: Located directly east of Chicago's Loop. Bounded on the north by Randolph Dr., on the south by McFetridge Dr., on the west by Michigan Ave., and on the east by Lake Michigan. Lake Shore Dr. runs north and south through the park.

Open daily, year-round, at all times. Fountain displays are presented daily, May 30–Labor Day, 11:30 A.M.–9:00 P.M.; major color displays 9:00–10:00 P.M..

For Additional Information:
Department of Public Information
Administration Building
Chicago Park District
425 E. McFetridge Dr.
Chicago, IL 60605
(312) 294-2492

Indian Boundary Park

Indian Boundary Park, tucked away in the northeastern corner of Chicago a few blocks inland from Lake Michigan, contains one of only two zoos in the city park system (the other is in Lincoln Park, which is described elsewhere). Because this minuscule, thirteen-acre park is little known and rarely crowded, and because the zoo is a small one, it is an ideal place to introduce young children to the wonders of wildlife without overwhelming them. Exhibits may change, since animals are sometimes brought here on loan from the parent Lincoln Park Zoo, but a representative population might include some spectacled bears, wolves, llamas, monkeys, arctic foxes, fishers, raccoons, goats, turkeys, swans, and assorted waterfowl. Occasionally migrating birds settle down on the park's lagoon to join resident ducks and geese. If you want to plan your visit around a feeding time, come at 1:00 P.M. Monday through Saturday for most animals; fowl are fed at 8:00 A.M..

Elsewhere in the park, there are tennis, basketball, and volleyball courts; a children's playground; and, in winter, an ice skating area.

How to Get There: From downtown Chicago, go north on I-90/94. When I-90 and I-94 separate, continue north on I-94 to Touhy Ave. Head east on Touhy Ave. to Sacramento Ave. and turn right (south). To reach zoo, proceed on Sacramento to Estes Ave. and turn left (east) to zoo entrance on right at 2555 W. Estes Ave. To reach main park entrance, continue south on Sacramento, past Estes Ave., to Lunt Ave. and turn left (east). Park entrance is at 2500 W. Lunt on the left side of the street.

Open daily, year-round, from sunrise to 10:00 P.M. Free.

For Additional Information:

Department of Public Information
Administration Building
Chicago Park District
425 E. McFetridge Dr.
Chicago, IL 60605
(312) 294-2492

Indian Boundary Park Zoo
2555 W. Estes Ave.
Chicago, IL 60645
(312) 274-0200

Jackson Park

One of Chicago's best-loved city parks, 543-acre Jackson Park lies along the Lake Michigan shoreline south of downtown Chicago. As much water as it is land, the park features a sheltered yacht harbor and picturesque lagoons bordered by cattails and other aquatic plants, in addition to Lake Michigan itself. The World's Columbian Exposition of 1893 was held here, and some of the buildings and gardens of the park today are legacies of the fair's grandeur.

For nature lovers, the most popular part of Jackson Park is the Paul H. Douglas Nature Sanctuary, a secluded island retreat that lies in the park's largest lagoon. Its plantings of deciduous trees and fruit-bearing shrubs attract wild birds; among the sightings are such locally rare birds as the sandhill crane, green heron, Bohemian waxwing, and evening grosbeak. Mallards that reside year-round on the lagoon are joined by more of their own kind, as well as other species of ducks, during spring and fall migration periods. In the spring, many small land birds pause to rest, sheltered by the dense shrubs.

The Japanese garden at the north end of the island is a restoration of the original, which was a gift of the Japanese government for the 1893 exposition. After years of neglect and an initial restoration that was thwarted by fire and vandalism, the current garden was dedicated in June 1981. Rocks, water, and plants are skillfully arranged to create a miniature version of such natural landscape features as mountains, lakes, and trees. Formerly known as Wooded Island, the 16 1/2-acre island was designed by Frederick Law Olmsted for the exposition and has been a favorite spot of Chicagoans ever since. It's accessible by a footbridge at the southern end of the lagoon.

The Windy City's most popular tourist attraction, the Museum of Science and Industry, is also in Jackson Park, situated on the wooded banks just north of the lagoon. The largest and most complete museum of its kind in the world, it offers an astonishing range of exhibits, many of which encourage visitors to experience them through participation. You may descend into a reconstructed coal mine, watch baby chicks as they hatch, and view Lake Michigan in a most unusual way—through the periscope of a captured German submarine. The museum is housed in another legacy of the exposition, the former Palace of Fine Arts.

Located in the west central part of the park is an elaborate formal garden that annually displays more than 180 varieties of flowering plants. Its floral displays, maintained from April until the first freeze in fall, include masses of tulips, hyacinths, narcissus, and chrysanthemums, as well as many flowering shrubs and trees.

You may also want to take a tree walk. Throughout the park, you'll find many unusual trees bearing labels in both English and Latin.

Among the many recreational facilities in the park are baseball and softball fields, basketball backboards, tennis courts, bowling greens, children's playgrounds, and an eighteen-hole golf course and driving range. Three swimming beaches line Lake Michigan, and there are many marine facilities where you may rent a boat or launch one of your own. Paths are laid out for bicycling and horseback riding, and winter brings cross-country skiers and ice skaters.

The Midway Plaisance, a narrow, landscaped strip of open space at Stony Island Avenue and 59th Street on the west side of Jackson Park, provides a pleasant route westward to Washington Park, another major city park that features a formal garden and an outdoor swimming pool.

How to Get There: From downtown Chicago, take Lake Shore Dr. (US 41) south to park; Lake Shore Dr. runs through park, and park roads lead off it. Watch for signs to Museum of Science and Industry, which lies at the north end of the park. Park near the museum or at the south end of the lagoon.

Park open daily, year-round, 6:00 A.M.–11:00 P.M. Free. Museum of Science and Industry open daily, year-round, except Christmas; 9:30 A.M.–5:30 P.M. daily, Memorial Day–Labor Day; 9:30 A.M.–4:00 P.M., Mon.–Fri., and 9:30 A.M.–5:30 P.M., Sat., Sun., and holidays rest of year. Free.

For Additional Information:

Department of Public Information
Administration Building
Chicago Park District
425 E. McFetridge Dr.
Chicago, IL 60605
(312) 294-2492

Museum of Science and Industry
57th St. and Lake Shore Dr.
Chicago, IL 60637
(312) 684-1414

Lincoln Park

Even people who have never been to Chicago have heard of Lincoln Park, a 1,212-acre expanse of greenery and beach that edges Lake Michigan in the heart of the Windy City. Called Lake Park when it was first established in 1846, it was renamed in honor of President Abraham Lincoln at the close of the Civil War in 1865.

Like all major city parks, Lincoln Park attempts to offer something for everyone, but its main attractions are its conservatory, its zoo, and the lakefront itself with its free beaches.

Occupying just thirty-five acres of parkland, the Lincoln Park Zoo claims to be the most visited zoo in the world with an estimated four million visitors annually. From its beginnings in 1868, when New York City's Central Park presented the city of Chicago with two pairs of swans, the zoo has increased the number of its wild residents to about 2,500 specimens. Its collection of primates, housed in a unique building that permits visitors to observe the apes close up from two viewing levels, is world-famous. Twice a day, simulated storms rain down on the tropical setting. Also notable is the Penguin and Seabird House, whose inhabitants share a re-created North Atlantic seacoast complete with waves and ocean mists; the world's first zoo-rookery, a man-made oasis for wild birds; and the beautiful endangered snow leopards.

The children's zoo is a special preserve for tame animals that children may pet. At a nursery for the newborn and orphaned, such animals as tigers, jaguars, leopards, and lions may be viewed through glass.

Chickens, dairy cows, and pigs live at the farm-in-the-zoo, a real working farm that gives city youngsters a look at rural life. They can watch chicks hatching, see cows being milked, and enjoy such special events as sheep-shearing, butter-churning, and cheese-making.

Besides being a home for wild animals, the zoo is a big, beautiful garden when its many trees and flowers—including cherry trees, dogwoods, redbuds, and lilacs—are in bloom. There are other gardens, too, in Lincoln Park. The charming grandmother's garden, which gaily displays such old-fashioned plants as columbine, iris, sunflower, chamomile, and meadowrue, is in bloom from very early spring until late fall. Containing formal plantings that are arranged in different patterns each year, the main garden presents a dazzling array of vivid colors, while the nearby rock garden is a pleasant retreat filled with a variety of trees, shrubs, and rock plants.

The most famous blooms of all are indoors, sheltered by the towering glass domes of the Lincoln Park Conservatory. Here, rare orchids, palm trees, ferns, thick vines, and banana trees grow in profusion all year.

Nearly all the birds that have ever been seen in the Chicago area, including the extremely rare Swainson's warbler and Ross's gull, have been sighted at one time or another in Lincoln Park. The park is located along a major flyway and includes a variety of habitats attractive to birds—open lawns, clusters of woodland, some nearly impenetrable thickets, a series of sheltered harbors and lagoons, beaches, and the expanse of Lake Michigan.

Visitors interested in natural history should seek out the original sandbar ridges that still exist near the south end of the park. Formed by windblown sand deposited atop low sandbars as Lake Michigan withdrew from its old shoreline, once ten miles farther inland, these dunes provide a glimpse of how the city looked some 150 years ago.

Two of the city's outstanding museums—the Chicago Academy of Sciences (described elsewhere) and the Chicago Historical Society—are located in the park.

In addition to the recreational facilities listed below, you'll find baseball, football, and soccer fields; basketball, volleyball, and tennis courts; a driving range, nine-hole golf course, and miniature golf course; an archery range; a trap-shooting range; a chess pavilion; and many picnic areas scattered throughout the park.

Bicycling, Horseback Riding, and Running Trails

Visitors may use a jogging path and a physical fitness trail. A bridle trail and bicycle path along the lakeshore permit magnificent views of Lake Michigan. Bicycles may be rented in the park, but there are no horse rentals in the park or nearby area.

Boating and Fishing

With all of Lake Michigan for a playground, boating is a prime activity in Chicago. Many marinas along the lake, including some in Lincoln Park, rent boats, and there are two launching ramps in the park. Rowboats may be rented for use on the park's boating lagoon. Another lagoon is reserved for shore fishing; it's adequate for beginners, but can't begin to compete with Lake Michigan. A fishing pier extends into the lake near Montrose Harbor.

Swimming

There are six free bathing beaches in the park, with three beach houses for changing into swimwear.

Winter Sports

Cross-country skiers may use park paths when snow cover is deep enough, and four ponds are open to ice skaters.

How to Get There: Located on Chicago's north side. The park borders Lake Michigan from North Ave. on the south to Hollywood Ave. on the north. Lake Shore Drive, which runs through the park in a north-south direction, is crossed by several park roads. Some parking available within park.

Park open daily, year-round, during daylight hours; later for special events. Beaches open 9:00 A.M.–9:30 P.M. daily, mid-June through Labor Day. Zoo grounds open 8:00 A.M.–5:15 P.M. daily, year-round; zoo buildings open 9:00 A.M.–5:00 P.M. Conservatory open daily, year-round, 9:00 A.M.–5:00 P.M. (during major shows, until 9:00 P.M.). Admission to all is free.

For Additional Information:
Department of Public Administration
Administration Building
Chicago Park District
425 E. McFetridge Dr.
Chicago, IL 60605
(312) 294-2200—Administration
(312) 294-4660—Zoo
(312) 294-4770—Conservatory

Marquette Park

One of the largest municipal rose gardens in the Midwest covers approximately one acre in Marquette Park, a refreshing oasis with a cattail-rimmed lagoon on Chicago's southwest side. From early summer through October, more than 4,000 roses, representing some eighty varieties, are in bloom. In the center of the garden is a pool with live swans and eighteen fountains.

Roses are Marquette Park's biggest drawing card, but there are other floral displays as well. In the early spring, some 15,000 tulips bloom. A trial garden, used primarily as a testing ground for new annuals and perennials, also contains a cactus and succulent garden, a rock garden with a picturesque pool, an herb garden, and a topiary garden.

Marquette's recreational facilities include ballfields, tennis and basketball courts, horseshoe pits, an archery range, a bicycle path, and a nine-hole golf course. From spring through fall, fishermen can angle for bass, carp, perch, and sunfish in the lagoon. Snow and cold weather lure cross-country skiers and ice skaters.

How to Get There: Located in southwest Chicago, not far from Midway Airport. From the intersection of IL 50 and 63rd St., which forms Midway's southeast corner, go south on IL 50 to Marquette Rd. and turn left (east). Proceed on Marquette Rd. to Marquette Park, which extends southeast from the intersection of Marquette Rd. and Central Park Ave.

Open daily, year-round, from sunrise to 10:00 P.M. Free.

For Additional Information:
Department of Public Information
Administration Building
Chicago Park District
425 E. McFetridge Dr.
Chicago, IL 60605
(312) 294-2492

Shedd Aquarium

The John G. Shedd Aquarium is said to be the largest "under-one-roof" aquarium in the world. Through special viewing windows visitors can watch more than 5,000 fish from all parts of the world, including schools of piranha, an octopus, and a 600-pound, seven-foot-long grouper.

Mammals, reptiles, and invertebrates live here, too, as do harbor seals, Humboldt penguins, and dolphins.

The aquarium, perched on a landscaped lawn at the edge of Lake Michigan, contains more than 150 exhibits displayed in six separate galleries. Each gallery contains fish from a specific habitat—saltwater and freshwater samples from tropical, temperate, and cold climates. At centerstage is the coral reef exhibit, opened in 1971 and inhabited by sharks and moray eels, tarpon and French angel fish, among others. At 11:00 A.M., 2:00, and 3:00 P.M. on weekends and at 11:00 A.M. and 2:00 P.M. each weekday, divers hand-feed the reef's residents and describe the action to viewers through built-in microphones in their masks.

An eight-minute slide show introducing the aquarium to visitors is shown every hour on the half hour in the auditorium. Both the general public and school groups may sign up for various educational programs. A marine library is open free to the public, by appointment.

How to Get There: Located next to Lake Michigan, on Chicago's near south side, at the intersection of Lake Shore Dr. and 12th St.

Open daily, 9:00 A.M.–5:00 P.M., May–Aug.; 10:00 A.M.—5:00 P.M., Sept., Oct., March, April; 10:00 A.M.–4:00 P.M., Nov.–Feb. Open to

9:00 P.M. every Friday, year-round; closed Christmas and New Year's Day. Nominal admission fee; free on Friday.

For Additional Information:
John G. Shedd Aquarium
1200 South Lake Shore Dr.
Chicago, IL 60605
(312) 939-2426

Part 2

Bill Thomas

Natural Attractions in
Illinois

ILLINOIS–WISCONSIN

1. Belmont Prairie **B/C–5**
2. Berkeley Prairie **C–3**
3. Blackwell Recreational Preserve **B–5**
4. Bluff Spring Fen **A–4**
5. Braidwood Dunes and Savannah **B–8**
6. Brookfield Zoo **C–5**
7. Calumet Forest Preserve Division **D–6**
8. Cantigny **B–5**
9. Cary Prairie **B–3**
10. Chain O'Lakes State Park **B–2**
11. Chicago Botanic Garden **C/D–3**
12. Churchill Woods Forest Preserve **B/C–5**
13. Crabtree Nature Center **B–3**
14. Des Plaines Forest Preserve Division **C–4**
15. Des Plaines River Trail **C–2**
16. Des Plaines State Conservation Area **B–7**
17. Dole Wildlife Sanctuary **B–4**
18. Fabyan Forest Preserve **A–5**
19. Fermilab Prairie **B–5**
20. Fullersburg Woods Nature Preserve **C–5**
21. Gensburg–Markham Prairie **D–6**
22. Glacial Park–Nippersink Trail **A–2**
23. Goodenow Grove Forest Preserve **D–7**
24. Goose Lake Prairie State Park **A–7**
25. Great Western Trail **A–4**
26. Greene Valley Forest Preserve **B–5**
27. Grosse Point Lighthouse Park **D–4**
28. The Grove **C–4**
29. Harrison–Benwell Conservation Site **A–2**
30. Hickory Grove **B–3**
31. Illinois and Michigan Canal State Trail **A–7**
32. Illinois Beach State Park **C–2**
33. Illinois Prairie Path **C–5**
34. Indian Boundary Forest Preserve Division **C–4**
35. Izaak Walton Preserve **D–7**
36. Kankakee River State Park **C–8**
37. Keepataw Forest Preserve **B/C–6**
38. Ladd Arboretum **D–4**
39. Lockport Prairie **B–6**
40. Maple Grove Forest Preserve **C–5**
41. McKinley Woods Forest Preserve **B–7**
42. Messenger Woods Forest Preserve **C–6**
43. Moraine Hills State Park **B–2**
44. Morton Arboretum **B/C–5**
45. Morton Grove Prairie **C–4**
46. Ned Brown Forest Preserve **C–4**
47. Nelson Lake Marsh **A–5**
48. Norris Woods **A–4**
49. North Branch Forest Preserve Division **C/D–4**
50. Palos and Sag Valley Forest Preserve Divisions **C–6**
51. Pilcher Park **B/C–6**
52. Powers State Conservation Area **D–6**
53. Pratt's Wayne Woods **B–4**
54. Queen Anne Prairie–Eckert Cemetery **A–2**
55. Raccoon Grove Forest Preserve **D–7**
56. Reed–Turner Woodland **C–3**
57. Ryerson Conservation Area **C–3**
58. Salt Creek Forest Preserve Division **C–5**
59. Shaw Woodlands and Prairies **C–3**
60. Silver Springs State Park **A–6**
61. Skokie Forest Preserve Division **C/D–3**
62. Thorn Creek Forest Preserve Division **D–6**
63. Thorn Creek Nature Preserve **D–7**
64. Timber Ridge Forest Preserve **B–5**
65. Tinley Creek Forest Preserve Division **C/D–6**
66. Trout Park **B–4**
67. Veterans Acres Park **A–3**
68. Volo Bog State Natural Area **B–2**
69. Waterfall Glen Forest Preserve **C–6**
70. West Chicago Prairie **B–5**
71. West DuPage Woods Forest Preserve **B–5**
72. Willowbrook Wildlife Haven **B–5**
73. Woodworth Prairie Preserve **C–4**
74. Bong State Recreation Area **B–1**
75. Hawthorn Hollow **C–1**
76. Petrifying Springs County Park **C–1**

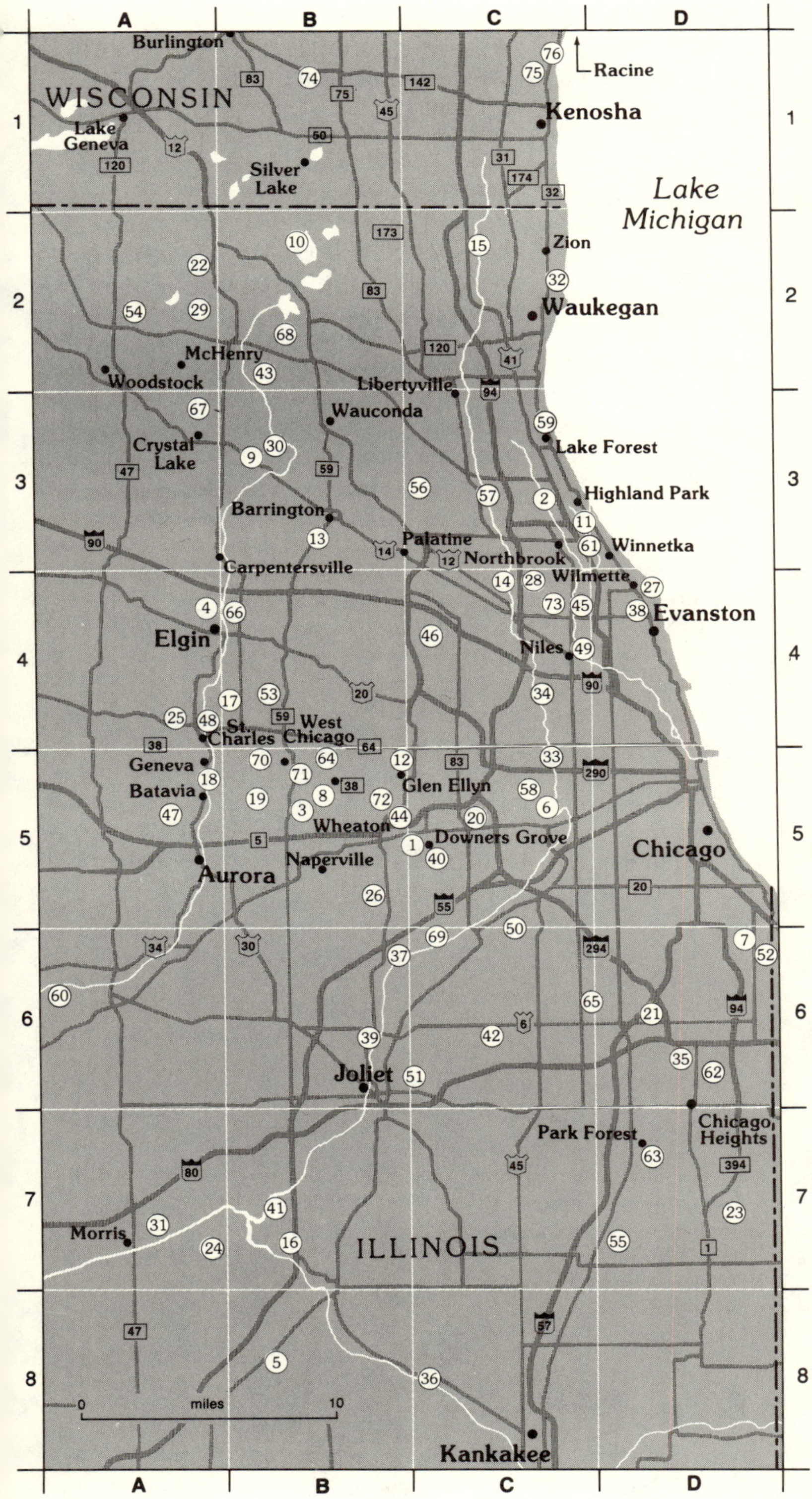
WISCONSIN
Burlington
Racine
Kenosha
Lake Geneva
Silver Lake
Lake Michigan
Zion
Waukegan
McHenry
Woodstock
Libertyville
Wauconda
Lake Forest
Crystal Lake
Highland Park
Barrington
Palatine
Northbrook
Winnetka
Carpentersville
Wilmette
Evanston
Elgin
Niles
St. Charles
West Chicago
Geneva
Glen Ellyn
Batavia
Wheaton
Downers Grove
Chicago
Aurora
Naperville
Joliet
Park Forest
Chicago Heights
Morris
ILLINOIS
Kankakee
miles
0
10

Argonne National Laboratory

See listing under Waterfall Glen Forest Preserve, p. 131.

Belmont Prairie

This tiny surviving parcel of Illinois tallgrass prairie perches on the rolling hills of the Valparaiso Moraine in central DuPage County.

The Belmont Prairie is noted for its displays of color from spring through fall. Here, growing among the tall prairie grasses, are such showy floral specimens as the shooting star, hoary puccoon, golden Alexander, and Culver's root. Plants that are rare in the Chicago region—the marsh betony, yellow gentian, scurfy pea, and Hill's thistle—thrive alongside the small white lady's slipper, a federally endangered species that exists here in abundance. Altogether, more than 120 species of native flowering plants have been identified within this ten-acre preserve, an amazing diversity for such a small area.

Also found at this spot are the brightly hued American painted lady butterfly, the sulfur-winged grasshopper, and the giant assassin fly.

Although groups are permitted here, a visit to Belmont Prairie is more rewarding if you visit alone or with your family. Dedicated as a state nature preserve in 1979, Belmont Prairie has no facilities. Activities are limited to nature study and hiking along a system of narrow trails. An excellent interpretive display on the natural history of the prairie stands at the trail entrance.

How to Get There: Located in the town of Downers Grove. From the intersection of US 34 (Ogden Ave.) and Belmont Rd. in northwestern Downers Grove, go south about one mile to Haddow Ave. (you'll see a schoolhouse where you turn). Turn right (west) onto Haddow Ave. and proceed to Cross St. Turn right (north) onto Cross St. and go approximately half a block to prairie entrance on left (west) side of the road. Small parking lot on site holds five cars.

Open daily, year-round, during daylight hours. Groups must obtain permission in advance to visit prairie. Guided tours available May through Sept. if prior arrangements are made. Free.

For Additional Information:

Administration Office
Downers Grove Park District
6801 Main St.
Downers Grove, IL 60515
(312) 963-1300
(312) 963-1304—Guided Tours Only

The Nature Conservancy
Illinois Field Office
79 W. Monroe St., Suite 708
Chicago, IL 60603
(312) 346-8166

Berkeley Prairie

Although this eighteen-acre prairie in southeastern Lake County has been disturbed in the past by farming and grazing, it is being restored to its natural state through a controlled burning program that deep-rooted prairie plants can survive and invading woody plants cannot.

Rare grasses, such as dropseed and prairie brome, are found here, along with a series of flowering plants. Golden Alexander and the minute blue-eyed grass begin the annual display each spring, succeeded by the rattlesnake master and the butterfly weed and followed in late summer by blazing stars, asters, and goldenrods.

An adjacent oak grove illustrates how prairie and woodland communities mixed in presettlement times. Yet another ecosystem, the floodplain, may be seen along the West Fork of the North Branch of the Chicago River, which flows southward at the prairie's western boundary.

Since this is being preserved as a natural area, there are no facilities other than a trail system, but you'll find other facilities and recreational opportunities at Ryerson Conservation Area (described elsewhere) and Wright Woods, two nearby Lake County forest preserves. Some guided tours are offered; staff members at Ryerson Conservation area use Berkeley Prairie as a focal part of natural history studies during some of their programs.

How to Get There: Located at the northeast corner of Deerfield. Permission to visit the preserve is required and may be obtained, along with exact directions, by contacting the Lake County Forest Preserve District.

Open daily, 8:00 A.M.–5:00 P.M., year-round. Free.

For Additional Information:

Lake County Forest Preserve District
2000 N. Milwaukee Ave.
Libertyville, IL 60048
(312) 367-6640

Edward L. Ryerson Conservation Area
3735 Riverwoods Rd.
Riverwoods, IL 60015
(312) 948-7750

The Nature Conservancy
Illinois Field Office
79 W. Monroe St., Suite 708
Chicago, IL 60603
(312) 346-8166

Blackwell Recreational Preserve

Starting with the purchase of a worked-out gravel pit in the early 1960s, the Forest Preserve District of DuPage County converted a local eyesore into one of the prime park sites in the Chicago area. Blackwell Preserve offers visitors the opportunity both to explore a fine natural environment and to experience a wide variety of outdoor recreational opportunities year-round.

When acquired, the gravel pit covered some 65 acres and was surrounded by fifty-foot-high limestone bluffs. The purchase of adjacent forest and meadowland increased the size of the preserve to more than 1,200 acres.

Over the years, the gravel pit was developed into seventy-acre Silver Lake, the focal point of the park. Two smaller lakes were built nearby—one for swimming and one for service as a reservoir.

Since DuPage County was desperately searching for a suitable location for a new landfill garbage dump at the same time land was being acquired here, the Forest Preserve District decided that such a landfill could be put to practical use on Blackwell Preserve. Refuse from the surrounding area soon reached a height of more than 150 feet, just right for transformation into a winter sports hill, which was called Mt. Hoy and is the highest point in the county. Monitored for environmental quality every step of the way, the hill was completed in 1973 and 2,000 trees planted on its slopes.

Blackwell is divided into two distinct parts. The larger southern portion contains the developed recreational facilities, including Mt. Hoy and the lakes mentioned previously, a campground, picnic areas, and an amphitheater where free nature films are presented on Friday evenings throughout the summer. A mix of forest, marsh, and open fields provides a scenic backdrop. Penetrating its boundaries are two streams, Springbrook and the West Branch of the DuPage River.

The latter also flows through a corner of the virtually undeveloped northern part of the park, where patches of prairie and marsh ecosystems blaze with native plants. Forty acres of wetland, designated a wildlife refuge, host both resident and migratory waterfowl. In 1977, this area made local headlines when over 300 pieces of bone excavated here proved to be the remains of a woolly mammoth more than 14,000 years old—the oldest such specimen yet found in northeastern Illinois. (These bones are occasionally displayed at Fullersburg Woods Nature Preserve, which is described elsewhere.) Also located here is an authentic one-room schoolhouse more than 100 years old, the last remnant of a now-vanished pioneer settlement.

Hawks and owls may be found throughout the park. Sandpipers, muskrats, and herons frequent the marshy regions, while the woodlands harbor woodpeckers, chipmunks, and squirrels. Deer, foxes, meadowlarks, woodchucks, and bob-o-links live in the meadows.

Hiking and Horseback Riding

More than seven miles of footpaths meander through the southern part of the preserve, while in the northern part some twenty miles of unmarked, mowed trails appeal to the more rugged hiker. Trails in the northern part double as bridle paths, but all horses must be registered with the district; no rentals. Part of the Illinois Prairie Path (described elsewhere) runs along the southern boundary of the preserve.

Boating and Fishing

Sailboats, rowboats, canoes, and kayaks less than twenty feet in length are permitted on Silver Lake; no rentals. The lake is periodically stocked with bass, crappie, walleye, and northern pike. In 1975, the Forest Preserve District placed old Christmas trees in concrete casings and sank them to the bottom, thus improving fish habitat. The West Branch of the DuPage River yields channel catfish, carp, and some crappie and bass; a canoe and raft launch is provided. A daily fee (payable at the park gatehouse) or an annual permit (available at the district office) is required to launch any type of boat.

Swimming

Swimmers and splashers will both find areas of the four-acre swim lake to their liking. A sand beach and large lawn attract sunbathers. Scuba divers are permitted to use the lake on Saturday and Sunday mornings from 9:00 to 10:30 A.M. Lifeguards on duty; change rooms provided. Swim area open daily, 11:00 A.M.–6:00 P.M., mid-June through Labor Day; nominal fee, under two free.

Camping

A family campground provides sixty sites for tents and recreational vehicles; no hookups. Open daily, Memorial Day through Labor Day; weekends only, spring and fall. Reservations must be made at least seventy-two hours in advance through district headquarters.

Winter Sports

Cross-country skiing is permitted on all trails; in northern portion of park, skiers are free to break their own trails. Silver Lake is used by ice skaters and ice fishermen. A special feature of the park is snow tubing on Mt. Hoy, offered from 9:00 A.M.–4:00 P.M. on winter weekends and holidays. Visitors must use inner tubes rented from district on site.

How to Get There: Located northeast of the intersection of Butterfield Rd. (IL 56) and IL 59 in west central DuPage County. From Wheaton, take Roosevelt Rd. (IL 38) west to IL 59; turn south to Butterfield Rd. (IL 56), then left to park entrance on left side of road. Ample parking on grounds.

Open daily, year-round, from one hour after sunrise to one hour after sunset. Entrance is usually free; nominal fees may be charged at certain times, and small fees are charged for some activities.

For Additional Information:
Forest Preserve District of DuPage County
P.O. Box 2339
Glen Ellyn, IL 60137
(312) 620-3800

Bluff Spring Fen

Bluff Spring Fen contains one of the most remarkable mixes of natural habitats and endangered plants in all of northern Illinois. Covering ninety acres in the Fox River Valley, the preserve has a rugged, diverse topography.

The steep, conical hills were formed long ago when glacial outwash was deposited here. At the bases of these hills, lime-laden spring water surfaces to feed alkaline wetlands and create rivulets that hurry through prairie and marsh to join Poplar Creek. It is in the alkaline water of these fens and seeps that such extremely rare plants as tufted hair grass, false asphodel, and shrubby cinquefoil thrive in abundance. On the hillsides, carpets of little bluestem and grama grasses mingle with prairie violets, fringed puccoon, and prairie smoke, while the low, wet prairie below nurtures taller prairie grasses and other plant species that so dominated the primeval Illinois landscape.

Perhaps the most interesting of all wildlife residents are the woodcocks, which nest beneath scattered willow shrubs and perform their spectacular aerial displays in the spring.

No facilities will be built here, and recreational use will remain limited, as it is currently, to hiking and nature study. Trails created by ORV traffic are now utilized only for pedestrians and allow visitors to observe examples of all preserve communities.

How to Get There: Located near the town of Elgin in Kane County. No casual visitation is allowed, but information about free guided tours may be obtained from the McGraw Wildlife Foundation.

For Additional Information:

McGraw Wildlife Foundation
% Friends of the Fen
P.O. Box 194
Dundee, IL 60118
(312) 428-6331

The Nature Conservancy
Illinois Field Office
79 W. Monroe St., Suite 708
Chicago, IL 60603
(312) 346-8166

Braidwood Dunes and Savanna

In the remote countryside of southwest Will County lies one of The Nature Conservancy's most important projects, the Braidwood Dunes and Savanna. This 205-acre site, the largest intact remnant of the inland sand dunes of the Kankakee River Valley, contains a priceless ecological heritage. As early as 1927, Chicago's pioneer land planners were urging that this area be preserved, but it wasn't until late 1978, when The Nature Conservancy purchased the property at a land auction, that this goal was finally realized.

Braidwood is a land of diversity, rich in rare vegetation and vanishing wildlife. Its crescent-shaped dunes, twenty feet high, support an open savanna of old black oaks that soar above an understory of such prairie grasses as little bluestem, porcupine grass, and June grass. Sassafras and huckleberry thrive alongside prairie plants like button blazing star, prairie coreopsis, and showy goldenrod, while a seasonal parade of beautiful legumes, from blue lupine to goat's rue to the partridge pear, colors the desertlike landscape. Animal residents include ground squirrels, racerunner lizards, hognose snakes, and the regal fritillary butterfly. A lucky visitor may spot a herd of white-tailed deer, a nesting whippoorwill, or the colorful eastern bluebird.

Below the dune tops are flat sand prairies, which grade into wet prairies and dense sedge marshes. Here thrives a curious mix of plants. Sedges and prairie species, like Indian and cord grass, marsh phlox, and white indigo, appear with plants of northern bogs, such as chokeberry and the very rare grass pink orchid. Plants more common on the Atlantic coast—lanceleaf violet, colicroot, and the tubercled orchid, designated a threatened species by the federal government—find suitable growing conditions here. Among the birds that pause to rest at Braidwood are the meadowlark, bob-o-link, dickcissel, and the elusive Virginia rail.

Today, Braidwood Dunes is an Illinois nature preserve, and ownership has been transferred to the Will County Forest Preserve District.

Hiking

The gentle slopes over most of the terrain permit easy hiking. There is no formal trail system at this writing, but one is planned. In the meantime, paths worn through the area before it became a nature preserve may be used.

How to Get There: Located one mile southeast of the town of Braidwood. Because access as of this writing involves the crossing of private lands, visitors must contact the Will County Forest Preserve District for permission to enter, accompanied by a naturalist. Precise directions will be given when you call or write. Parking is available near the site.

For Additional Information:

Will County Forest Preserve District
Cherry Hill Rd. and Rt. 52, R.R. 4
Joliet, IL 60433
(815) 727-8700

Plum Creek Nature Center
Box 241, R.R. 2
Beecher, IL 60401
(312) 946-2216

The Nature Conservancy
Illinois Field Office
79 W. Monroe, Suite 708
Chicago, IL 60603
(312) 346-8166

Brookfield Zoo

In the Salt Creek Forest Preserve of Cook County, just west of downtown Chicago, is one of the most imaginatively created

The Brookfield Zoo in Cook County, just west of downtown Chicago *Bill Thomas*

zoological parks in the nation. Brookfield Zoo, located on some 200 wooded acres sprinkled with open meadows, officially opened during the summer of 1934 and was called the Chicago Zoological Park. Located in the suburb of Brookfield, it has become popularly known as the Brookfield Zoo and has more than two million visitors annually.

The zoo is noted for the breeding and conservation of rare or endangered animals from throughout the world, often attaining success with species that have not bred well elsewhere in captivity. In fact, some species now on exhibit are already extinct in the wild. The original Brookfield collection began with a contribution of 143 mammals, 123 birds, and four reptiles from one donor's private collection. Today over 2,000 specimens, representing more than 650 species, live here in re-creations of their natural habitats. Besides the caged animals, several native mammals, including the raccoon, opossum, gray and red fox, skunk, woodchuck, muskrat, and the thirteen-lined ground squirrel or gopher, live here by choice.

Among the rare animals found here are the Galapagos tortoise, second largest turtle in the world; Przewalski's horse, the same proud creature that carried the armies of Ghengis Khan in their sweeping victories across China and Russia, but which numbers only about twenty animals in the wild today; the black rhinoceros, the hairy-nosed wombat, the snow leopard, Father David's deer of China, now extinct in the wild; and the okapi, a rare relative of the giraffe, that wasn't even known by man to exist before 1900.

Tropic World, a life-size re-creation of a tropical rain forest, is the largest indoor zoo exhibit in the world. Some seventy-five feet tall, it creates a realistic environment shared by such creatures as lowland gorillas, a pygmy hippo, and monkeys.

The lake and its surrounding terrain in the far western end of the park are preserved in their natural states. Many large and small trees native to the area, including oak, ash, hackberry, hickory, black cherry, hawthorn, linden, elm, and prairie crab, thrive here. Some of the huge oaks are more than 150 years old. During spring, the forest floor is carpeted with a profusion of wildflowers. The area has changed little since the days when Indians were the only people roaming the countryside; there's even a herd of bison grazing on the prairie.

Near the north entrance is a large circular flower bed utilizing colorful annuals to depict the logo of the Chicago Zoological Society. More than 20,000 plants are used in that display, all from cuttings of the previous season's plants propagated over the winter in the zoo's own greenhouses.

When you tire of walking the cool, tree-shaded paths, hop aboard the Motor Safari for a narrated tour of the zoo or ride a narrow-gauge steam railroad around the park's periphery through parts of the zoo not normally open to visitors. Both operate from early spring to early fall.

How to Get There: Located in Brookfield at the intersection of First Ave. and 31st St. From I-90, go south at First Ave. exit; from I-55, go north at First Ave. exit.

Open daily, 10:00 A.M.–6:00 P.M., May–Sept.; 10:00 A.M.–5:00 P.M., Oct.–April. Nominal admission fee, except on Tues., when admission is free; under 6, free at all times. Nominal parking fee every day. Also nominal fees for some special exhibits, steam railroad, and Motor Safari.

For Additional Information:
Brookfield Zoo
8400 W. 31st St.
Brookfield, IL 60513
(312) 242-2630—Chicago number
(312) 485-0263—Suburban number

Calumet Forest Preserve Division

Actually composed of six unconnected preserves, some of which are inside the Chicago city limits, the Calumet Division of the Cook County Forest Preserve District lies south of the downtown area. Most of the preserves border the Little Calumet or Grand Calumet rivers; one edges the northern shoreline of Wolf Lake, a state-owned site described elsewhere as Powers State Conservation Area.

The latter stretch of woodland includes the Wolf Lake Overlook and Eggers Grove, one of the few places in Cook County where you can see native sassafras trees. Also noted as a bird-watching area, Eggers Grove is at its best during spring migration when great numbers of warblers, thrushes, sapsuckers, vireos, and kinglets stop here. Black-crowned night herons fly overhead throughout the summer, and in winter, several species of owls inhabit the forest. Well-defined trails lead around and through the woods and to a marsh where long-billed marsh wrens nest.

In another division preserve south of Wolf Lake, thirty-five-acre Powderhorn Lake lies in a picturesque, swampy area that is scheduled for dedication as a state nature preserve. The marsh at the northern end of the lake, ringed by a profusion of cattails and tall marsh grasses, is managed as a wildlife refuge. Just to the west is a large tract of undisturbed, wet meadow where myriads of wildflowers bloom much of the year. Some, including the prickly pear cactus, are locally rare. In the swampy areas, water and marsh birds congregate in great numbers. Pied-billed grebes, least bitterns, black and Forster's terns, and yellow-headed blackbirds have nested here on occasion, and red-winged blackbirds are seen with their young every spring.

Elsewhere, near Dan Ryan Woods, there is an overlook that provides a remarkable, little-known view of the Chicago skyline. And although there are no established hiking trails in this division, it is possible in places to stroll along the wooded shorelines of the Little Calumet River.

Boating and Fishing

Boating is allowed on Powderhorn Lake and the Little Calumet River. Known by boaters and canoeists as one of the better waterways in the area, the Little Calumet is both gentle and beautiful. Private watercraft of all types with motors may be launched on the river free of charge at the Calumet and Beaubien boating centers on division lands. Canoes, sailboats, and rowboats are permitted on Powderhorn Lake; there's a free launch ramp, but only electric motors are allowed here. No rentals.

Two Calumet Division lakes, Powderhorn and Flatfoot, are stocked for fishing. Both offer largemouth bass, bluegill, sunfish, bullhead, carp, goldfish, perch, and crappie; Powderhorn also features northern pike and channel catfish. Shoreline fishing only is available at Flatfoot; no fishing is permitted in the wildlife refuge in the northernmost waters of Powderhorn.

Boating and fishing at Wolf Lake are described elsewhere in a description of the Powers State Conservation Area.

Picnicking

Picnic areas are available in all the preserves of the Calumet Division. All areas have drinking water and tables; some have grills. A prime family picnic area is located alongside the Calumet River near Dixmoor and Kickapoo playfields. Groups of twenty-five or more must obtain advance permits in person from the Permit Office, Room 230, County Building, 118 N. Clark St., Chicago.

Winter Sports

Sledding and tobogganing may be enjoyed at Dan Ryan Woods in the division's northernmost preserve. Toboggan slides are open daily 10:00 A.M.–10:00 P.M. when weather conditions permit. Both Powderhorn and Flatfoot lakes are open to fishermen, and a section of Powderhorn Lake is reserved for ice skaters.

How to Get There: Located in and near the southern part of Chicago. Most areas lie along the banks of the Little Calumet or Grand Calumet rivers; all areas lie between 82nd St. on the north and 147th St. on the south. Since each division of the Cook County Forest Preserve District features several recreation areas and attractions, crisscrossed by many roads and in some instances disconnected, it's best to obtain division maps, directions for getting there, and other pertinent information from district or division headquarters before visiting one. To reach Calumet Division headquarters from downtown Chicago, go south on I-94 (Dan Ryan Expwy.) to 87th St. and turn west to Dan Ryan Woods, which extends north and south from 87th St. just east of Western Ave. The headquarters building is located south of 87th St.; look for signs. Parking on site.

Preserve lands open daily, year-round, sunrise to sunset; free. Headquarters offices open Mon.–Fri., year-round, 8:30 A.M.–5:00 P.M.; closed major holidays.

For Additional Information:
Calumet Division Headquarters
Cook County Forest Preserve District
Dan Ryan Woods
87th St. and Western Ave.
Chicago, IL 60620
(312) 233-3766
(312) 233-3767

Conservation Department
General Headquarters
Cook County Forest Preserve District
536 N. Harlem Ave.
River Forest, IL 60305
(312) 261-8400—Chicago number
(312) 366-9420—Suburban number

Cantigny

Cantigny is renowned for both its historical associations and its natural qualities. The Robert R. McCormick Museum is the central attraction of the 500-acre estate, but nearby are 10 acres of lovely gardens and more than 200 acres of wild woodlands to explore.

The gardens of Cantigny, rated among the finest in America, are divided into seventeen areas. Drawing upon the Japanese art of creating "alive rooms," the landscape architect designed each garden as a self-contained unit. The plants, several of which had never been tested in the Chicago environs before, were selected to provide color and drama throughout the year. More than 85,000 plants are grown annually in Cantigny's greenhouses for display in the gardens.

Self-guided tours are enhanced by a brochure that describes points of interest along the way. In a grove of rare trees, you'll see the dawn redwood, thought for many years to be extinct until it was rediscovered in China in 1945. The Chicago Peace Rose was first developed at Cantigny and now adorns gardens throughout the world. Near the end of your tour, pause to admire a massed bed of 4,000 begonias, grown here from seed so minute that all 4,000 could be piled on one dime.

Once you've toured the floral displays, take time to wander through the natural woodlands via a system of well-defined trails. Picnicking is also permitted on the grounds. The areas provided are among the cleanest you'll find anywhere.

The magnificent Georgian mansion that was the McCormick home is also open to the public. Another attraction here is the First Division Museum, which depicts the history of this famous combat unit during two world wars and in Vietnam. Colonel McCormick was deputy commander of one of the division's artillery battalions during World War I, a fact of which he was very proud, but he is best known in the Chicago area for his tenure as editor and publisher of the *Chicago Tribune*.

How to Get There: From Wheaton, go west on Roosevelt Rd. (IL 38) to Winfield Rd., then turn left. Entrance is on left side of Winfield.

Grounds and gardens open daily during daylight hours. McCormick Museum (housed in McCormick mansion) open daily, noon–5:00 P.M., Memorial Day–Labor Day; noon–4:00 P.M., Wed.–Sun., rest of year; closed in Jan. First Division Museum open daily, 9:00 A.M.–5:00 P.M., Memorial Day–Labor Day; 10:00 A.M.–4:00 P.M., except Mon., rest of year; closed in Jan. Parking on grounds. Everything is free.

For Additional Information:
Cantigny
1 S. 151 Winfield Rd.
Wheaton, IL 60187
(312) 668-5161

Cary Prairie

This three-acre prairie that adorns a hillside next to the junior high school in the village of Cary is one of the few remaining remnants of virgin prairie around Chicago. Although small in size, the grassland supports approximately sixty varieties of prairie plants. The best known stands of rattlesnake master and leadplant in McHenry County find room to thrive here among big bluestem and tall Indian grass.

Discovered in 1978 by a science teacher, this prairie is now a valued possession in which the whole community takes pride, and the general public is invited to share it. You may wander through it at your leisure, or participate in some of the guided walks offered each summer.

How to Get There: Located at the edge of the village of Cary in southeastern McHenry County. From the intersection of US 14 and First St. just west of Cary, go north on First St. to Sunset St. Turn right (east) and proceed on Sunset to Crest St. At Crest St., turn left (north) and go to Oriole Trail. Turn right (east) onto Oriole and proceed to the junior high school on Oriole. Park at west end of school parking lot, and walk south about 50 yards to prairie.

Open daily, year-round, during daylight hours. Free. If possible, the school would appreciate a call first.

For Additional Information:
Principal
Junior High School
Oriole Trail
Cary, IL 60013
(312) 639-2148—During School Year

Administration Office
School District #26
Oak Knoll School
First St.
Cary, IL 60013
(312) 639-7788—During Summer Months

Chain O'Lakes State Park

The largest concentration of natural lakes in Illinois lies in the vicinity of Chain O'Lakes State Park just south of the Wisconsin border. Fed by the beautiful Fox River, which flows through the park from north to south, the ten connected lakes have a combined surface area of more than 6,000 acres and a shoreline of nearly 500 miles. Grass, Bluff, and Marie lakes touch the state park's eastern border, while the other seven (Fox, Catherine, Nippersink, Redhead, Channel, Petite, and Pistakee) are located just outside park boundaries. Except for Lake Michigan, this network of lakes formed by the last great glacier comprises the finest water playground in northeastern Illinois.

On most weekdays, in contrast to the hectic weekend scene,

the park offers a semblance of solitude. Birds and animals that take refuge during the weekend reappear, and the marsh areas come alive with the sounds of the natural world.

The entire region is chiefly freshwater bog overlying peat deposits. Of the park's 5,581 acres, 3,230 acres are set aside as a conservation area. Most of the land is covered with sparse to dense stands of timber that include hickory, oak, elm, birch, sumac, black cherry, Scotch pine, and spruce. Ground squirrels, gophers, chipmunks, white-tailed deer, cottontail rabbits, skunks, raccoons, foxes, and mink find shelter in the forest. In spring, the lake and marsh areas attract large numbers of songbirds, while in autumn, migrating waterfowl gather here. Saw-whet and great horned owls are occasionally seen in the area, and on a small lake about four miles west of Fox Lake, black terns nest every year.

Adding to the natural beauty of the park are the lotus beds of Grass Lake. Many people come to this park just to view the exquisite blooms. Since blossoming times vary, you may want to check with the superintendent's office before coming.

In the park's headquarters town of Spring Grove, a few miles west of the park itself, an Illinois State Fish Hatchery is open to the public free of charge. The bass, bluegill, sunfish, and Chinook salmon raised here are used primarily to stock state-owned waters and Lake Michigan.

This part of Illinois is also of historic interest. In the late seventeenth century, French voyageurs canoed down the placid Fox River, seeking furs to trade. The Sauk and Fox Indians lived here then, residing in wigwam villages the year round. During the Black Hawk War of 1831–32, Abraham Lincoln and Jefferson Davis served with the U.S. Army in the Chain O'Lakes area.

Hiking and Horseback Riding

A marked 2¼-mile nature trail loops through the woods. Although there are some hills, it provides an easy walk, and there's a shortcut available if you don't want to go the entire distance. A short circular trail has been designed especially for the handicapped. Horseback riders will find some 8 miles of trails; no rentals, but a special parking area is provided at the trail head.

Boating, Canoeing, and Fishing

The ten connected lakes and the river provide some fine boating experiences. Two public launch ramps are provided, and rentals are available. No limit on motor size on any lake.

One of the best ways to explore the lakes and the Fox River itself is by canoe. Because you may encounter heavy boat traffic on weekends, it's best to plan a canoe trip on other days.

Fishermen catch bluegill, bass, crappie, northern pike, walleye, catfish, and bullheads. River and bank fishing is permitted in certain areas, and some fishing piers are provided.

Camping

Three separate areas are available for camping; fourteen-day limit each thirty-day period. Only one area has hot showers. Electricity available at some sites; two sanitary stations.

Picnicking

Six separate picnic areas have tables, grills, water, and restrooms. Some playground equipment is available.

Winter Sports

A six-mile trail is open to cross-country skiers in season; part of the main office is used as a warming house. Sledding, ice skating, and ice fishing are also popular.

How to Get There: Located in Lake and McHenry counties. From the town of Fox Lake, take US 12 northwest to State Park Rd. and turn right. Follow signs to park entrance.

Open daily, year-round, during daylight hours. Free admission.

For Additional Information:
Superintendent
Chain O'Lakes State Park
729 E. State Park Rd.
Spring Grove, IL 60081
(312) 587-5512

Chicago Botanic Garden

Until 1965, this land was a desolate, polluted marsh, visited primarily by mosquitoes. Now it is a living, growing garden atop 300 acres of landfill. The insect-infested swamp has been transformed into a showplace, composed of low, wooded hills, carefully groomed lawns, placid lagoons, and an island-studded lake with shooting fountains.

Also a peaceful sanctuary for wildlife, the garden is home to wild ducks and geese, white-tailed deer, raccoons, opossums, foxes, and squirrels. Mute swans and a whistling swan, rarely seen in the Chicago region, have been sighted here in winter among the many water birds that are forced to seek food elsewhere when the waters of Lake Michigan are frozen over.

Owned by the Forest Preserve District of Cook County and managed by the Chicago Horticultural Society, the garden offers visitors a pleasant educational encounter with thousands of species of plants, shrubs, trees, and flowers, many of them rare, in varied habitats.

A fifteen-acre natural woodland known as Turnbull Woods has been enhanced with the addition of wildflowers, rhododendrons, ferns, and evergreens native to the northeastern United

States. Winding nature trails are bordered by labeled plants. In spring, the forest floor is carpeted with the beautiful pure white blossoms of the large-flowered trillium.

Any garden representative of the Illinois landscape would not be complete without a prairie. An ongoing restoration of this unique habitat will include samplings of unusual wildflowers and native grasses found in various types of prairies throughout the Midwest.

In a special "Trees of Illinois" section, you'll see some of the 110 species native to the state.

One of the most serene spots is Sansho-En, a cluster of three tiny islands planted as Japanese gardens.

Come here, too, for a reprieve from Chicago winters. Even on the coldest days, you'll see orchids blooming, and it's a good time to learn something about the cacti, succulents, ferns, and tropical flowers that are nurtured year-round in the greenhouses.

In the massive education center that is the hub of activity here, you'll find a gift shop, food service area, museum of botanical art, an exhibition hall with changing exhibits, and open courtyards with displays of bonsai. Narrated tram tours of the grounds depart here on a regular basis from mid-April through October, and special programs and lectures are scheduled throughout the year. Also on the grounds are demonstration gardens, a research area, and home landscape center.

How to Get There: Located at the northeastern tip of Cook County. From the intersection of US 41 (here called Edens Parkway) and Lake Cook Rd. (at the Lake–Cook County line), head east on Lake Cook Rd. to the garden on the right. Parking on site.

Open daily, year-round, except Christmas. Grounds open 8:00 A.M.–5:00 P.M., Nov. 1–March 31; 8:00 A.M.–6:00 P.M., April 1–Memorial Day and Labor Day–Oct. 31; and 8:00 A.M.–8:00 P.M., Memorial Day–Labor Day. Education Center open daily 9:00 A.M.–4:00 P.M., year-round, except weekends Memorial Day–Labor Day, when it's open 9:00 A.M.–6:00 P.M. Free admission; nominal fee for tram tours.

For Additional Information:

Chicago Botanic Garden
P.O. Box 400
Glencoe, IL 60022
(312) 835-5440

Conservation Department
Cook County Forest Preserve District
536 N. Harlem Ave.
River Forest, IL 60305
(312) 261-8400—Chicago number
(312) 366-9420—Suburban number

Chicago Zoological Park

See listing under Brookfield Zoo, p. 25.

Churchill Woods Forest Preserve

A linear park containing some 250 acres, Churchill Woods lies along the sinewy shoreline of the East Branch of the DuPage River. Dense oak woods cover most of the terrain, luring songbirds and small mammals in abundance. Making the area even more attractive to wildlife are several open ponds, patches of marsh, and fishing lagoons. Three islands in the river are accessible by foot.

In the northernmost part of the preserve, the march of time has been reversed. A forty-five-acre prairie restoration recreates the landscape of chest-high grasses and nodding flowers seen by the first white settlers in this area.

Hiking and Horseback Riding

The Churchill Prairie Trail winds through woods and prairie. A steep hill along the way provides an observation point with a spectacular view of the surrounding territory. The Illinois Prairie Path for hikers and bicyclists (described elsewhere) passes near the southeast corner of the preserve. Horseback riders will find a trail through the woods for their use. No rentals; annual registration is required.

Fishing

Shoreline fishing in park waters yields sunfish, carp, goldfish, largemouth and smallmouth bass, crappie, bluegill, and bullhead.

Picnicking

Picnic tables are provided in several locations, with drinking water and toilets close by. Both a shelter and an entire picnic area may be reserved in advance for a fee.

Winter Sports

Ice skating and fishing are permitted when ice is at least three inches thick. Although there are no marked trails, cross-country skiers may break their own.

How to Get There: Located near the center of DuPage County, just northeast of Glen Ellyn. From the intersection of IL 53 and IL 38 (Roosevelt Rd.) in Glen Ellyn, go north on IL 53 to St. Charles Rd. Turn left (west) on St. Charles and proceed to park. Churchill Woods lies on both sides of St. Charles Rd., about half a mile west of IL 53. Parking on site.

Open daily, year-round, from one hour after sunrise to one hour after sunset. Free.

For Additional Information:
DuPage County Forest Preserve District
P.O. Box 2339
Glen Ellyn, IL 60137
(312) 620-3800

Fullersburg Woods Nature Center
3609 Spring Rd.
Oak Brook, IL 60521
(312) 620-3843

Crabtree Nature Center

One of the finest holdings of the entire Cook County Forest Preserve District, Crabtree Nature Center is a delight for nature lovers. Situated in the far northwest corner of the county, the center lies atop some 1,100 acres of gently rolling hills dotted with lakes, ponds, groves of woodland, meadows, marsh, and prairie.

This wilderness preserve is intended only for nature study and education. Near the parking lot, overlooking Sulky Pond, is an interpretive building that houses a fine natural history museum. In the middle of the large exhibit room is a man-made pond filled with rocks, goldfish, and reeds of grass. The displays that surround it include dioramas that explore such natural wonders as the migratory travels of monarch butterflies and Canada geese, the integral character of a marsh, and the history of glaciers. Freshwater fish tanks permit you to view the watery world of largemouth bass, bluegill, sunfish, and bullhead. Enchanting butterfly mobiles hang from the ceiling, and a live fox snake lies curled in its cage.

Just outside the back door, a resident flock of wild Canada geese sometimes struts boldly along the sidewalk. Wild and free-flying, the geese are but one of the more than 70 species that nest here. All are included on a checklist of nearly 250 types of birds that have been sighted at the nature center since 1964, soon after the forest preserve district began purchasing this land. During spring and fall, the sanctuary teems with waterfowl, lured here by several areas of open water and by some 200 acres of cultivated cropland that provide food for them. An observation blind that overlooks 75-acre Crabtree Lake is a good place from which to view the thousands of ducks and geese that settle down on the lake during migration. Even during winter, when part of the surface of Crabtree Lake is kept free of ice by water pumps, the waterfowl number in the hundreds. Wading birds favor secluded Bulrush Pond, which is bordered by woods and marsh.

As you walk the trails of Crabtree, you'll see many kinds of wildlife grown bold with the growing realization that no one here will harm them and that they can raise their young in peace. You may spot white-tailed deer, red and gray foxes, ground squirrels, raccoons, mink, or opossums.

One of the best places to see many of these species is in the relatively isolated stretch of prairie, a faithful reconstruction begun in the late 1960s that closely resembles the native grasslands that so awed the pioneers. Some sixty acres of ground were seeded with grasses that, due to a limited local supply, were brought in from Nebraska, and with wildflowers that were hand-harvested from a few surviving prairie remnants in nearby areas.

Two fine natural areas, both designated state nature preserves, lie near the nature center. Just to the northwest is 560-acre Spring Lake Preserve, a wildlife refuge known for its scenic beauty. The natural lake is fed by Spring Creek as it lazily winds its way northward through a broad valley. Along its shores lie picturesque cattail marshes that attract myriads of waterfowl, broad open meadows, and mesic prairie where rare flora thrive.

Shoe Factory Road Preserve, a nine-acre remnant of gravel-hill prairie, lies not far south of Crabtree. Totally fenced in for protection, it offers an unusual combination of plant species seldom found in this area. The side-oats grama, little bluestem, and many-flowered scurfy pea that generally are found on hill or bluff prairies flourish among the blazing stars, compass plant, prairie dock, rattlesnake master, and downy gentian that are indicative of wetter grasslands. To visit both preserves, you must first obtain permission from the naturalist at Crabtree Nature Center. Directions will be given at that time.

Northeast of Crabtree is Deer Grove Forest Preserve, nearly 1,000 acres of woods, marsh, and lakes that offer picnicking, fishing, hiking, and winter sports. All of the aforementioned preserves are part of the Cook County Forest Preserve District's Northwest Division. Made up of several widely scattered properties, including Ned Brown Forest Preserve (described elsewhere), it is the district's newest division and is still being organized.

Hiking

The 1$^{2}/_{3}$-mile-long Phantom Prairie Trail leads past Sulky Pond and through the woods to the center's prairie reconstruction. A printed trail guide includes illustrations of some of the plants you will see along the way. The Crabtree Lake waterfowl sanctuary is one of the highlights of the Bur Edge Trail, which also takes you through bur oak woodlands, past two ponds, across prairie and meadow, and around a marsh along its 1$^{1}/_{3}$-mile-long loop route. Part of the trail guide for this latter hike is changed monthly to depict its most interesting features at the time. Both trails are level and easy to walk.

Picnicking

Although no picnicking is allowed at Crabtree Nature Center itself, picnic facilities are available at Deer Grove Forest Preserve 2$^{1}/_{2}$ miles northeast of Crabtree. Tables and drinking water are available, but you'll have to bring your own grill.

How to Get There: Located in northwestern Cook County. From the intersection of US 14 and Palatine Rd. in the village of Palatine, go west on Palatine Rd. to Crabtree Nature Center on the right (north) side of the road. To reach Deer Grove from Crabtree's entrance road, head east on Palatine Rd. to Barrington Rd. and turn left (north). Proceed on Barrington Rd. to Dundee Rd. and turn right (east). Continue on Dundee to Deer Grove's entrance road on the left (north) just after you pass US 14. Parking on both sites.

Crabtree open daily, year-round, from 8:00 A.M. to about half an hour before sunset; closed Thanksgiving, Christmas, and New Year's Day. Exhibit building open 9:00 A.M.–5:00 P.M., March–Oct.; and 9:00 A.M.–4:00 P.M., Nov.–Feb. All free. Group visits are encouraged; reservations should be made in advance by calling the Forest Preserve District Conservation Department. Deer Grove open daily, year-round, sunrise to sunset. Free.

For Additional Information:
Crabtree Nature Center
Rt. 1, Box 334
Stover Rd.
Barrington, IL 60010
(312) 381-6592

Conservation Department
Cook County Forest Preserve District
536 N. Harlem Ave.
River Forest, IL 60305
(312) 261-8400—Chicago number
(312) 366-9420—Suburban number

Northwest Division Headquarters
Cook County Forest Preserve District
Golf Rd. and Frontage Rd. East (I-290)
Rolling Meadows, IL 60008
(312) 437-8330

Deer Grove Forest Preserve

See listing under Crabtree Nature Center, p. 36.

Des Plaines Forest Preserve Division

This lovely division of the Cook County Forest Preserve District, noted for its maple trees, primarily borders the Des Plaines River and preserves much of the stream's wooded shoreline between the Cook–Lake County line to the north and the district's Indian Boundary Forest Preserve Division (described elsewhere) to the south. Together, the two divisions offer a quiet riverside retreat more than twenty miles in length.

The River Trail Nature Center near the division's midsection is filled with exhibits that will delight people of all ages. Outside, you may saunter along trails whose markers inform you of the area's Indian and pioneer history. A prairie restoration recaptures the splendor of the area's original landscape, and life in an Indian village is depicted in a display that includes a tepee.

There are gardens galore here—a wild birdseed garden, a moss garden, a garden of herbs that were cultivated by the early white settlers of the region, another garden containing the herbs the Indians used for medicinal purposes, a unique Eurasian weed garden with plants similar to those of the prairie community. Working beehives stand in the midst of a small orchard. Each fall, during the nature center's annual Harvest and Honey festival, you may watch as the honey is removed from the hives, strained, and put into jars. The honey is then sold to the public, along with honey apples, hot buttered sweet corn, Indian corn, pumpkins, and gourds. It all takes place against a background of gorgeous fall colors.

In the spring, usually in late March, a Maple Syrup festival is held at the center.

Near the west end of one of the center's parking lots, along the banks of the Des Plaines River, you may feed a flock of wild ducks that makes its home here year-round. More ducks visit the center's "Ye Olde Fishing Hole," whose muddy waters harbor bass, catfish, northern pike, and bluegill. Two small creeks wind through the nearby woods.

Across the road from the exhibit building, such animals as a coyote, raccoon, skunk, opossum, and bobcat cavort in their outdoor cages. More wildlife is exhibited inside the pioneer-style museum that serves as the center's headquarters. Since emphasis here is placed on the importance of seasonal changes to both man and wildlife, many exhibits change as the year progresses.

Elsewhere in the division, the Camp Pine Woods and Lake Avenue Woods are noted for the abundance and variety of their spring wildflowers. A picturesque pioneer cabin at Camp Pine Woods is nestled in a grove of huge cottonwoods, and the remains of some Indian charcoal pits may be seen along the east bank of the Des Plaines River just south of the Cook–Lake County line.

There are many scenic spots in the division, but the areas known as Dam No. 1 Woods and Dam No. 2 Woods, belying their plain names, are particularly beautiful, especially in the fall.

Hiking, Bicycling, and Horseback Riding

One main trail extends from one end of the preserve to the other. At its south end, it connects up with the trail in the adjoining Indian Boundary Division. From its southern terminus to the Dam No. 1 picnic area, a distance of about 10 miles, the trail is designed for use by hikers, bicyclists, and horseback riders (no rentals; annual horse registration and rider's license required); north of Dam No. 1, hikers may continue another two miles to the Cook–Lake County line. Two nature trails at the

River Trail Nature Center, one ³/₄-mile long, the other ¹/₂-mile long, lead to interesting natural and historical attractions.

Boating and Fishing

All types of watercraft and motors are allowed on the Des Plaines River; two free launch ramps for canoes and rowboats are located in the southern third of the division. Canoes, sailboats, and rowboats may be launched at the free ramps provided at E. J. Beck and Big Bend lakes; electric motors only are allowed. There are no boat rentals at this division.

The waters of the Des Plaines River are cleaner within the boundaries of this division than elsewhere in Cook County and therefore offer the best fishing. Northern pike, largemouth bass, yellow bass, bluegill, channel catfish, and crappie are among the species that lure anglers here to fish from boats and shoreline alike. Big Bend, Belleau, and E. J. Beck lakes, as well as Pottawatomi Pond, are stocked with many of the same species. Shoreline fishing only is permitted at Belleau Lake and Pottawatomi Pond. From May through September, the nature center sponsors a fishing contest, giving prizes for record catches from "Ye Olde Fishing Hole."

Picnicking

The quiet woodlands of this division offer some lovely picnic areas on both banks of the Des Plaines River. Most include shelters and grills; and you'll find parking space, drinking water, and toilet facilities near all of them. Groups of twenty-five or more must obtain a permit in advance by personally visiting the Permit Office, Room 230, County Building, 118 N. Clark St., Chicago.

Winter Sports

Pottawatomi Pond is cleared for ice skating, while ice fishermen use Belleau and E. J. Beck lakes. Cross-country skiers may use any part of division trails and lands except the grounds of the nature center.

How to Get There: Located along the banks of the Des Plaines River near Mount Prospect in northeastern Cook County; bounded on the north by the Cook–Lake County line and on the south by Touhy Ave. Since each division of the Cook County Forest Preserve District features several recreation areas and attractions, crisscrossed by many roads and in some instances disconnected, it's best to obtain division maps, directions for getting there, and other pertinent information from district or division headquarters before visiting one. To reach Des Plaines Division headquarters from the intersection of IL 83 (Main St.) and Central Rd. in Mount Prospect, head east on Central Rd. to Wolf Rd. and turn left (north). Continue on Wolf Rd. to Foundry Rd. and turn right (east). Go east on Foundry Rd. to its terminus at Des Plaines River Rd. The entrance road to division headquarters is on the east side of Des Plaines River Rd. opposite Foundry Rd. To reach the River Trail

Nature Center from the intersection of Foundry Rd. and Des Plaines River Rd., go north on River Rd. to Milwaukee Ave. (US 45/IL 21) and turn right (southeast). Proceed on Milwaukee Ave. across the Des Plaines River to the nature center's entrance road on the right (west) side.

Preserve lands open daily, year-round, sunrise to sunset; free. Headquarters offices open Mon.–Fri., year-round, 8:30 A.M.–5:00 P.M.; closed major holidays. Grounds at River Trail Nature Center open Mon.–Fri., 8:30 A.M.–5:00 P.M.; and on Sat., Sun., and most holidays, 9:00 A.M.–5:30 P.M.; exhibit building closed half an hour earlier than grounds Sat.–Thurs. and all day on Fridays, Thanksgiving, Christmas, and New Year's Day; free.

For Additional Information:
Des Plaines Division Headquarters
Cook County Forest Preserve District
801 N. River Rd..
Mount Prospect, IL 60056
(312) 824-1900
(312) 824-1883

Conservation Department
General Headquarters
Cook County Forest Preserve District
536 N. Harlem Ave.
River Forest, IL 60305
(312) 261-8400—Chicago number
(312) 366-9420—Suburban number

Des Plaines Game Farm

See listing under Des Plaines State Conservation Area, p. 42.

Des Plaines River Trail

The Des Plaines River has become increasingly popular as a source of recreation in recent years. Because of this, the Lake County Forest Preserve District is attempting to acquire as much land along the riverbanks as possible, both to create more access to the river and to permit the area to return to its natural state. One part of this project is the creation of a county-long trail that parallels the stream, and recently the first segment of that trail was opened to the public.

Beginning near the Wisconsin border, the 6.3-mile-long trail is used by hikers, horseback riders, and cross-country skiers. For the most part it follows the west bank of the river and is accessible at several points along the way. The northern terminus of the trail lies near Sterling Lake in the Van Patten Woods Forest Preserve, where visitors will find car and trailer parking, drinking water, pit toilets, and an 80-acre lake stocked with largemouth and smallmouth bass, northern pike, crappie, yellow perch, and panfish. In another part of the 908-acre Van Patten Woods Preserve are some picnic areas and a short nature trail.

The Wadsworth Prairie, an intriguing area of marsh and wet prairie limited to pedestrians only, supports a wealth of flora and fauna on its 140 acres. It is accessible from the Des Plaines River Trail, and although there are no improved trails, hikers are welcome to explore this lovely natural area.

At Wadsworth Road, near the southern terminus of the trail, there are more visitor facilities—car and trailer parking, drinking water, pit toilets, a canoe launch, and a fishing dock that extends into the Des Plaines River.

The trail is wooded along much of its length and attracts a variety of birds. Since the river itself is a migration route, birdwatching is particularly good in the spring and fall. Bald eagles and Swainson's hawks, both extremely rare, are occasionally seen along the river, and the wooded areas are home to several species of owls.

How to Get There: Located along the Des Plaines River in northeastern Lake County. The northern terminus of the trail begins along the shoreline of Sterling Lake in Van Patten Woods Forest Preserve. From the intersection of US 41 and IL 173, west of Zion, go north on US 41; a park road turns right off US 41 just north of this intersection. Look for signs. To gain access to the trail near its southern terminus, go south on US 41 from the same intersection. At Wadsworth Rd., turn left. The trail crosses Wadsworth Rd. on the west bank of the river. Parking is available at both sites. Before using the trail, horseback riders must obtain a permit from the district office; there are no rentals on preserve lands. A free trail guide is available from the district office.

Open daily, year-round, from 8:00 A.M. to sunset. Free.

For Additional Information:
Lake County Forest Preserve District
2000 N. Milwaukee Ave.
Libertyville, IL 60048
(312) 367-6640

Des Plaines State Conservation Area

The Des Plaines State Conservation Area southwest of Chicago, acclaimed as one of the most popular outdoor playgrounds in Illinois, offers a diversity of natural features and recreational opportunities. Encompassing more than 4,200 acres, including some 200 acres of water, the conservation area is a mecca for nature lovers. Its mixed habitat harbors a rich variety of flora and fauna.

Along the area's southern boundary, the broad, slow-flowing Kankakee River creates a 1 1/2-mile-long shoreline, while the Des Plaines River briefly touches the area's northern border. The backwaters of both rivers, several ponds, creeks, and Milliken Lake lie within the conservation area and attract great concentrations of ducks and geese during migratory periods. Part of the backwater area is designated a waterfowl refuge.

Fields of fertile farmland are planted in crops favored by such wildlife as pheasants, white-tailed deer, rabbits, doves, and waterfowl. Woodlands and pockets of swamp are also part of the environment here.

In addition, there are two expanses of native prairie that support an abundance of prairie flora. The larger tract, the 78-acre Grant Creek Prairie, has been set aside as a state nature preserve. Within its boundaries are both mesic and wet prairie communities where more than 100 plant species thrive. The wet prairie is dominated by bluejoint grass, sedges, and cordgrass, while the mesic supports big bluestem, prairie dropseed, and Indian grass.

Adjacent to the conservation area is the 320-acre Des Plaines Game Farm. The 80,000 pheasants raised here annually are used for stocking hunting areas throughout Illinois. Visitors are welcome.

Hiking

Although there are no designated hiking trails, visitors may roam freely throughout the conservation area. There are several secondary roads with numerous parking spots and trails used by hunters and fishermen.

Boating, Canoeing, and Fishing

Boating and canoeing are permitted on the Kankakee River and on the backwaters of both the Kankakee and Des Plaines rivers; none is allowed on Milliken Lake. Boats in the backwaters are limited to a maximum of ten horsepower, but there is no horsepower limitation for boats launched on the Kankakee River, where free boat ramps are provided. Although there are no rentals on state-owned lands, the Three Rivers Marina is located on the Des Plaines River shoreline near the conservation area's northern boundary.

Milliken Lake, various ponds, and river backwaters offer largemouth bass, channel catfish, and panfish. The Kankakee River provides the same species, along with walleye and northern pike.

Camping

Camping facilities for tents only are provided in designated areas. Water, chemical toilets, and picnic tables are available. Campsites closed November through February.

Picnicking

One picnic area lies west of I-55 (which bisects the conservation area), and another is located adjacent to Milliken Lake on the east side of I-55. Tables, stoves, shelters, playground equipment, and chemical toilets are provided.

Winter Sports

Ice fishing is as popular here as warm-weather, open water angling.

How to Get There: Located in Will County. From Joliet, go west on I-80 to I-55. Turn south on I-55 and proceed to the Wilmington exit (last exit before crossing the Kankakee River); this exit is also known as Co. Rd. 304/44 and as River Rd. The conservation area extends both east and west of this exit. To reach the office, turn west; it lies on the right side of River Rd.

Open daily, year-round, except Christmas and New Year's Day, during daylight hours. Free.

For Additional Information:

Superintendent
Des Plaines Conservation Area
R.R. 3, Box 167
Wilmington, IL 60481
(815) 423-5326

Superintendent
Des Plaines Game Farm
R.R. 3, Box 189
Wilmington, IL 60481
(815) 476-6741

Dole Wildlife Sanctuary

In keeping with its nature-oriented purposes, the Illinois Audubon Society has established its headquarters on thirty-five acres of land that form an ideal wildlife habitat. The ecosystems at Dole Sanctuary include an open pond with a small island near its center, a meandering creek, an alkaline fen, patches of woodland that contain both hardwoods and evergreens, a broad meadow, a prairie restoration project, and an area aptly named Skunk Cabbage Bottom. Here, totally unhindered, birds and animals roam at will, wildflowers run rampant, and ferns and trees grow lush and full.

The Audubon Society has opened the parklike grounds of its sanctuary to the public for bird-watching, nature study, and photography. Also available, to members and nonmembers, are a continuing series of educational programs, a small gift store, and an ornithology/conservation research library.

Hiking and Horseback Riding

A marked trail loops and crisscrosses throughout the sanctuary for a total of 1 1/2 miles. Every habitat on the grounds may be observed from this pathway. Equestrians may bring their own horses and follow a shorter trail that skirts the western and southern boundaries of the area.

How to Get There: Located near the town of Wayne, which straddles the DuPage–Kane County line.

Open daily, year-round, during daylight hours. Grounds are always free, but the society requests that you call for an appointment before you visit. Exact directions will be given to you when you phone. Nominal fees are charged for some programs; nonmembers pay more than members.

For Additional Information:
Office Manager
Illinois Audubon Society
P.O. Box 608
Wayne, IL 60184
(312) 584-6290

The Ecology Center
See listing under Ladd Arboretum, p. 78.

Elgin Botanical Garden
See listing under Trout Park, p. 126.

Elsen's Hill Winter Sports Area
See listing under West DuPage Woods Forest Preserve, p. 133.

Fabyan Forest Preserve
A mix of woods and landscaped lawns, Fabyan Forest Preserve covers some 260 acres on both sides of the Fox River just south of Geneva. Once part of the estate of Colonel George Fabyan, the park also contains a number of historic features.

The estate's main house, now a museum that reflects the varied interests of Colonel Fabyan, was designed by Frank Lloyd Wright. Not far away, in a quiet setting enhanced by mature trees, is a small Japanese garden with reflecting pools, winding pathways, an arched bridge, and a teahouse. The entrance gate is kept locked most of the time, but the garden may easily be viewed from the picturesque fence that encloses it. Groups of ten or more may enter the garden if they request permission in advance, and it may also be reserved for weddings.

On the east side of the river is an authentic Dutch windmill, one of a handful in Illinois. Colonel Fabyan purchased it in 1914 for $8,000, then had it disassembled, transported to his home, and reconstructed there for an additional cost of $70,000. Estimated to be more than 130 years old, it's now on the National Register of Historic Places.

A small island in the Fox River, accessible by a footbridge, has an interesting lighthouse on it.

Beyond the preserve's buildings and open fields are dense woodlands that may be explored on foot or, in places, on a bicycle. Great horned owls congregate in the forest from December to May, while warblers and shorebirds gather here in April and May. In late November and December, snow and blue geese often fly over the river, and goshawks regularly visit the river's environs in winter.

Boating and Fishing

The Fox River is one of the most beautiful and most popular canoe streams in northeastern Illinois. A free launch ramp is available on the west bank of Fabyan Preserve. Fishermen pursue their sport from small boats or the shoreline, hoping to catch the bluegill, crappie, largemouth bass, and catfish that lurk in the depths of the river.

Picnicking

Tree-shaded tables along the river's edge and a shelter house are provided. Restrooms and drinking water are nearby.

Winter Sports

Ice skaters, ice fishermen, and cross-country skiers use the preserve in winter.

How to Get There: Located just south of Geneva in east central Kane County. To reach park on east bank of the Fox River: from the intersection of IL 38 (here called State St.) and IL 25 (here called Bennett St.) in Geneva, go south on IL 25. Preserve borders both sides of IL 25 about one mile south of intersection. To reach park on west bank of the Fox River: follow directions above. Continue past east park entrance to Fabyan Pkwy. and turn right (west). Proceed on Fabyan Pkwy. across the Fox River to IL 31 and turn right (north) again. Entrance to west park is a short distance north on the right (east) side of IL 31. Parking on both sides of the river in park.

Open daily, year-round, 8:00 A.M.–9:00 P.M., May 1–Sept. 15; 8:00 A.M.–8:00 P.M., Sept. 16–April 30. Windmill open 1:00–5:00 P.M., Sun. and holidays, June 1–Sept. 1. All free.

For Additional Information:
Kane County Forest Preserve District
719 Batavia Ave.
Geneva, IL 60134
(312) 232-1242

Fermilab Prairie

Although prairie restorations are not uncommon in the Midwest, the restored grassland at the Fermi National Accelerator Laboratory (Fermilab for short) is unique in one respect. It is enclosed by an atom smasher. While atomic fragments whirl about in a four-mile-long proton accelerator heading toward their destiny as tools for the investigation of matter, the rich earth the accelerator encircles nurtures a native prairie ecosystem.

The project had its beginnings in 1974 when The Nature Conservancy approached Fermilab, a federal nuclear research facility, with a plan to rebuild a portion of this area's original tall-

The Chinese Garden in the Fabyan Forest Preserve   *Bill Thomas*

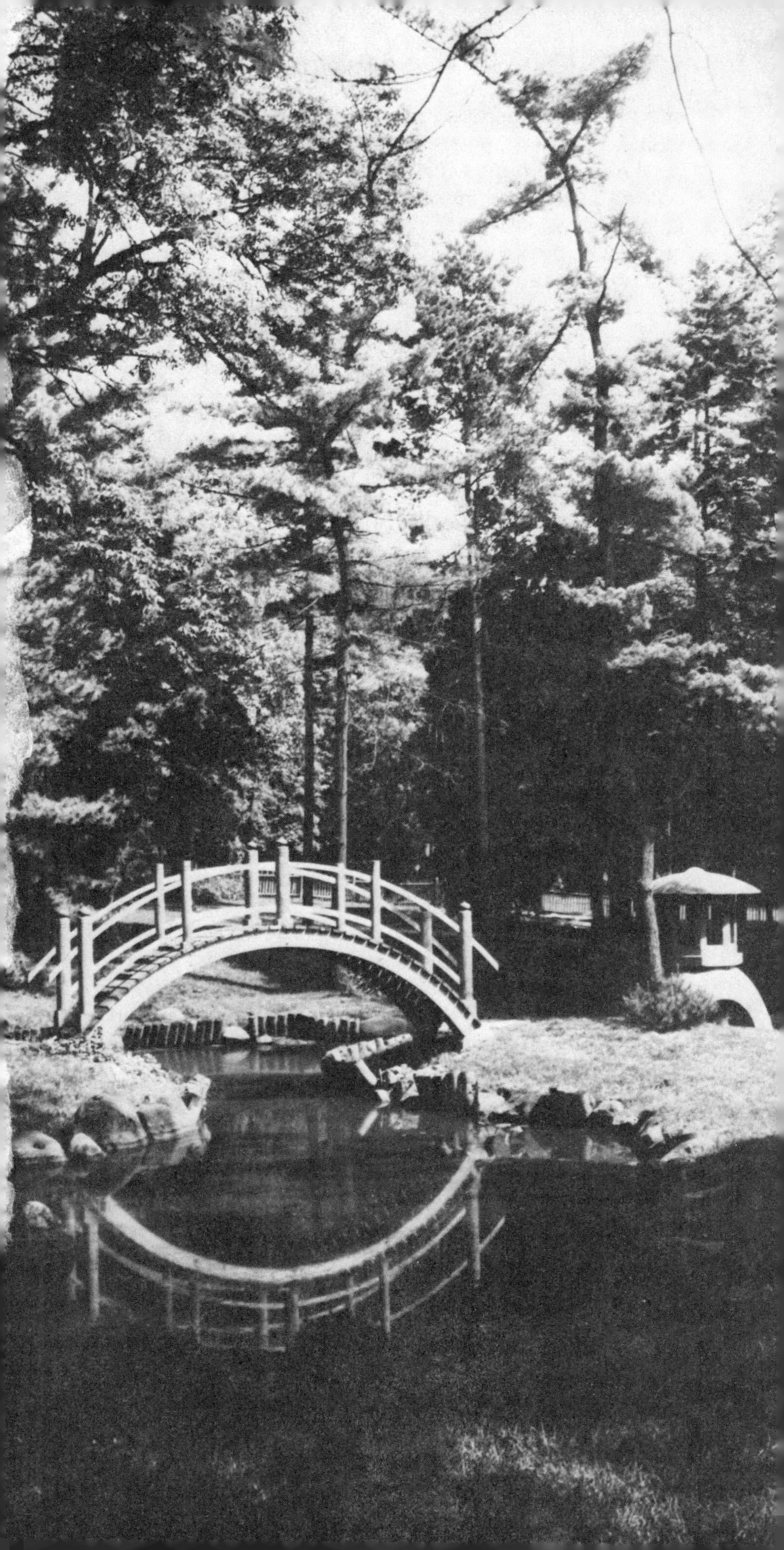

grass prairie landscape. Since the 640 acres within Fermilab's main accelerator ring are enclosed by a berm of earth that covers the underground accelerator, as well as a canal that supplies cooling water used in the acceleration process, they provided favorable conditions for such a project. Fire is an essential ingredient in the ecology of a prairie because it winnows out intruding plants and encourages the growth of true prairie species. Setting such a fire inside a circular canal helps to contain the flames. In addition, this site was historically a prairie marsh and still contains such remnants from the past as a bur oak grove, patches of marsh, and some small lakes.

Rebuilding began with the planting of prairie seed on an eight-acre section near the bur oak grove in June 1975. In order to simulate the original landscape as closely as possible, all seed was harvested from such undeveloped lands as old cemeteries and railroad rights-of-way within a fifty-mile radius. The first plants to be started were the big and little bluestem, Indian, and switch grasses, since they were the predominant species of the original Illinois prairie. Over the years, the prairie has gradually been enlarged to about 250 acres, with some new plant species being added each year. Plans call for the entire circle to be filled by the mid–1980s.

Animals, too, are part of a real prairie. It is expected that some will establish themselves on the preserve, while other creatures, such as certain prairie insects, may be introduced.

Architects of the landscape at Fermilab have created a parklike atmosphere on the facility's entire 6,800 acres. A second grassland, the Prairie Demonstration Plot, covers a forty-foot by forty-foot area. Existing groves of trees have been preserved, and new trees have been planted, providing shelter for the white-tailed deer and small game that live here. Several artificial lakes, developed to collect surface water, and two ponds in which heated water from the accelerator cools down combine with the marshy areas to provide habitat for a sizable population of geese, ducks, and swans. A herd of nearly fifty buffalo roams a pasture near the center of the facility.

In Wilson Hall, the hub of activity at Fermilab, visitors may enjoy a lush indoor garden. The atrium here, one of the world's largest, features plants and shrubs that thrive year-round in prevailing light conditions. History buffs will want to see a display of stone tools, arrowheads, and pottery shards dating back to 7,000 B.C., all discovered on the Fermilab site by local residents. Also notable are the distinctive architectural designs and several pieces of sculpture, some of which are located outside. From time to time, special exhibits are shown in the second floor gallery of Wilson Hall; and Fermilab sponsors a variety of cultural and scientific activities (schedules are available from the Public Information Office) that are open to the public.

How to Get There: Located in Kane and DuPage counties. From Batavia, go east on Wilson Rd. to Kirk Rd. and turn right. Proceed to Fermilab's main entrance on the left side of Kirk Rd. (opposite Pine St.).

Open daily, 8:30 A.M.–5:00 P.M., year-round for self-guided tours (no more than six people in a group). Since some parts of Fermilab are closed to the public, be sure to pick up a free tour pamphlet at the reception desk in Wilson Hall. Guided tours for groups of ten or more, ninth-grade age and over, are available Monday through Friday by appointment only; at least three months notice is advised. Free.

For Additional Information:
Public Information Office
Fermilab
P.O. Box 500
Batavia, IL 60510
(312) 840-3351

Ferson's Creek Marsh

See listing under Norris Woods, p. 94.

Forest Preserve Districts of Northeastern Illinois

The forest preserve districts of northeastern Illinois are similar to county park departments in other states. Although several of their properties are described separately throughout this book, space does not permit the listing of every one. In addition, these districts are continually acquiring new park areas and adding new facilities to existing parks. Among them are some of the most beautiful green spaces and choicest natural areas in the Chicago region. Readers who would like to know more about such sites should contact each district office.

For Additional Information:
Cook County Forest Preserve District
536 N. Harlem Ave.
River Forest, IL 60305
(312) 261-8400—City
(312) 366-9420—Suburban

DuPage County Forest Preserve District
P.O. Box 2339
Glen Ellyn, IL 60137
(312) 620-3800

Kane County Forest Preserve District
719 S. Batavia Ave.
Geneva, IL 60134
(312) 232-1242

Lake County Forest Preserve District
2000 N. Milwaukee Ave.
Libertyville, IL 60048
(312) 367-6640

McHenry County Conservation District
6512 Harts Rd.
Ringwood, IL 60072
(815) 338-1405
(815) 678-4431

Will County Forest Preserve District
US 52 and Cherry Hill Rd., R.R. 4
Joliet, IL 60433
(815) 727-8700

Fullersburg Woods Nature Preserve

Each spring, visitors throng to Fullersburg Woods Nature Preserve to view a pile of bones. The bones, some 300 of them, belonged to a woolly mammoth who roamed these parts 14,000 years ago and were discovered in 1977 at another DuPage County preserve (see Blackwell Recreational Preserve).

The mammoth made big news when it was accidentally discovered by a bulldozer operator because scientists had believed for years that the woolly mammoth had never been in this part of the world. Now the remains are kept in storage at Fullersburg and exhibited briefly once a year. The Forest Preserve District plans to put them on permanent display as soon as a suitable place can be found at one of its preserves.

But Fullersburg Woods is noted for much more than woolly mammoth bones. This 200-acre tract is home to the Environmental Education Center of the Forest Preserve District of DuPage County. As such, it is dedicated to depicting local ecology and natural history through a wide range of nature programs and attractions.

Salt Creek, which flows through the heart of the preserve, is heavily polluted, but improving, and makes an interesting study area. Duck blinds are provided for observation and photography. There's a "history-rock" garden, and free weekend lectures and field trips are oriented to the entire family.

One unique feature is a living freshwater marsh, complete with frogs, salamanders, and the appropriate insects, that has been constructed indoors for year-round observation.

The tiny creatures that freely roam the woodlands and marsh outdoors include chipmunks, foxes, woodchucks, indigo buntings, and Baltimore orioles.

At the southernmost tip of the preserve are the Old Graue Mill and Museum. This 1850 waterwheel grist mill still operates, and visitors may purchase stone-ground yellow cornmeal to take home. The museum occupies the second and third floors of the mill, with exhibits on local farm life of the 1800s. If you're with a group, you may make advance reservations for spinning and weaving demonstrations.

Hiking and Horseback Riding

A 1½-mile loop trail provides easy walking along part of Salt Creek. Rented headsets provide sound interpretation through a series of lively programs that change with the seasons. Another trail approximately ¾-mile long leads in the opposite direction along Salt Creek, but you must return the same way you came. There's also a brief Woodland Wildflower Walk in an oak woods near the preserve's amphitheater; the first flowers usually appear in late April. A bridle trail encircles the preserve, a distance of about 3½ miles; no rentals. All riders must obtain a permit from the district office.

Picnicking

A small area with tables has been provided here so visitors may enjoy a picnic lunch as part of a day's outing; no fires permitted.

Winter Sports

Trails are open to cross-country skiers during snow season; sledding and tobogganing are also popular.

How to Get There: Located in east central DuPage County. From Glen Ellyn, take Roosevelt Rd. (IL 38) east to IL 83. Turn south to Ogden Ave. (US 34), then left to Spring Rd., and left again to park entrance on right. Parking on grounds.

Preserve open daily, year-round, from one hour after sunrise to one hour after sunset. Environmental center open daily, 9:00 A.M.–5:30 P.M., year-round; closed holidays and on winter weekends from Halloween to Feb. 15. Mill and museum open daily, 10:00 A.M.–5:00 P.M., from early May to late Oct. Preserve and center free; nominal admission fee to mill and museum.

For Additional Information:
Environmental Education Center
Fullersburg Woods
3609 Spring Rd.
Oak Brook, IL 60521
(312) 620-3843

Forest Preserve District of DuPage County
P.O. Box 2339
Glen Ellyn, IL 60137
(312) 620-3800

Gensburg–Markham Prairie

Less than twenty-five miles from the Chicago Loop, in the village of Markham, is a remarkable 120-acre stretch of open prairie. Classified as a lacustrine prairie, it lies on one of the few untouched remnants of the bed of ancient Lake Chicago.

The diverse composition of its rich soil supports a prairie plant community of more than 400 species. Such rare and unusual plants as small sundrops, grass pink orchid, colicroot, yellow-eyed grass, narrow-leaved sundew, and screwstem thrive alongside prairie dock, marsh phlox, coreopsis, and leadplant. The bobwhite quail, green prairie snake, regal fritillary butterfly, and red fox are rarely seen in this section of Illinois, but populations of them persist at Gensburg–Markham.

When the prairie's existence was first discovered in the early 1960s, the tract had been subdivided as a prelude to development. Neighborhood children used it as a playground, commercial florists gathered wildflowers—especially the popular *Liatris*—and some area residents dumped their garbage here. Once, just before a community game on Memorial Day, lawnmowers were brought in to create a baseball diamond in the midst of the compass plant, rattlesnake master, and thick prairie cordgrass.

This rare natural area in the heart of a town was saved for posterity because Dr. Robert Betz, one of the country's most noted prairie authorities, decided to take an after-dinner stroll while in the neighborhood visiting relatives. He went out and found himself confronted with a virgin prairie. From that point, it was a matter of getting the attention of the right people. The Gensburg family donated sixty acres of the tract, and The Nature Conservancy negotiated the purchase of the rest of the land.

Currently owned and managed by Northeastern Illinois University, where Dr. Betz is a member of the faculty, the preserve is open to the public for nature study.

Hiking

More than two miles of trails allow visitors to view the prairie. The flat dirt paths make for easy hiking.

How to Get There: Located south of Chicago in Markham. From I-57 near the west edge of Markham, take US 6 (195th St.) east to Troy Ave. and turn left to an entrance gate on the right side of the road, at the corner of Troy and 155th St. To reach another entrance gate, go east on US 6 from I-57, past Troy Ave., to Whipple St. and turn left to dead end at prairie fence.

Open Sat., Sun., and holidays from 10:00 A.M. to sunset; additional hours by appointment. Hours sometimes vary, so it's best to call or write Northeastern Illinois University before coming here. Prairie can be viewed through fence at any time. Free.

For Additional Information:

Department of Biological Sciences
Northeastern Illinois University
5500 North St. Louis Ave.
Chicago, IL 60625
(312) 583-4050

The Nature Conservancy
Illinois Field Office
79 W. Monroe St., Suite 708
Chicago, IL 60603
(312) 346-8166

Glacial Park–Nippersink Trail

Glacial Park, located near the village of Ringwood in northeastern McHenry County, contains 393 acres of peat bog, forested hills, natural marsh, and such glacial landforms as kettles, kames, eskers, and outwash plains. Much of the park borders Nippersink Creek, which meanders along the site's western boundary and through the northernmost reaches.

The unobstructed view from atop the treeless kames (ridges) is one of the main attractions here. Visitors may also learn the difference between a prehistoric bog and a marsh. In addition, Glacial Park offers a variety of outdoor recreational opportunities.

If you'd like to obtain literature and up-to-date information about all lands owned and/or managed by the McHenry County Conservation District, stop at their headquarters near the main entrance. The district, established in 1971, is in the process of acquiring and developing several new sites that will be open to the public in the future.

Hiking and Horseback Riding

A variety of hiking trails combine to provide a total length of $9^1/_2$ miles. Shortest is the Coyote Loop Trail, an easy walk of $^3/_4$ of a mile through old pastures and forest, past a marsh and a bog. An excellent self-guiding interpretive brochure for this trail can be picked up in the parking lot near the trailhead. The Deerpath Trail departs from the Coyote Loop Trail and circles through a hillier, more wooded section of the park for just over 2 miles before rejoining Coyote Loop Trail near its terminus. Those who hike Deerpath Trail will have several opportunities to view the surrounding countryside from atop glacial ridges. The longest trail in the park follows Nippersink Creek for $5^1/_2$ miles. Known as Nippersink Trail, it's also open to horseback riders (no rentals). Drinking water is available near the midway point along this trail, and farther north there's a shelter with picnic tables, fire rings, and restrooms.

Canoeing and Fishing

Nippersink Creek is also popular with canoeists. It is possible to launch a canoe in Glacial Park and follow the creek to its junction with the Fox River, then continue south to a pull-out point at the district's Hickory Grove site (described elsewhere). The Glacial Park launch is east of the intersection of Bernard Mill and Keystone roads at the park's western boundary. Restrooms and a parking lot here are open during the spring and summer only. Two other public parks are located between Glacial Park and Hickory Grove, and canoeists may pull out or put in at either. One is the Lyle C. Thomas Park and Landing (until recently known as Spring Grove Park Landing), a small, 13-acre area in the village of Spring Grove with picnic tables, playground equipment, and restrooms (no drinking water). Farther downstream, near the confluence of Nippersink Creek and the Fox River, is the Nippersink Canoe Base, a 71-acre mix of woods and marsh where canoeists will find picnic tables, restrooms, and drinking water. This area is closed in the winter. You will spend approximately thirteen hours canoeing the entire route from Glacial Park to Hickory Grove. For details on portages, special precautions, what you will see along the way, passing through the McHenry Dam locks on the Fox River, etc., check with district headquarters before starting out.

Bank fishing is permitted at designated areas along the Nippersink Trail in Glacial Park, in the backwaters and along the creek bank at Nippersink Canoe Base, and at Hickory Grove. Crappie, sunfish, bluegill, and northern pike are among the resident fish.

Picnicking

Picnic tables with fire grates are available near Glacial Park's main entrance.

Winter Sports

All trails are open to cross-country skiers in winter. Beginners and experts will both find something to their liking here. Maps with trail descriptions and ratings are available at district headquarters.

How to Get There: Located at 6512 Harts Rd., Ringwood. From Ringwood, go north on IL 31 to Harts Rd. and turn left. Harts Rd. ends at park entrance. Parking at lot near district headquarters.

Park open daily, year-round, 8:00 A.M.–sunset. Headquarters office open 8:30 A.M.–5:00 P.M., Mon.–Fri.; closed some holidays.

For Additional Information:
McHenry County Conservation District
6512 Harts Rd.
Ringwood, IL 60072
(815) 338-1405
(815) 678-4431

Goodenow Grove Forest Preserve

Covering 400 acres in eastern Will County, Goodenow Grove offers a variety of outdoor recreational opportunities. Plum Creek snakes its way through the northwestern corner of the preserve, while a smaller tributary creek flows north through Goodenow Grove's midsection. In addition to these streams, visitors will find a small lake, marsh, open fields, and woodlands to explore.

The hub of all activity here is the Plum Creek Nature Center, which offers educational and recreational activities all year long. Along with historical displays and interpretive slide programs, there are some fascinating exhibits on wild foods and medicines. Children will love the Discovery Den, a place designed just for them where they may use puzzles, touch boxes, and color sheets to learn basic concepts of nature and science.

Each summer, campfire get-togethers are scheduled on a regular basis. Nature programs are combined with singalongs and marshmallow roasts to create an evening the whole family will enjoy.

Hiking and Nature Trails

A combination of hiking trails leads through the woods and along the banks of both creeks for approximately one mile. Across from the nature center, a quarter-mile nature trail meanders through old fields and a marshy area. Naturalist-led interpretive hikes are available upon request.

Camping

Seven family and twelve group sites are available for tent campers only from May 1 through Oct. 31. Drinking water and toilets are provided. All sites must be reserved in advance.

Picnicking

Several tree-shaded picnic areas are located near the nature center. Drinking water and toilets are close at hand.

Winter Sports

A steep hill just north of the nature center is used by sledders when the snow is four or more inches deep. Cross-country skiers will find marked trails. When it gets a bit chilly, you'll find a warm fire and coffee bar in the nature center. Special winter programs are offered for both young and old on Sundays.

How to Get There: From Crete, go south on IL 1 (Dixie Hwy.) to Goodenow Rd. Turn left (east) on Goodenow Rd. and proceed to S. Park Ave. Turn left (north) and follow Park Ave. into preserve. Parking on site.

Open daily, year-round. Preserve open 8:00 A.M.–8:00 P.M., May–Oct.; 8:00 A.M.–5:00 P.M., Nov.–April; nature center open 10:00 A.M.–4:00 P.M., Tues.–Sun., closed Mon. Free admission to preserve and nature center; nominal fee for campsites.

For Additional Information:
Plum Creek Nature Center
Goodenow Grove Nature Preserve
Box 241, R.R. 2
Beecher, IL 60401
(312) 946-2216—Office
(312) 946-2215—Campground Reservations

Forest Preserve District of Will County
US 52 and Cherry Hill Rd., R.R. 4
Joliet, IL 60433
(815) 727-8700

Goose Lake Prairie State Park

Several remnants of the tallgrass prairie that once covered more than seventy percent of Illinois have been preserved, but few are large enough to convey effectively what man must have felt when he first gazed upon those vast grasslands. Goose Lake Prairie, the largest tract of protected prairieland in the Prairie State, is such a place. Here you can stand in the midst of a native grassland that offers the same feast for the senses that our ancestors experienced. The whispering wind, the sweet scent of prairie blooms, and the billowing grasses stretching unbroken to the horizon combine to re-create the prairie of yesterday.

Some 1,500 of the park's 2,366 acres have been dedicated as a state nature preserve. Besides the dry, wet, and mesic prairies found here, natural features include extensive thickets of hawthorns and prairie crab apples, groves of trees, ponds, potholes, and more than 200 acres of marsh. The variety of wildlife and vegetation supported by such diverse habitats provides a rich environmental study area that attracts scientists from all over the country.

More than 300 species of plants are known to exist on Goose Lake Prairie. Among them are such rarities as the rattlesnake master, several species of gentians, a hybrid of the aster and goldenrod that today is found nowhere else in the United States, and, of course, the prairie grasses, taller in some places than a man's head. Wildflowers are in bloom most of the year. The violet shooting star and blue-eyed grass that blossom forth in the spring give way in summer to false indigo and blazing star and in autumn to sunflowers, goldenrods, and asters.

Birdwatchers may see the Henslow's sparrow (rare elsewhere but common here), Bell's vireo, three species of rails, quail, ring-necked pheasant, upland sandpiper, pied-billed grebe, Traill's flycatcher, the yellow-billed cuckoo, and various warblers. In the spring and fall, wild ducks and geese concentrate on the marshland. Representatives of the animal kingdom include the muskrat, mink, white-tailed deer, coyote, the plains pocket gopher, and western harvest mouse. The broad-winged skipper and fritillary butterflies add color and beauty to the landscape.

Goose Lake Prairie is also interesting historically. At one time, it was home to the buffalo, prairie chicken, otter, and wolf. Several Indian tribes lived in the area, including some moundbuilders. In the mid-nineteenth century, fifty pioneer families formed a community called Jugtown in what is now a part of the park and began making pottery from area clay. The industry existed only a few years, but the old drying shed, kiln, and a building believed to have been the school still stand. Goose Lake itself, drained near the turn of the last century, contained 1,000 acres of surface water, so covered with waterfowl much of the time that the water was not visible—hence its name.

Visitors may learn more about the geology, flora, fauna, and history of the park at the interpretive center. Year-round programs include guided hikes, lectures, and slide shows.

Nature Trail

The Tallgrass Nature Trail, which begins near the interpretive center, loops 1 1/2 miles through the prairie and its potholes and marshes. A cutoff is available for those who don't want to walk the entire distance. Trail guides may be picked up at the trailhead.

Picnicking

Two areas with tables, grills, and toilets are provided. One, the Prairie Picnic Grove, also has water and shelters.

Winter Sports

Nearly seven miles of trails are maintained for cross-country skiers; a warming house is located at the interpretive center.

How to Get There: Located in Grundy County. From Morris, go south on IL 47 (Division St.), across the Illinois River, to Pine Bluff Rd. and turn left. Continue on Pine Bluff (also known locally as Lorenzo Rd.) to Jugtown Rd. and turn left again. Proceed to park entrance on right side of Jugtown Rd.

Open daily, year-round, during daylight hours, except Christmas and New Year's Day. Hours for the interpretive center vary with the seasons.

For Additional Information:
Site Superintendent
Goose Lake Prairie State Park
5010 N. Jugtown Rd.
Morris, IL 60450
(815) 942-2899

Great Western Trail

Beginning on the doorstep of the city of St. Charles and extending westward for seventeen miles, the Great Western Trail might best be described as a linear wildlife refuge. It offers some of the finest outdoor experiences in Kane County.

The trail, covered with finely crushed limestone to provide a smooth surface for both hikers and bicyclists, begins at the Leroy Oakes Forest Preserve in Kane County. From there, it follows a stretch of right-of-way for the old Great Western Railway to Community Park in Sycamore, just across the DeKalb County line.

Several designated natural areas border the pathway, including Murray Prairie. It covers only 2 1/2 acres within the Oakes Forest Preserve, but it is such an outstanding example of dry prairie that scientists use it as a gauge by which to evaluate other dry prairies in the northeastern Illinois region. Nearby, several acres of wetlands provide a productive habitat for wildlife.

Elsewhere along the trail, you will pass other wetlands and cross small streams where duck, coot, and the great blue heron nest and raise their young. Shrubs such as dogwood, blackberry, and hazelnut mingle with scattered patches of native prairie. In the wooded areas, hickory, walnut, various types of oak, and linden trees tower above an understory of ironwood, hawthorn, black cherry, and sumac. Beyond them, rich prairie soils are decorated with growing crops in summer and magnificent farm structures year-round.

Deer, fox, skunk, rabbit, beaver, opossum, and raccoon make their homes nearby. Woodchucks burrow in the old railroad embankment and occasionally sun themselves along the path.

Although you will pass some commercial and manufacturing enterprises, as well as subdivisions, the path for the most part is a natural, quiet place.

Be sure to obtain a map of the trail from the Kane County Forest Preserve Commission before you start out; it notes points of interest to nature lovers and history buffs, as well as facilities and services offered along the way. It also includes a list of shops in the vicinity of the trail where bicycles and cross-country ski equipment may be rented or purchased.

Picnicking

Picnic tables, shelters, water points, and restrooms are located at points along the trail. In addition, there are picnic areas just off the trail at Leroy Oakes Forest Preserve where the trail begins, at Campton Forest Preserve near the town of Wasco, and at the trail's end. Food may be obtained at several places along the way at restaurants or general stores, or you may carry your own with you.

Winter Sports

Cross-country skiers may use the trail in the winter; area shops sell and/or rent equipment.

How to Get There: The trail begins in St. Charles. From the Fox River, which flows through the heart of town, head west on Main St. (IL 64) to Dean St. Turn right and proceed to the Leroy Oakes Forest Preserve, which borders both sides of Dean St. The main entrance to the preserve is on the right; access to the trail is through preserve lands on the left. From here, the trail leads west.

Access to the western terminus of the trail is in Community Park in Sycamore. From the downtown area, proceed east on IL 64 to Airport Rd. and turn right. The park is on the right side of Airport Rd.

Parking available on both sites.

Trail open daily, year-round, during daylight hours. Free.

For Additional Information:
Kane County Forest Preserve District
719 Batavia Ave.
Geneva, IL 60134
(312) 232-1242

Greene Valley Forest Preserve

Greene Valley, sprawling over 1,431 acres of rolling hills, pockets of dense woodlands, and broad meadows, is one of the largest forest preserves in DuPage County. The East Branch of the DuPage River flows southward through the entire length of the preserve, then crosses the DuPage–Will County line that forms Greene Valley's southern boundary.

Birds and wildflowers are exceptional here. During spring and fall migrations, migratory waterfowl follow the river, and songbirds by the hundreds flock to a wooded bird sanctuary in the northern portion of the preserve.

Among the fine facilities found here are athletic fields, a dog training and exercise field, a polo field where games are played every Sunday afternoon throughout the summer and fall, and youth group campsites for year-round use. A sanitary landfill currently under construction will, when completed, become a winter sports site similar to Mt. Hoy at Blackwell Recreational Preserve (described elsewhere).

Hiking, Horseback Riding, and Nature Trails

A self-guided tree identification nature trail, open to the general public, is located at the Thunderbird Youth Camp area in the southwestern corner of the preserve. Five miles of marked trails, some strenuous, lead hikers throughout the preserve and along the riverbank. The same trails are used by horseback riders. No rentals; annual registration is required.

Fishing

Anglers fish the DuPage River for crappie, sunfish, largemouth and smallmouth bass, carp, goldfish, bluegill, and bullhead.

Winter Sports

Five miles of marked cross-country ski trails are available. When the ice is at least three inches thick, ice fishing is allowed.

How to Get There: Located just west of IL 53 in south central DuPage County. From Lisle, head south on IL 53 to Hobson Rd. Turn right (west) on Hobson, proceed to Greene Rd., and turn left (south). Follow Greene Rd. to a parking lot on the left side of the road near the polo field; or continue south on Greene to 79th St. Turn right (west), follow 79th St. to Yackley Ave., and turn left (south). A small lot with limited parking is located on the left (east) side of Yackley near the ranger's office.

Open daily, year-round, from one hour after sunrise to one hour after sunset. Free.

For Additional Information:
DuPage County Forest Preserve District
P.O. Box 2339
Glen Ellyn, IL 60137
(312) 620-3800

Fullersburg Woods Nature Center
3609 Spring Rd.
Oak Brook, IL 60521
(312) 620-3843

Grosse Point Lighthouse Park

This small park in Evanston combines nature and history in a lovely lakeside setting.

Visitors may study the plants, birds, insects, animals, and minerals native to this area at the Lighthouse Nature Center, housed in a former fog signal house just east of the lighthouse itself. In another fog house nearby, there's a visitor center with a museum that's designed to interpret the maritime heritage of the Great Lakes.

The Center for Natural Landscaping consists of a greenhouse surrounded by wildflower gardens that demonstrate the beauty of Illinois's native plants. In the northern part of the park, several wooded areas are being preserved as refuges where wild flora and fauna may thrive. A park brochure points out such trees as the ginkgo, silver maple, horse chestnut, cottonwood, European purple beech, and an ancient black oak, as well as a patch of wild onions.

Steps lead down to the beach, where you'll have a fine view of migrating birds in season. Of particular interest are the hawks, which pass through in September, October, and November.

On a promontory overlooking Lake Michigan, the lighthouse for which the six-acre park is named still operates, although it has been modernized since it was built in 1873. Tours of the lighthouse, which is now on the National Register of Historic Places, include a climb to the top of the 113-foot-tall tower and an unusual view of Lake Michigan and its shoreline.

Other points of interest include a vernal pond, a grotto pond, a group of purple martin houses, an organic cooperative garden, and a dune restoration project. While on the grounds, you may also want to visit the Evanston Art Center. Located in a mansion built in the 1920s, it offers exhibitions in visual arts and a gift shop.

Nature Trail

A winding nature trail, half a mile long, leads you past 17 tree species and some 200 species of woodland wildflowers.

Picnicking

A picnic shelter is available, but an advance permit is required for its use. Nearby is a children's playground with equipment made of wood.

How to Get There: Located in northeastern Evanston along the Lake Michigan shoreline just north of Northwestern University. From downtown Evanston, follow Sheridan Rd. north; the park is located at 2535 Sheridan Rd.

Grounds open daily, year-round, during daylight hours. Nature center and maritime museum open daily, 2:00–5:00 P.M., July and Aug.; 2:00–5:00 P.M., Sat. and Sun., May to Oct. Lighthouse open 2:00–5:00 P.M., Sat. and Sun., May to Oct. All hours may vary from time to time. Group tours may be arranged through the Evanston Environmental Association, which also sponsors many environment-related classes and field trips. Admission to park free; donation requested for EEA tours.

For Additional Information:
Lighthouse Nature Center
2600 Sheridan Rd.
Evanston, IL 60201

Evanston Environmental Association
2024 McCormick Blvd.
Evanston, IL 60201
(312) 864-5181 (Nature Center and EEA)

The Grove

Tucked away in a wooded corner of Glenview is a beautiful estate of about ninety acres known as The Grove, so idyllic a setting that it is sometimes called Walden West. Its rich history has resulted in its being designated a national historic landmark, but it remains an attraction little known outside the immediate area in which it's located.

Originally The Grove was the home of the Kennicotts, a pioneer family who settled here in 1836 and were noted for their involvement in horticulture and natural history research. During the century the Kennicotts lived at The Grove, various family members were involved in the early exploration of Alaska, the development of modern floriculture, popular understanding of and interest in nature, Central American anthropology, and early Smithsonian Institute collections.

Robert Kennicott, who was just a year old when his parents moved to The Grove, was the founder and first curator of the Chicago Academy of Sciences (described elsewhere). As a young man, he inventoried the wildlife that lived at The Grove and in the surrounding area. Then the bison, black bear, wildcat, weasel, wolf, coyote, beaver, and passenger pigeon all resided on this land. Although the species represented by today's wild residents are not nearly so varied, the populations are numerous because of their protected status. Among the birds and animals you may see here are white-tailed deer, opossums, rabbits, red foxes, great horned owls, red-tailed hawks, flycatchers, vireos, and golden-throated warblers.

The Kennicotts' love of nature shows in the way they maintained the grounds of their home. On the back fifty acres, the forest grove for which the estate is named still thrives, dotted with kettle holes and patches of virgin woodlands that have survived untouched over millennia. Nature trails intertwine and loop through these natural areas, leading to Willow Slough, Redfield Island, and the park's interpretive center where exhibits depict the flora and fauna of this part of Illinois. On the first and third Saturday of each month, visitors of all ages participate in guided walks that explore the ecology and history of The Grove. There are other special activities, too—an annual Folk Fest, a writers' workshop, a pioneer arts and skills workshop, and programs especially planned for young people.

Besides the interpretive center, two other buildings are open to the public—the Kennicott house, now a museum, and the Redfield Cultural Center, once the home of descendants of the Kennicotts. The lawns are dotted with gardens, flowering shrubs, and huge old trees, some of which were growing here when the Kennicotts came to this area. In keeping with the overall historical theme, new plantings of roses, fruit trees, and perennial flowers, as well as the methods used to care for them, are limited to those known to exist during the period when The Grove was a private residence.

Naturalist and writer Donald Culross Peattie lived here for a while and was so impressed with its ecological significance that he commemorated The Grove in his book *A Prairie Grove*. His wife, a Kennicott descendant named Louise Redfield, was herself a noted author during the first half of this century; her novel *American Acres* is set in The Grove, where she was born and reared.

How to Get There: Located in northern Cook County in Glenview. From the intersection of Golf Rd. (IL 58) and Milwaukee Ave. (IL 21) in Glenview, go north on Milwaukee Ave. to The Grove on the right side of the road at 1421 Milwaukee Ave. Look for some wooden gates and a sign; foliage sometimes makes them difficult to spot until you're right next to them. Parking on site.

The interpretive center and grounds are open weekdays, 8:00 A.M.–4:30 P.M., year-round; weekends 10:00 A.M.–4:00 P.M., April 15–Nov. 15; closed weekends, Nov. 16–April 14. Free.

For Additional Information:

The Grove
1421 Milwaukee Ave.
Glenview, IL 60025
(312) 299-6096

Grove Heritage Association
P.O. Box 484
Glenview, IL 60025
(312) 298-7497

Glenview Park District
1930 Prairie St.
Glenview, IL 60025
(312) 724-5670

Harrison–Benwell Conservation Site

This eighty-acre site in northeastern McHenry County, although small, is a lovely getaway spot. Consisting primarily of a mature oak woodland, it also has a small creek wandering through it, a marsh, and open fields. It is a place to camp, hike, picnic, study nature, or just relax. If you occasionally yearn for something a little more active, there's a cleared play area where you can toss a ball or set up a badminton net.

Much of Harrison–Benwell is moist underfoot, but a series of short bridges allows visitors a close-up view of the ecology of the marsh. Willows and aspens compete with wetland grasses for supremacy in the marsh, while the surrounding forest of oak, walnut, cherry, and hickory trees is gradually encroaching upon the wetland area.

For many years, cattle grazing in the forest here kept young trees from growing up and joining ranks with the old giants, which explains the age gap in the trees you see today. Now the older trees, with no strong middle-aged ones to help buffer the force of the winds, are being uprooted or snapped off at an accelerating rate.

Hiking

A self-guided interpretive nature walk, the Trail of the Big Oaks, circles through the native timber and marsh for $2^1/_2$ miles. It's possible to shorten your hike to about 1 mile by using a shortcut.

Camping

A primitive campground occupies a small clearing near the creek and marsh. Restrooms are nearby, and drinking water may be obtained near the park entrance. A written permit must be obtained from the district office at least one week in advance.

Picnicking

Picnic tables are nestled among the bur oaks. Drinking water and restrooms are close at hand.

Winter Sports

Cross-country skiers follow the snow-covered Trail of the Big Oaks, while sledders enjoy the gentle slopes of the park.

How to Get There: From the town of McHenry, go north on IL 31 to McCullom Lake Rd. and turn left. Proceed to park on left side of road at 7055 McCullom Lake Rd. There's a parking lot adjacent to the roadside; no roads enter the site itself.

Open daily, year-round, 9:00 A.M.–sunset. Free.

For Additional Information:
McHenry County Conservation District
6512 Harts Rd.
Ringwood, IL 60072
(815) 338-1405
(815) 678-4431

Hickory Grove

This 220-acre conservation site just east of Crystal Lake in McHenry County offers a variety of outdoor recreation. It combines a large natural marsh, open fields, dense hardwood forest, a 6-acre lagoon, and 1,000 feet of frontage on the beautiful Fox River.

Near the center of the park is a stretch of native prairie that gives visitors a sense of the natural history of this land. Migratory waterfowl and such wading birds as the great blue heron are attracted to the lagoon, and muskrat are sometimes seen near the shoreline. In the woodlands, you may surprise a gray squirrel or cottontail rabbit as you walk the loop trail.

During the summer, a special environmental experience introduces participants to "The Living Land." A nominal fee is charged, and reservations are necessary.

Lyons Prairie, a nature preserve, adjoins Hickory Grove, but it is not open to the public at this time.

Hickory Grove, a green haven in the midst of a heavily populated area, became public property in 1974, and facilities are still being added.

Hiking and Horseback Riding

This park is divided into two sections by Hickory Grove Rd. The northern portion borders the Fox River, and a short trail leads to the riverbank. Two miles of interpretive nature trails and more than three miles of horse trails (no rentals) loop through the forest and prairie in the larger southern part of the park.

Camping

Primitive camping for groups of twenty-five or more is available; a written permit must be obtained at least one week in advance.

Picnicking

Facilities for family picnicking are provided with tables, drinking water, and restrooms. One area overlooks the lagoon; another is located in the woods near the main entrance. There is also a place to picnic midway along the bridle path.

Fishing

You will find excellent bass fishing in the lagoon.

How to Get There: Located in southeastern McHenry County. From Crystal Lake, go east on Crystal Lake Ave. to Rawson Bridge Rd. Turn left on Rawson Bridge Rd. to Hickory Grove Rd., and turn right to park entrance at 500 Hickory Grove Rd.

Open daily, year-round, 9:00 A.M. to sunset. Free.

For Additional Information:
McHenry County Conservation District
6512 Harts Rd.
Ringwood, IL 60072
(815) 338-1405
(815) 678-4431

Illinois and Michigan Canal State Trail

The citizens of Chicago were elated when, in the mid-1800s, a canal was constructed between Lake Michigan and the Illinois River. Cut in the bed of an ancient river that is believed to have flowed down the same route about 8,000 years ago, the ninety-six-mile-long waterway signaled the beginning of Chicago's growth and its emergence as a commercial power in the Midwest. Today, remnants of that canal still exist, and parts of it are currently being restored. The towpath along its north side, known as the Illinois and Michigan Canal State Trail, is being developed as a major recreation pathway for hikers and bicyclists. When completed, it will run sixty-one miles from Joliet to LaSalle. The canal itself, which generally parallels the north banks of the Chicago, Des Plaines, and Illinois rivers, is open in part to canoeists.

Visitors who travel the pathway will have the opportunity to sample both natural and historical aspects of the Prairie State. Channahon, Goose Lake Prairie, Gebhard Woods, William G. Stratton, Buffalo Rock, Illini Starved Rock, and Matthiessen state parks, as well as the McKinley Woods Forest Preserve of Will County either border or are not far from the trail. (Goose Lake Prairie State Park and McKinley Woods Forest Preserve are described elsewhere.) Even alongside private landholdings, much of the canal is edged with forest where great horned owls signal even during the daytime, and where redheaded woodpeckers and a wide variety of warblers are found in abundance.

History buffs will find several places of interest in addition to the canal itself. Several canal locks may be seen along the way; two of them and a lockkeeper's house are in Channahon State Park. In Gebhard Woods State Park, a stone aqueduct built to carry the canal over Nettle Creek has been restored. Another aqueduct crosses AuxSable Creek. Buffalo Rock State Park is in the heart of an area rich in Indian and French history. Although it's now privately owned, a barn once used to house the mules that pulled barges down the canal is visible from the trail. The history of the canal may be explored further at the LaSalle County Historical Museum in Utica, originally a general store that served the needs of early pioneers and traffic along the canal, and at the Illinois Waterway Visitor Center just south of Utica.

On-site rangers at park headquarters in Gebhard Woods State Park periodically present slide shows that inform viewers about the ecology and the historical significance of the canal's corridor.

Hiking and Bicycling

Thus far, approximately thirty miles of the trail are open to hikers—a stretch of twenty-five miles between Channahon and Seneca, and another section of about five miles between Utica and LaSalle. Bicyclists may now use a fifteen-mile section between Channahon and Morris and the section between Utica and LaSalle. Water, toilets, parking, and canoe launch facilities are available along the section between Channahon and Morris. The wide, flat pathway makes for easy walking, and the views along the way are pleasant and scenic. When completed the trail will offer facilities along its full sixty-one-mile length. Check at park headquarters for maps and up-to-date information.

Canoeing and Fishing

Approximately twenty-eight miles of the canal are filled with water and are open to canoeists. (Current plans call for the rest of the canal to be left dry.) Launch facilities are available at the towns of Channahon and LaSalle, at AuxSable Creek just east of Morris, and at Gebhard Woods State Park in Morris.

Anglers will find bass, crappie, bluegill, catfish, and bullhead in canal waters. Visitors to three state parks that border the canal will find additional fishing waters. Channahon State Park is along the DuPage River. The Illinois River forms part of the boundary of William G. Stratton State Park. In Gebhard Woods State Park, youngsters will find four ponds for their exclusive use; adults may use Nettle Creek.

Camping

Primitive camping is permitted at Channahon and Gebhard Woods State Park along the canal. Campsites are accessible only by foot, and a permit must be obtained from park offices before entering the campground. All groups of more than twenty-five persons must obtain permission in advance to camp. A nominal fee is charged per campsite; youth groups pay a nominal fee per person. Campsites with electricity and vehicular access are available at Illini and Starved Rock state parks not far south of the canal.

Picnicking

Tables and grills are available at various locations along those parts of the trail now open. Shelters have been built at Channahon, Gebhard Woods, and Buffalo Rock state parks.

Winter Sports

The fifteen-mile stretch of towpath between Channahon and Morris serves as a cross-country ski trail for beginners; a ten-mile trail from Morris to Seneca is recommended for experts. Skiers will find a warming house at Gebhard Woods State Park on the canal's banks.

How to Get There: Headquarters for the I&M Canal State Trail are located at Gebhard Woods State Park in Morris. From the intersection of I-80 and IL 47 just north of Morris, head south on IL 47 to Jefferson St. Turn right and proceed to Ottawa St. Turn left on Ottawa and proceed a quarter of a mile across Nettle Creek to park entrance on left. Parking on site.

Open daily, year-round, during daylight hours; closed Christmas and New Year's Day. Free admission.

For Additional Information:
Site Superintendent
Illinois & Michigan Canal State Trail
P.O. Box 272
Morris, IL 60450
(815) 942-0796

Illinois Beach State Park

Edging Lake Michigan just south of the Wisconsin-Illinois border lies Illinois Beach State Park, a blend of sand and gravel beach, low dunes, deciduous and coniferous forests, prairie, marsh, and the sluggish Dead River. The 5,400-acre park extends along the shore of Lake Michigan for 7 1/2 miles and offers a multitude of recreational opportunities as well as a great diversity of natural habitats.

In the mid-1960s, when more than 1,000 natural areas were inventoried and evaluated for inclusion in Illinois's newly established nature preserve system, several hundred acres in this park were ranked at the head of the list. They contain sixteen different natural communities and offer an intriguing study of plant succession from sandy shore to forest. In October 1964, the site was dedicated as the state's first nature preserve, and its importance as a natural resource was further recognized in 1980 when it became a National Natural Landmark. Today, it encompasses nearly 900 acres and includes a nature center with a full-time interpretive staff.

More than sixty types of plants and animals in the preserve are threatened or endangered in Illinois. Two of the more interesting plants growing here are the Waukegan juniper, a species found nowhere else in the world, and the prickly pear cactus. The virgin sand prairie supports such unusual plants as the prairie aster, fringed gentian, and Indian paintbrush.

Among the 150 kinds of birds that sometimes use the preserve are the knot and the ruddy turnstone, rarely seen in Illinois except during migration periods; the piping plover, a summer resident; the varied thrush, western kingbird, and hummingbird. The bald eagle, osprey, peregrine falcon, and cliff swallow are occasionally spotted in the spring and fall, and bluebirds nest in the dead trees.

The insect population, too, is unusual. One eminent entomologist described the area as having "one of the most extraordinary communities of caddis flies in Illinois." A unique butterfly known as the *Gallophrys polios* that is abundant here is seen nowhere else in Illinois.

Perhaps the most interesting part of the preserve, however, is the Dead River, a slow-moving stream whose waters are clogged with a profusion of aquatic plants. Just $2^1/_2$ miles long, it originates at a few small lakes in adjoining marshland, then twists its way through the dunes as though undecided which way to go. During most of the year, it's actually a shallow, elongated pond that stops just short of Lake Michigan, its mouth blocked by a sandbar that is continually built up by storm waves. Occasionally, when the stream is swollen by rainfall and runoff waters from surrounding parklands, the river breaks through the sandbar and spills into the lake.

A native deciduous forest in the park is dominated by black oak, interspersed with white oak, bur oak, cottonwood, and quaking aspen. Although many of the trees are more than a century old, they appear scrubby and unhealthy, due in part to the lack of nutrients in the sandy soil. A second forest, planted nearly 100 years ago to help stabilize the dunes, contains various kinds of pine trees.

The geologic history of the park is quite complex. Once it lay entirely beneath the ice of different glacial periods and later, when the glaciers melted, beneath the waters of ancient Lake Chicago. As the lake receded, it gradually dropped from its highest level of about 640 feet above sea level, staying at each succeeding level for a few hundred years until it reached its present level of 580 feet. Each level created new shorelines and beaches that can still be discerned today by the differences in plant growth.

The park is divided into two zones that lie north and south of the Zion nuclear power plant. Until recently, only the south end was open to the public. It contains the nature preserve, the park's 106-room lodge, a campground, and numerous recreational facilities. The north zone, opened in the summer of 1982, currently offers picnicking, fishing, and beach access.

Located just forty miles north of downtown Chicago, Illinois Beach is the most popular playground in Illinois's state park system, luring more than $1^1/_2$ million people annually.

Hiking

There are many designated trails throughout the park, some intersecting with others so that hikers may walk virtually any distance they choose. Within the nature preserve itself, there is a 3½-mile system with markers along the way that interpret some of the basic natural features of a sand dune and of the Dead River. All trails in the preserve begin near the nature center, where a free printed trail guide is available for self-guided hikes. If you prefer to take a guided hike, the park interpreter conducts regularly scheduled nature walks year-round.

Fishing

Fishing is permitted along the beach area in both the north and south zones, except in the swimming area and the nature preserve. Lake Michigan produces northern pike; lake, rainbow, and German brown trout; coho and chinook salmon. Some small fishing ponds in the park are stocked with bluegill, catfish, and crappie.

Swimming

The star attraction for most visitors to this park is the swimming beach, which stretches for 1,000 feet along the Lake Michigan shoreline. Several bathhouses provide bathers with hot showers, toilets, and dressing rooms. Lifeguards protect the beach from 11:00 A.M. to 7:00 P.M. daily during the summer season. A children's playground is also located on the beach, and refreshments are available at a park concession.

Camping

Both tent and trailer camping are permitted year-round. Of 400 sites, 175 have electricity. A campground utility building contains hot showers and toilets, and a sanitary dump station is located nearby. Supplies are available at a camper store. Advance registration is required for a special youth group camping area.

Picnicking

Picnicking is allowed at both the north and south zones. Tables and stoves are provided; visitors may bring their own firewood or charcoal or purchase them at the park concession.

Winter Sports

Six miles of trails are open to cross-country skiers. Ski rentals and lessons are available in the park.

How to Get There: Located in northeastern Lake County along the Lake Michigan shoreline. The new north zone lies north of the Zion nuclear power plant; the south zone is south of the same plant. From Zion, go south on IL 173 (Sheridan Rd.) to Wadsworth Rd. and turn left. Wadsworth Rd. leads to the park's main entrance in the south zone; ask at gate for directions to north zone.

Open daily, year-round, 7:00 A.M.–10:00 P.M. Admission free.

For Additional Information:
Site Superintendent
Illinois Beach State Park
Lake Front
Zion, IL 60099
(312) 662-4811
(312) 662-4828

Illinois Prairie Path

One of the finest trails in the state is the Illinois Prairie Path, a 45-mile-long pathway that winds through portions of Cook, DuPage, and Kane counties. It is an outstanding recreational facility, a bird observatory, a natural science laboratory, and a link among many municipal parks and county forest preserves for nonmotorized travel. Open all year long, the path is used by hikers, backpackers, joggers, bicyclists, birdwatchers, equestrians, science students, cross-country skiers, and even commuters. History and nostalgia buffs also enjoy it, since the trail follows the right-of-way of the former Chicago, Aurora & Elgin Railway, which suspended operations in 1957.

Beginning at First Avenue in Maywood, the path leads westward through Glen Ellyn to Wheaton. There it forks, with one leg leading northwest to Elgin, the other southwest to yet another fork. If you follow the trail to the left at this latter fork, you'll head for Aurora. The trail to the right leads to Batavia, then follows the lovely Fox River north to St. Charles.

Surfaced with fine limestone gravel and dirt, the path is well marked and easy to follow. The eastern section, between Maywood and Wheaton, takes you through a series of built-up areas, but from Wheaton on, it enters scenic, more rural land and passes through or near some county forest preserves. If you decide to take the northwest branch, you'll see mostly flat farmland and an occasional marsh, while the southern spur leads past picturesque horse farms and across a stile. The northern section of the second fork skirts the wooded boundaries of Fermilab (described elsewhere), dips into a canyon where you may have to ford a stream, and passes some huge boulders that are a legacy of the Ice Age. A turn to the south at this second fork will lead you to a park on the banks of the Fox River.

Much of the trail, especially west of Wheaton, is bordered by trees, and more trees as well as prairie flowers are constantly being planted. Although there are no facilities on the path itself, you'll find drinking water, restrooms, and picnic tables at local parks and in DuPage and Kane county forest preserves along the way. A few DuPage County forest preserves offer a limited number of campsites, but they must be reserved in advance.

Formally established in 1966, the Illinois Prairie Path is managed by a nonprofit organization. The trail is open to the public free of charge at all times, but several types of path memberships are available. Members receive a quarterly newsletter, special notification of organized walks and other special events, and the right to help establish use policies. All dues payments are used to cover overhead expenses and to help develop any new additions to the trail.

Before embarking for an outing on the Prairie Path, contact the corporation for a map, an update on facilities, and trail regulations. A thirty-one-page booklet, *The Illinois Prairie Path—A Guide,* is available for $1.25 (less for quantity orders). In addition to discussing the history and geology of the area, it provides illustrations of the wildflowers, trees, and animal tracks seen along the way.

How to Get There: The eastern trailhead lies near the west bank of the Des Plaines River in Maywood, which is located directly west of downtown Chicago not far from the Cook–DuPage County line. From the intersection of I-290 and 1st Ave. in Maywood, proceed north on 1st Ave. to the trailhead on the left (west) side of the road. The trail leads westward from this point. You'll find several access points to the Prairie Path along its length, and parking is available near most of them.

Open daily, year-round, at all times. Free.

For Additional Information:
Illinois Prairie Path
P.O. Box 1086
Wheaton, IL 60187
(312) 665-5310

DuPage County Forest Preserve District
P.O. Box 2339
Glen Ellyn, IL 60137
(312) 620-3800

Kane County Forest Preserve District
719 S. Batavia Ave.
Geneva, IL 60134
(312) 232-1242

Indian Boundary Forest Preserve Division

A long, narrow corridor of green space, the Indian Boundary Division of the Cook County Forest Preserve District touches both banks of the Des Plaines River between the communities of Park Ridge and River Forest. Another stretch of parkland along the river (the Des Plaines Forest Preserve Division, described elsewhere), extends northward from Indian Boundary Division to the Cook–Lake County line. Together, they offer some twenty-five miles of tree-draped shorelines.

It is an area so rich in Indian history and steeped in lore that a walk through the woods can be a near-mystical experience, with the knowledge that you are passing the sites of former Indian villages, prehistoric mounds, and burial grounds. Only one place remains as a visible reminder of these former inhabitants—a small Indian cemetery that contains the remains of Chief Robinson (the English name of Che-Che-Pin-Qua, a half-breed Indian chief of the Ottawa-Chippewa-Pottawatomi confederation known as "Three Fires") and his family.

Angling through the southern half of the division in a northeast-southwest direction is the imaginary line for which the division is named. It represents the northern limit of the Indian Boundary Line, a twenty-mile-wide strip of land extending from Lake Michigan to the town of Ottawa on the Illinois River that was ceded to the whites by the Pottawatomi Indians in 1816.

In the extreme southern part of the division is the Trailside Museum, the oldest nature center in the Cook County Forest Preserve District. There are no nature trails on the center's thirty-five acres, but you may stroll over tree-shaded grounds where an extensive collection of local wildlife is housed in cages. Inside the exhibit building there are more animals, some of them patients in an animal hospital.

Indian Boundary is a lovely place to visit in the spring, when the wildflowers run rampant in sun-drenched meadows and wet pockets of the lowlands, and the fresh green forest echoes with birdsong.

Hiking, Bicycling, and Horseback Riding

A hiking trail, developed for most of its length, extends northward on the east side of the Des Plaines River through the entire length of the division, a distance of about 10¾ miles. In several places, it closely parallels the banks of the twisting stream. That portion of the trail near Trailside Museum in the southern part of the division is a footpath used by hikers only, but the developed portions, including some branches that lead off the main trail, are also used by bicyclists and equestrians (no rentals; annual horse registration and rider's license required). The trail system in this division connects with the trail in the Des Plaines Division just to the north.

Boating and Fishing

All types of boats and motors use the Des Plaines River. A free launch ramp for canoes and rowboats is available on the west bank of the river near Dam No. 4 South.

Many species of fish, including northern pike, largemouth bass, yellow bass, bluegill, channel catfish, bullhead, and crappie, tempt river anglers. Axehead Lake near the division's northern boundary and a small lagoon near Trailside Museum are stocked with rainbow trout, perch, bluegill, and largemouth bass for shore fishermen. The pond at Schiller Woods North, recovering from a damaging winterkill in the late 1970s, is stocked with largemouth bass, bluegill, crappie, and bullhead.

Picnicking

Picnic areas are found in every part of the division. Although they lie on both sides of the river, the majority are located on the east side. Most sites have grills, and there are many shelters. The shelter at Maywood Grove resembles a concrete mushroom; it was experimental and the only one of its kind in the forest preserve district. All areas have drinking water, toilet facilities, and parking space close at hand. Groups of twenty-five or more must obtain a permit in advance by personally visiting the Permit Office, Room 230, County Building, 118 N. Clark St., Chicago.

Winter Sports

Cross-country skiers follow the trail system or break their own paths across open fields and through the woods. Axehead Lake offers ice fishing, while ice skaters take to the frozen surfaces of the lagoons in Schiller Woods North and near Trailside Museum. There are also some slopes suitable for sledding at Schiller Woods North.

How to Get There: Located directly west of the northern third of Chicago, along both banks of the Des Plaines River; bounded on the north by Touhy Ave. and the Des Plaines Division of the Cook County Forest Preserve District, on the south by Madison St. Since each division of the Cook County Forest Preserve District features several recreation areas and attractions, crisscrossed by many roads and in some instances disconnected, it's best to obtain division maps, directions for getting there, and other pertinent information from district or division headquarters before visiting one. Indian Boundary is the division closest to the district's general headquarters, which are located approximately one mile east of the division, on the west side of Harlem Ave. just north of the intersection of Harlem Ave. and Lake St. in River Forest. Park on street. To reach Trailside Museum from this same intersection, proceed west on Lake St. to Thatcher Ave., turn right (north) onto Thatcher, and continue to museum on the southwest corner of the intersection of Thatcher and Chicago Ave. To reach Indian Boundary Division headquarters from Trailside Museum, head west on Chicago Ave. to Fifth Ave. and turn right (north). Proceed on Fifth Ave. until it ends at Des Plaines River Rd. and turn left (northwest). Continue on Des Plaines River Rd. to Belmont Ave. and turn right (east), across the river, to the headquarters building on the left (north) side of the road. Parking on site.

Preserve lands open daily, year-round, sunrise to sunset; free. Headquarters buildings open Mon.–Fri., year-round, 8:30 A.M.–5:00 P.M.; closed major holidays. Trailside Museum open Fri.–Wed., year-round, 10:00 A.M.–5:00 P.M.; closed Thurs. and major holidays; free.

For Additional Information:
Indian Boundary Division Headquarters
Cook County Forest Preserve District
8800 W. Belmont Ave.
Chicago, IL 60634
(312) 625-0606
(312) 625-0607

Conservation Department
General Headquarters
Cook County Forest Preserve District
536 N. Harlem Ave.
River Forest, IL 60305
(312) 261-8400—Chicago number
(312) 366-9420—Suburban number

Izaak Walton Preserve

Some 14,000 years ago, the land upon which Chicago now stands and much of the surrounding area lay beneath the waters of a great inland sea known as Lake Chicago. This ancient lake, created by melting glaciers, extended inland about fifteen miles from the present edge of Lake Michigan. When the waters eventually receded, they left behind a rich deposit of sand and gravel.

Although some of this glacial repository was excavated during modern times for use in a construction project, a remnant of it has been preserved since the late 1940s by the Homewood chapter of the Izaak Walton League. The sand pits left here by the digging are now filled with water, and small islands in the lake thus formed serve as refuges for wildlife. Much of the surrounding terrain has been reforested with such tree and shrub species as bur oak, sugar maple, highbush cranberry, bush honeysuckle, dogwood, willow, wild black cherry, walnut, red pine, and raspberry.

The Homewood dunes are just northwest of the preserve. Their sandy slopes support dense stands of maple, oak, and cherry trees. On the north side of the dunes lies a small prairie where such unusual plants as latrium and compass plant thrive.

Although small, containing just thirty-eight acres, the Izaak Walton Preserve is a lovely spot in which to study geological history and to enjoy a high-quality natural experience. Some recreational facilities and activities are available only to members, but the general public is welcome on a limited basis. Please remember that this is a very fragile area, and treat it gently. No motorized traffic is allowed beyond the parking lot.

Hiking and Bicycling

Trails lead throughout the entire preserve and along the shorelines of the lakes. Visitors may walk or ride their bicycles along any portion of the trails, but none of the trails are marked. Stop at the league's chapter house on the preserve for directions.

Picnicking

A shelter and picnic tables not far from the parking lot may be used by the public, provided that advance arrangements are made by telephone.

Winter Sports
Cross-country skiers may take to the trails in winter.

How to Get There: Located in southern Cook County, in the northeast corner of the town of Homewood. From the intersection of I-80 and IL 1 northeast of Homewood, go south on IL 1 (known here as Halsted St.) to Ridge Rd. Turn right and proceed to preserve at 1100 Ridge Rd. on the right side of the road. Parking on site.
   Open daily, year-round, 9:00 A.M.–5:00 P.M.

For Additional Information:
Izaak Walton Preserve
1100 Ridge Rd.
Homewood, IL 60430
(312) 798-1850

Kankakee River State Park

Astride the beautiful stream from which it takes its name lies Kankakee River State Park, a 3,783-acre preserve that is a haven for wildlife, home of one of the rarest plants in North America, and a year-round playground for outdoor recreation enthusiasts.

   A featured scenic attraction is Rock Creek, which flows southward through a deep canyon before spilling into the Kankakee River. Hemmed in by precipitous limestone walls etched with the scars of time, the stream tumbles over a sudden drop to form a miniature cascade. The canyon's haunting loveliness, enhanced by a profusion of colorful plants and gnarled cedars that cling tenaciously to the rocky crevices, lures many photographers and artists.

   Areas of special geological and vegetative significance are abundant throughout this linear park, which extends along both banks of the river for about eleven miles. Wind-blown sand dunes, relatively undisturbed forests, limestone outcroppings, gently flowing sloughs, and a prairie glade are all part of the topography here.

   Although several types of rare plants grow here, the most noted is a summer-blooming wildflower known as the Kankakee mallow, or *iliamna remota*. The only place in the world where this species occurs as a native plant is on Altorf Island (sometimes called Langham Island) in the Kankakee River. Managed as a state nature preserve, the island is one of several that lie within park boundaries. The plant, which grows to a height of three to six feet and somewhat resembles a hollyhock, is highly protected, and permission to visit the island must be obtained from the park superintendent.

   In the woods of Kankakee River State Park, the catalpa, cottonwood, elm, basswood, birch, chestnut, walnut, hickory, willow, cedar, and sycamore grow undisturbed. Bluebirds live in the park, along with cardinals, hummingbirds, meadowlarks, hawks, owls, quail, ducks, and wild turkeys. Although they are seldom seen, coyotes inhabit the parklands, while badgers and beavers are drawn to park waters.

A visitor center provides such displays as fish aquariums, stuffed wild animals, antique farm equipment, and seasonal exhibits. You may also learn more about the Kankakee mallow here.

From June to September, special interpretive programs are scheduled. They include nature hikes, hayrides, Saturday night movies, and two festivals—Watermelon Day and Corn Boil Day. Playfields are available for baseball, volleyball, and badminton. A concession stand near the main entrance sells refreshments and ice from May to September.

Once this park was the site of the Little Rock Pottawatomi Indian village, then later the location of the Shaw-waw-nas-see Indian Reservation. Pottawatomi women were allowed to sit in on tribal councils, an unusual custom in those times, but they could not speak. In this way, it was hoped, tribal history would be preserved if the men perished in battle.

A bit of area history may be seen just inside the main entrance to the park, where the aged and unusual tombstones of an old cemetery stand behind a board fence.

Hiking and Bicycling

Several miles of trails wind throughout the forest and along the banks of Rock Creek and the Kankakee River. The most popular are those that follow Rock Creek; one is approximately 3 miles round trip and features steps that lead down the canyon wall at intervals along the way. Near the concession stand, there's a short trail designed for the handicapped. Trail maps may be obtained at the office. A posted bicycle trail runs parallel to the north bank of the Kankakee River for 3 1/2 miles. It begins near the Pottawatomi Campground at the east end of the park, crosses a suspension bridge over Rock Creek Canyon, and ends at Chippewa Campground.

Boating and Fishing

The Kankakee River is one of the finest canoe streams in northern Illinois. Canoes may be rented at the concession stand in the park; pick them up in the town of Kankakee and turn them in at the concession stand. Call (815) 937-0048 for reservations, and be sure to arrange transportation back to your car. Several other concessions in the area also rent canoes and provide transportation to and from the river as well. A boat ramp is located at Chippewa Campground. Motors are permitted, but are limited to a maximum of ten hp. Exercise caution; much of the river in the park is shallow with a rocky bottom, but there are dropoffs and holes up to eighteen feet deep.

Both the Kankakee River and Rock Creek are open to fishing. Bass, bluegill, carp, crappie, catfish, gar, grass pickerel, northern pike, sunfish, and walleye are native to the park. Ice and bait are sold at the park concession.

Camping

Two family campgrounds and one youth camping area are available year-round. Pottawatomi Campground offers electricity, showers, water, a dump station, and tree-shaded sites. Chippewa Campground has water, pit toilets, a dump station, a few sites with electricity, and some walk-in sites for tent campers. Only water and pit toilets are available in the youth group area. No reservations are accepted, but very large groups must have advance permission from the office to camp.

Picnicking

Several shaded picnic areas with tables and stoves are scattered throughout the park. Six open pavilions, three small shelters in the woods along Rock Creek, drinking water, toilets, and playground equipment are also available. Groups of twenty-five or more must obtain a permit at least two weeks in advance.

Winter Sports

Beginning cross-country skiers may use the bicycle trail during winter months. A trail for intermediate and expert skiers lies in the westernmost part of the park on the north side of the river. The system totals about seven miles, and a warming house is available. Ask for a map at the office. Other favorite cold weather sports are ice fishing and tobogganing.

How to Get There: From the town of Kankakee in central Kankakee County, head north on US 52/45 to IL 102 and turn left. Proceed on IL 102 to main park entrance on left side of road; the office is located here.

Park open daily, year-round, 6:00 A.M.–10:00 P.M. Office open daily, year-round, 8:00 A.M.–5:00 P.M.; adjacent visitor center open daily, 9:00 A.M.–5:00 P.M. Admission free.

For Additional Information:
Site Superintendent
Kankakee River State Park
R.R. 1
Bourbonnais, IL 60914
(815) 933-1383

Keepataw Forest Preserve

Sprawling over 184 acres in northern Will County, this preserve is a mix of upland oak woods, cliffs, springs, sloughs, marshes, wet prairies, and quarry ponds. The Des Plaines River flows along the park's southern edge. Within this diverse habitat, both people and wildlife find a retreat in a portion of the Chicago area that is otherwise highly developed.

Some exposed bedrock in the river valley, a type uncommon in northeastern Illinois, and eroded bluffs more than 100 feet high that display several different layers of glacial deposits are of interest geologically.

Visitors will find that the wildlife here is readily seen. More than 200 species of birds, including migratory sandhill cranes, use the preserve, while fallow and white-tailed deer, raccoons, squirrels, and muskrats roam the land throughout the year. Fresh water sponges have been found in quarry ponds.

From 1889 to 1918, the Western Stone Company operated on this site, and the remains of their kilns and cottages may still be seen. Ornamental shrubs, colonies of day lilies, and such herbs as burdock, catnip, and lion's tail still grow around the crumbling foundations, bearing mute testimony to human occupancy in generations past.

Hiking

Hiking trails lead visitors through this undeveloped preserve. Guided nature hikes are offered in the spring and fall.

How to Get There: Located in northern Will County. From Romeoville, go northeast on IL 53 to a fork in the road. At the fork, take the road to the right, which is County Road 66 (Joliet Cutoff Rd.). Proceed northeast on this road to Bluff Rd. and turn right (east) to preserve entrance on right (south) side of road. Parking on site.

Open daily, year-round, 8:00 A.M.–8:00 P.M., May–Oct.; 8:00 A.M.–5:00 P.M., Nov.–April. Free.

For Additional Information:
Plum Creek Nature Center
Goodenow Grove Nature Preserve
Box 241, R.R. 2
Beecher, IL 60401
(312) 946-2216

Forest Preserve District of Will County
US 52 and Cherry Hill Rd., R.R. 4
Joliet, IL 60433
(815) 727-8700

Ladd Arboretum

This narrow outdoor tree museum stretches for three-quarters of a mile along the North Shore Channel of the Chicago River in Evanston. Within its twenty-three acres, trees and shrubs of many varieties are arranged and labeled according to their plant family. Among them are an oak grove and pine knoll, as well as collections of legumes, nut trees, maples, birches, and trees that belong to the rose family.

Habitats are also demonstrated. An open meadow has been

rimmed by plantings typically found at the edge of an open, grassy area. Along the channel banks, there's a prairie restoration that flowers from spring to fall. As many as seventy species of plants bloom at one time during the peak period in June. In the bird sanctuary, you'll see trees and shrubs that were selected and landscaped to provide food and shelter for wildlife.

One of the special features of the arboretum is the Ecology Center, home of the Evanston Environmental Association. Designed as a working demonstration of the effectiveness of alternative energy sources, it includes a solar heating system, a solar greenhouse, solar water heater, and two wind generators. Visitors will also find a reference library and small bookstore here. To further the cause of environmental education, the EEA sponsors a number of workshops, classes, field trips, nature walks, and other programs.

Another point of interest is the North Shore Channel itself. Dug in 1908, it was part of a project then considered one of the seven engineering wonders of the world. Chicago needed a sewage disposal system that would not pollute Lake Michigan, and so it reversed the normal flow of the Chicago River. Instead of emptying into the lake, the sewage-laden stream coursed westward to the Mississippi River. However, an ever-increasing population has taxed the capacity of this system, and a 120-mile-long tunnel is currently being constructed 200 feet below ground level to hold any overflow. Two of the drop shafts are within Ladd Arboretum. The hope is that eighty percent of the channel pollution will be cleaned up by 1988 and the full potential of the arboretum as a riverside park can be realized. Plans call for it to link up with an additional twenty-four miles of water and hiking trails through urban wilderness.

Canoeing

The North Shore Channel, bounded by extensive public lands, may be canoed from the Sheridan Road bridge in Wilmette to its confluence with the North Branch of the Chicago River. This includes the section that borders the arboretum, where a canoe landing is available. One of the first northern Illinois streams to open in late winter, the channel is an early season favorite of canoeists.

Picnicking

Although picnicking is not allowed in the arboretum, it is available in Eggleston Park just to the northwest across McCormick Boulevard and in the Channel Lands Parks on the opposite side of the channel.

How to Get There: From the intersection of Green Bay Rd. and McCormick Blvd. in northern Evanston, go southwest on McCormick Blvd. to Bridge St. on your left. Turn left onto Bridge St., which lies within the arboretum. Parking on site.

Grounds open daily, year-round, during daylight hours. Ecology Center open 9:00 A.M.–4:30 P.M., Tues.–Sat., year-round. Admission free.

For Additional Information:
Ladd Arboretum
% The Ecology Center
2024 McCormick Blvd.
Evanston, IL 60201
(312) 864-5181

Lighthouse Nature Center

See listing under Grosse Point Lighthouse Park, p. 60.

Lockport Prairie

Thriving among the glades of this 120-acre grassland is the leafy prairie clover, a federally endangered plant so rare that it is not known to grow anywhere else in the Midwest and exists elsewhere in this country only in a few populations in Alabama and Tennessee. This alone would be reason enough to preserve this tract of land along the Des Plaines River, but other rare and unusual plants are also found here—prairie satin grass, turtlehead, nodding ladies' tresses orchid, swamp betony, Ohio goldenrod.

Even the land is unique, a remnant of a type of prairie that has been almost totally eradicated by commercial exploitation. Known as a mesic prairie, it contains shallow soils atop limestone that was popular for flagstone and gravel.

Fens, marshes, several large springs, and a narrow band of floodplain forest provide a diversity of habitat that attracts such wildlife as hawks, green herons, common gallinules, coots, and common egrets. From spring through autumn, the land is ablaze with the color of more than 100 species of plants. Lockport Prairie is a place to wander free, a visual and spiritual delight in all seasons.

Nature Trail

A short nature trail meanders through the preserve. Groups must obtain a permit in advance to enter the prairie. A plant list is available from the district naturalist at Plum Grove Nature Center.

How to Get There: The prairie is located along the west bank of the Des Plaines River, just west of Lockport and directly east of the Stateville Correctional Center. From Lockport, go south on State St. to Division St. Turn right (west) on Division St. and proceed 1 1/4 miles to prairie on the left (south) side of the street. Park along roadside.

Open daily, year-round; 8:00 A.M.–8:00 P.M., May–Oct.; 8:00 A.M.–5:00 P.M., Nov.–April. Free.

For Additional Information:
Plum Creek Nature Center
Goodenow Grove Nature Preserve
Box 241, R.R. 2
Beecher, IL 60401
(312) 946-2216

Forest Preserve District of Will County
US 52 and Cherry Hill Rd., R.R. 4
Joliet, IL 60433
(815) 727-8700

Maple Grove Forest Preserve

A walk through the depths of these hushed woods is akin to a journey through the forest primeval. Except for a narrow trail, the casual observer might think that man had never before intruded here.

Although this small preserve covers just eighty-four acres, it encompasses some extraordinary natural riches, not the least of which are its magnificent sugar maples and ancient oaks. The gently rolling landscape also contains several bowl-shaped depressions known as glacial kettles and a tiny clearing that once was part of Illinois's vast prairie wilderness. In the far northwest corner of the preserve, spanned by a footbridge, St. Joseph Creek twists its way past tree-shaded banks.

A low, narrow ridge that rises not far southwest of the bridge and runs in a southwest direction to the preserve's boundary line poses a mystery that has never been satisfactorily solved. Park officials are uncertain of its origin, but its extreme straightness suggests that it was man-made. Although its soil composition is of very poor quality, the ledge is topped by a variety of trees. One huge red oak nearly ten feet in circumference and more than 100 years old is proof that the ridge has existed undisturbed since at least the latter part of the last century.

Drinking water and toilets are located near the preserve entrance.

Hiking and Nature Trail

Visitors have the opportunity to sample the natural features of Maple Grove along a self-guided nature trail. An activity sheet guides walkers on a nature treasure hunt, suggesting things to look for along the way that demonstrate the process of succession. Although St. Joseph Creek and the mysterious ridge mentioned above do not lie along a marked trail, you may explore these features by following a map available at Fullersburg Woods Nature Preserve.

Winter Sports

Cross-country skiers may take off through the woods.

How to Get There: The preserve is located in southeastern DuPage County. From the intersection of IL 5 (East-West Tollway) and IL 53 in Lisle, go south on IL 53 to Maple Ave. Turn left (east) onto Maple and proceed to park entrance on left (north) side of the road. Parking on site.

Open daily, year-round, from one hour after sunrise to one hour after sunset. Free.

For Additional Information:
DuPage County Forest Preserve District
P.O. Box 2339
Glen Ellyn, IL 60137
(312) 620-3800

Fullersburg Woods Nature Center
3609 Spring Rd.
Oak Brook, IL 60521
(312) 620-3843

McHenry Dam State Park

See listing under Moraine Hills State Park, p. 84.

McKinley Woods Forest Preserve

This small preserve in a horseshoe bend of the Des Plaines River combines some striking natural features with a bit of local history.

An oasis in the midst of agricultural fields and housing developments, the rugged terrain of McKinley Woods is composed of open meadows, a mature forest, and a segment of the Illinois and Michigan Canal (described elsewhere). The steep ravines are the products of hundreds of years of erosion, carved out as countless raindrops fell on the uplands, then made their way to the Des Plaines River below.

Paralleling the north bank of the river is the old I&M Canal, built during the 1830s to connect Lake Michigan with the Illinois River. The narrow strip of land between the canal and the river served as a towpath where mules once pulled barges laden with goods destined for the Gulf of Mexico. When the railroads were first established in this area in 1848, the canal was discontinued as a shipping lane. Today, its surviving remnants have been preserved as a state park.

The wild animals that occupy McKinley Woods include white-tailed deer, raccoons, squirrels, woodchucks, and foxes. Although they are somewhat shy and may not easily be seen, their tracks, holes, nests, and droppings are evident to observant visitors. Among the many birds who make their home here, the woodpeckers, cardinals, chickadees, and blue jays are most numerous. Red-tailed and sparrow hawks scout the terrain for prey, and at night great barred owls call from the woodland.

Hiking, Bicycling, and Nature Trails

A rugged, 1/4-mile hiking trail, the Trail of the Old Oaks, follows a challenging loop route to the upland forests atop the ravines. The less strenuous Heritage Nature Trail, a self-guided, 1/2-mile loop that partially borders the north bank of the I&M Canal, offers seventeen numbered markers that are keyed to a free interpretive brochure. Between the canal and the Des Plaines River, the canal towpath now serves as a trail for hikers and bicyclists; this segment is part of a 17-mile stretch that runs from Channahon to Morris. Guided interpretive nature hikes are sometimes scheduled in the park; contact the site manager for more information.

Canoeing and Fishing

A canoe launch is provided for access to the I&M Canal. Fishermen may try their hand at catching bass, crappie, bluegill, catfish, and bullhead in the canal.

Picnicking

Picnic tables and a shelter are available near the parking lot. A playfield is close by. Groups of more than twenty-five must obtain a permit from the district office in advance of their outings; the shelter may be reserved for a fee.

How to Get There: From Channahon, take US 6 west for nearly a mile. Look for a sign and a gravel road on the left (south) side of the highway. Turn left onto the gravel road and proceed about two miles to the park.

Open daily, year-round, 8:00 A.M.–8:00 P.M., May–Oct.; 8:00 A.M.–5:00 P.M., Nov.–April. Free.

For Additional Information:
Will County Forest Preserve District
US 52 and Cherry Hill Rd., R.R. 4
Joliet, IL 60433
(815) 727-8700—District Office
(815) 476-2084—Site Manager

Messenger Woods Forest Preserve

Messenger Woods, a 206-acre haven in northern Will County, puts on one of the most exceptional displays of spring wildflowers in the Chicago region. Such species as squirrel corn, blue-eyed Mary, and the large-flowered trillium are not only unusual in this part of the country, but spectacularly beautiful as well. In a spring-fed stream in one of the park's ravines is a thriving colony of locally rare heart-leaved plaintain. Other rare and uncommon species found along these rolling glacial hills include the sweet-scented bedstraw, tall bellflower, wood sandwort, yellow honeysuckle, and sessile trillium.

North of Spring Creek, which flows westward through the

preserve, is a remnant of old-growth forest that has miraculously survived the development of the land surrounding it. The oak-dominated woodland is one of the few unaltered forests in northeastern Illinois, making this one of the best sites in the area for nature study.

Hiking

Hiking trails lead visitors throughout a terrain that includes gentle hills, steep-sided ravines, and a narrow stream valley. Guided nature hikes are offered in the spring and fall.

Picnicking

Both picnic tables and shelters are available. Drinking water and restrooms are nearby.

Winter Sports

Cross-country skiers are permitted to use preserve land, but there are no marked trails.

How to Get There: From Lockport, go east on IL 7 (159th St.) to Parker Rd. and turn right (south). Proceed about 1 1/2 miles on Parker Rd. to preserve on right side of road. Parking on site.

Open daily, year-round; 8:00 A.M.–8:00 P.M., May–Oct. 1; 8:00 A.M.–5:00 P.M., Nov.–April. Free.

For Additional Information:
Plum Creek Nature Center
Goodenow Grove Nature Preserve
Box 241, R.R. 2
Beecher, IL 60401
(312) 946-2216

Forest Preserve District of Will County
US 52 and Cherry Hill Rd., R.R. 4
Joliet, IL 60433
(815) 727-8700

Moraine Hills State Park

One of the loveliest pockets of unspoiled wilderness in the Chicago area is Moraine Hills State Park. Many types of outdoor recreation are available here, but if you bring your camera along, you may be so busy taking pictures you won't have time for anything else.

Within the park's 1,676 acres are marsh, fen, bog, forest, prairie, four small lakes, and a portion of the Fox River. Just as the topography is diverse, so is the plant and animal life.

Thousands of years ago, retreating glaciers left huge deposits of gravel to form the kames that are now seen in hills and ridges throughout the park. Lake Defiance, one of the few undeveloped natural glacial lakes in Illinois, was formed when a gigantic block of ice separated from the main body of a glacier and melted on the site. Now covering forty-eight acres, it's the largest lake in the park, but it is gradually filling in with peat from the unstable soils along the shoreline. The marshes and bogs of the park were similarly created by smaller ice chunks.

Leatherleaf Bog in the northern part of the park contains a large floating mat of sphagnum moss and leatherleaf surrounded by an open moat of water. In the southeastern corner of the parkland, a peat-filled basin known as Pike Marsh supports several rare plants, as well as the largest known colony of pitcher plants in Illinois. These two unique natural areas, which together cover about 242 acres, have been designated a state nature preserve.

From spring through fall, the park is sprinkled with such wildflowers as the shooting star, Greek calerian, bladderwort, round-lobed hepatica, Joe-Pye weed, bellwort, bird's-foot violet, and wild geranium. Water lilies adorn the surface of Lake Defiance. In the autumn, the forests of red, black, and white oak, hickory, hawthorn, ash, dogwood, and cherry are brilliant.

Wildlife is more visible in this park than in many other Chicago-area preserves. Blue and green heron are attracted to the marshy areas, while the open water lures wood ducks, mallards, teal, Canada geese, and other waterfowl. More than 100 species of birds have been identified here, and the upland forests are home to white-tailed deer, mink, red foxes, eastern cottontails, opossums, and raccoons.

Originally, this park was known as McHenry Dam State Park, named for the dam and locks that lie across the Fox River. When more land was acquired in the 1970s, the park was given its present name. The old name, however, still appears on some maps.

The park office, located on the north shore of Lake Defiance, houses an interpretive center that offers various displays and a brief slide show that depicts the features of the park.

Concession stands near the office and at McHenry Dam offer a variety of refreshments, and there are two playgrounds for young children.

Hiking, Bicycling, and Nature Trails
A total of 11 miles of hiking/bicycling trails, surfaced with crushed limestone, wander through the park; bicycles may be rented in the park. A 4-mile-long trail encircles Lake Defiance. The path around Leatherleaf Bog runs for $3^1/_2$ miles, while a $2^1/_2$-mile trail leads by the Fox River and McHenry Dam. All three are loops, with spurs leading to various day-use areas for hikers who don't want to follow the entire routes. The two nature trails lead visitors over floating boardwalks. At Lake Defiance, the trail is half a mile in length, while the other penetrates Pike Marsh for a distance of 0.7 miles. Printed guides are available for each nature trail.

Boating and Fishing

Boating is permitted on all lakes in the park, as well as on the Fox River. Because there are no launching facilities and there is not enough parking space to accommodate trailers, only canoes and boats transported on car tops may be brought into the park. Motors are not allowed on any of the lakes, but motors of twenty-five hp or less are permissible on the Fox River. Boats must be carried in to the northern lakes area (Tomahawk, Warrior, and Wilderness lakes). No private boats of any kind are allowed on Lake Defiance, but a limited number of rental boats are available specifically for use on this lake on a first-come, first-serve basis; contact the park office for more information.

All park waters are open to fishermen. Lake Defiance is stocked with largemouth bass, bluegill, and northern pike. The three northern lakes offer bullhead, green sunfish, largemouth bass, and bluegill; two of them, Tomahawk and Warrior, are also stocked with northern pike and channel catfish. In the Fox River, anglers will find yellow perch, yellow bass, largemouth and smallmouth bass, northern pike, walleye, bluegill, crappie, channel catfish, bullhead, and carp. Bank fishing is permitted in all waters except Lake Defiance. Bait and tackle are available at park concession stands.

Picnicking

Ten major day-use areas contain picnic tables in both open and shaded settings. Parking, drinking water, and restrooms are available at each. There's a shelter at the Pine Hills day-use area, and children will find playground equipment at the McHenry Dam and Moraine Hills areas.

Winter Sports

A one-way cross-country ski trail implements the eleven miles of hiking/bicycling trails. Ski rentals and clinics, as well as a warming house and concession stand, are available. Ice fishing is allowed in the park's four lakes and in the Fox River.

How to Get There: Located in eastern McHenry County. From the town of McHenry, head east on IL 120. Just after you cross the Fox River, turn right onto River Rd. and proceed to the park, which lies on both sides of River Rd. The main park road, which leads to Lake Defiance and the park office, will be on your left.

Open daily, year-round, except Christmas, from sunrise to sunset. Free admission.

For Additional Information:
Superintendent
Moraine Hills State Park
914 S. River Rd.
McHenry, IL 60050
(815) 385-1624

Canada geese make a stopover in Morton Arboretum   *Bill Thomas*

Morton Arboretum

The Morton Arboretum, a 1,500-acre outdoor museum of plants, is one of the Chicago area's great natural showplaces. Established in 1922 as part of a private estate, it was a labor of love for its owner, Joy Morton. His interest in trees came about quite naturally. J. Sterling Morton, his father, was Secretary of Agriculture under President Grover Cleveland, an avid conservationist, and the originator of Arbor Day. As an adult, Joy founded the profitable salt company that still bears his name and began planning the arboretum that would grace the grounds of his home. The younger Morton died in 1934, endowing the arboretum with funds to operate as a nonprofit scientific foundation. Today, the arboretum is a renowned research and education center, as well as a quiet beauty spot that attracts thousands of visitors annually.

Set among rolling hills, lakes, ponds, marshes, streams, and tracts of natural forest that have remained virtually undisturbed since 1922, the arboretum contains approximately 4,800 kinds of trees and shrubs, and additional species are still being added. The purpose of this living museum is to bring together in one place, for both study and enjoyment, every type of native and introduced woody plant that will thrive in the northern Illinois climate.

Although it is popular at all times, the arboretum is most crowded on weekends in May, when the lilacs and crab apples are in bloom, and again at the height of the fall foliage season in October.

Collections and habitats have been created here, interspersed with natural land forms. Among them are some fine plantings of spruce, pine, and fir; gardens containing hedges, dwarf shrubs, wild and cultivated flowers; a European forest reminiscent of locales in France; a woodland made up of trees native to Illinois; an area where the trees and shrubs of Japan have been planted; and a prairie restoration, open only after midsummer during the peak of the blooming season. Many trees and shrubs throughout the entire grounds are labeled for identification.

Bird-watchers declare that this is the best winter birding spot in the Chicago region. Cold-weather visitors may see long-eared and saw-whet owls, hairy and downy woodpeckers, purple finches, and tufted titmice. In May, waves of warblers pass through, and migrating waterfowl use Arbor Lake. At least three rare species have been sighted here—the black-backed three-toed woodpecker, the pileated woodpecker, and the varied thrush. The plantings also attract an abundance of small mammals, including red and gray foxes, woodchucks, and skunks.

Visitors may drive or hike through the arboretum. If you'd like to combine the two, there are several parking lots near foot trails throughout the grounds.

A horticultural library, open Tuesday through Saturday, extends borrowing privileges to the public. Just outside the library is a charming reading garden that contains plants associated with the history of botany. A plant clinic in the administration building is available to help with plant identification, diagnose wood plant ailments, and offer advice on the selection of plants for landscaping.

Some outstanding classes and field trips for adults and family groups are offered year-round, and schools are encouraged to use the teaching facilities.

It's best to start your visit at the visitor center, where you can obtain trail guides and other publications, see botanical exhibits, and view get-acquainted photographic programs in the theater. Although no picnicking is allowed within the arboretum, a small area has been set aside where bag lunches may be eaten from 11:00 A.M. to 3:30 P.M., mid-April through October. A restaurant, open daily during peak visitor hours, is located at the visitor center; groups of twelve or more should make advance reservations (under certain circumstances such as bad weather, this facility may close without notice).

Hiking and Nature Trails

Approximately twelve miles of trails circle through the arboretum. You may start your walk at the visitor center, or drive to one of the parking lots along arboretum roads and begin your hike there. You will be given a map of the grounds when you enter the arboretum, and you may purchase (for a nominal fee) a more detailed map and description of the walking trails at the visitor center. The most popular walk is the Illinois Trees Nature Trail, a series of three loops that enable you to adjust the length of your hike from 0.6 mile to 2.9 miles. Other trails, ranging in length from 0.1 mile to 1.3 miles, include the Ground Cover Path, Viburnum Path, Big Rock Trail, Forest Trail, East Woods Trail, Evergreen Trail, Joy Morton Trail, and the Changing Lands Nature Trail. The Prairie Trail, open only after midsummer to protect the fragile grassland through which it passes, is carefully regulated. Be sure to pick up a special guide leaflet at the visitor center before exploring this part of the arboretum.

How to Get There: Located just north of Lisle at the intersection of IL 53 and the East-West Tollway (IL 5). From this intersection, go north on IL 53. The arboretum grounds lie on both sides of IL 53, but the main entrance is on the right side of the road.

Grounds open daily, year-round, 9:00 A.M.–5:00 P.M. when standard time is in effect, 9:00 A.M.–7:00 P.M. when daylight savings time is in effect; may be closed in bad weather. Visitor center open 9:30 A.M.–5:00 P.M., Mon.–Sat.; noon–5:00 Sun., April–Nov.; 9:30 A.M.–4:00 P.M., Mon–Sat.; noon–4:00 Sun., Dec.–March; closed Thanksgiving Day, Dec. 24 and 25, Dec. 31, and Jan. 1. Nominal parking fee per car; no additional admission charge. During May and Oct., an open-air bus takes visitors on guided tours at 2:00 P.M. weekdays and at 1:00, 2:00, and 3:00 P.M. Sat.; tickets may be purchased at the visitor center.

For Additional Information:
Morton Arboretum
Lisle, IL 60532
(312) 968-0074

Morton Grove Prairie

This minute grassland in the community of Morton Grove is a piece of true primeval wilderness. Covering just 1½ acres, it proudly represents the ¹/₁₀,₀₀₀ of Illinois prairies that have survived to modern times. Even among the survivors, it is unusual, because it is a rare black soil mesic type.

Growing in the rich earth here are some sixty species of plants found only on a true prairie. These were the plants that were prolific during the time the Indians and first white settlers lived here, plants that began to disappear with the advent of the plow.

Although it is surrounded by protective fencing, the prairie may easily be viewed from a path that encircles it. A park brochure describes both the human and natural history of the prairie, as well as the plants and colorful wildflowers it supports. Because the prairie is so special, it has been officially designated a state nature preserve.

Picnicking

A small city park that adjoins the prairie has picnic tables, restrooms, and drinking water.

How to Get There: The prairie is located in the village of Morton Grove in northeastern Cook County. From the intersection of I-294 and US 14 (Dempster St.), go east on US 14 to Waukegan Rd. Turn left (north) onto Waukegan and proceed to Churchill St. Turn right (east) and continue on Churchill to park on left side of road. Morton Grove Prairie is located in the northeastern portion of Prairie View Park, a city-owned facility.

Park open daily, year-round, at all times. Free.

For Additional Information:

Dr. Thomas Conway, Professor
Cluster II
Oakton Community College
1600 E. Golf Rd.
Des Plaines, IL 60016
(312) 635-1600, Ext. 1862

Morton Grove Park District
6834 Dempster St.
Morton Grove, IL 60053
(312) 965-1200

The Nature Conservancy, Illinois Field Office

The primary objective of The Nature Conservancy is to locate and preserve outstanding natural areas, and many of the areas described in this book were saved through the efforts of this private, nonprofit organization. Since its incorporation in 1951, The Nature Conservancy has established the largest system of privately owned nature sanctuaries in the world. Most of them are open to the general public free of charge for hiking and nature study.

Although the Conservancy retains and manages approximately sixty percent of all its acquisitions throughout the nation, it also helps public agencies acquire ecologically significant lands. Such agencies do not always have the necessary funds on hand when a desirable piece of property comes on the market, so the Conservancy makes the purchase for them and holds the property in trust until those funds are available.

Lovers of nature might consider a membership in this organization. Fees are nominal, and as a member, you will receive a printed guide to all Nature Conservancy areas in your state, a monthly newsletter from your state field office that will keep you apprised of ongoing state projects, and a bimonthly magazine published by The Nature Conservancy's national headquarters that will inform you of Conservancy activities in all parts of the country.

While most Conservancy areas in this book are in Illinois, Michigan, Indiana, and Wisconsin also have active chapters. You may contact any of them or the national office for further information about membership. The local offices can also supply information about the preserves in their respective states.

For Additional Information:

The Nature Conservancy
Illinois Field Office
79 W. Monroe St., Suite 708
Chicago, IL 60603
(312) 346-8166

The Nature Conservancy
Indiana Field Office
4200 N. Michigan Rd.
Indianapolis, IN 46208
(317) 923-7547

The Nature Conservancy
Michigan Field Office
Suite E, 531 N. Clippert St.
Lansing, MI 48912
(517) 332-1741

The Nature Conservancy
Wisconsin Field Office
1045 E. Dayton St., Rm. 209
Williamson
Madison, WI 53703
(608) 251-8140

The Nature Conservancy
National Office
1800 N. Kent St.
Arlington, VA 22209
(703) 841-5300

Ned Brown Forest Preserve

Ned Brown Preserve is a lovely mix of woods, meadows, and the largest lake in the Cook County Forest Preserve District. Lying within its 1,700-acre sprawl is Busse Forest, a 440-acre woodland of such high natural quality that it is both a state nature preserve and a national natural landmark. Here the maples, oaks, and elms, undisturbed for many years, tower high above you. Each year, on the forest floor, the rare nodding trillium and its showy cousin, the large-flowered trillium, add their beauty to the spring landscape. A cattail swamp provides additional habitat for migratory and resident wildlife, found here in a diversity and abundance unusual for such an urbanized area.

One of the most popular species to be seen is a once-native animal that is no longer indigenous to this area. Confined in a fourteen-acre enclosure comprised of pasture and woodland is a herd of magnificent elk.

The preserve's biggest drawing card, however, is island-studded Busse Lake, a 590-acre reservoir that impounds the waters of Salt Creek. In its northernmost reaches, 25 acres of marshland have been set aside as a wildlife refuge. The rest of the lake, its arms twisting outward like tentacles, is open to boaters.

Ned Brown Preserve is part of the newly organized Northwest Division of the Cook County Forest Preserve District, and division headquarters are located in the preserve's northwest corner. For descriptions of more district properties in the Northwest Division, see Crabtree Nature Center, p. 36.

Hiking and Bicycling

Many miles of hiking trails lead through the woods and meadows, past marshlands, and along the lakeshore. Approximately three miles of bicycle trails are open at present, with nine more miles being planned.

Boating and Fishing

Canoes, rowboats, and sailboats, as well as electric trolling motors, are allowed on all parts of the lake except the wildlife refuge. You may rent rowboats from April through October, or bring your own watercraft; free launching ramps are provided.

Six fishing walls along the shoreline, including one in the wildlife refuge, are adjacent to deep-water areas. Boat fishermen may cruise the main or south pools of the lakes. Although the lake is stocked with largemouth and smallmouth bass, bluegill, redear, brown bullhead, channel catfish, and crappie, it is most noted for the northern pike it yields.

Picnicking

Thirty picnic groves and sixteen shelters are provided throughout the preserve. Nearby facilities include parking, drinking water, and toilet facilities. Bring your own grill. Groups of twenty-five or more must obtain a permit in advance by personally visiting the Permit Office, Room 230, County Building, 118 N. Clark St., Chicago.

Winter Sports

All preserve trails are open to cross-country skiers. When ice is at least four inches thick, a special ice skating area is cleared on the north pool (wildlife refuge). Designated ice fishing areas are so posted on the south and main pools of the lake.

How to Get There: Located in northwestern Cook County, south of Arlington Heights and northwest of Elk Grove. From the intersection of US 14 (Northwest Hwy.) and Arlington Heights Rd. in Arlington Heights, head south on Arlington Heights Rd. to Higgins Rd. and turn right (west). Higgins Rd. bisects Ned Brown Preserve, and several park roads lead off of Higgins. To reach the Northwest Division headquarters, where you may obtain information about this and other preserves in the Northwest Division, continue on Higgins Rd. to the western boundary of the preserve and turn right (north) toward the I-290 entrance ramp. Instead of taking the entrance ramp to the left, continue north on Frontage Rd. to the headquarters building on the right (east) side of the road. Parking on site.

Preserve open daily, year-round, sunrise to sunset. Free.

For Additional Information:
Northwest Division Headquarters
Cook County Forest Preserve District
Golf Rd. and Frontage Rd. East (I-290)
Rolling Meadows, IL 60008
(312) 437-8330

Conservation Department
General Headquarters
Cook County Forest Preserve District
536 N. Harlem Ave.
River Forest, IL 60305
(312) 261-8400—Chicago number
(312) 366-9420—Suburban number

Nelson Lake Marsh

At nearly 200 acres, Nelson Lake Marsh is the largest natural area in Kane County. It is also one of the most ecologically diverse in the entire Chicago region. Situated in a glacial kettle hole, the low, level marshland is rimmed on three sides by a gently rolling terrain topped with forests and farmland. The pastoral countryside and large size of the preserve evoke a sense of wilderness that is rarely experienced in northern Illinois.

At the south end of the marsh is a shallow, forty-acre lake that is adorned with white water lilies in midsummer. It is all that remains of a larger lake that has been filled in over the years by the gradually advancing vegetation of the marsh. The open water gives way to floating islands of reeds, bulrushes, and wild rice, which in turn fuse together to form a cattail marsh.

A fen at the marsh's edge provides habitat for such rare plants as bog birch, bog willow, poison sumac, and bog arrow grass. In late summer, the fen is splashed with the colors of the Ohio goldenrod, swamp thistle, Joe-Pye weed, and fringed gentian.

The vast wetland supports sizable populations of muskrats, mink, and snakes, but it is best known to wildlife observers as a bird refuge. Among the many threatened or endangered species that have been sighted here are the osprey, American bittern, black crowned night heron, yellow-beaked blackbird, great egret, black tern, and yellow-bellied sapsucker. If you come here in early spring or near dusk, when the eerie calls of the coot and sora pierce the air, you will find this place haunting and unforgettable.

Hiking

An old road serves as a mile-long trail at present. Two branches of this trail cross wet, fragile, peaty soils and provide observation points for the major features of the marsh.

How to Get There: Located in southeastern Kane County. From the intersection of IL 31 and Main St. in Batavia, go west on Main St./Batavia Rd. about 3 miles to Nelson Lake Rd. Turn left (south) and proceed about 1/4 mile to the entrance road on the right (west) side of Nelson Lake Rd. Park on entrance road.

Open daily, year-round, during daylight hours. Groups must obtain permission from the Kane County Forest Preserve District before visiting. Free.

For Additional Information:

Kane County Forest Preserve District
719 Batavia Ave.
Geneva, IL 60134
(312) 232-1242

Nelson Lake Advocates
1141 Woodland Ave.
Batavia, IL 60510
(No phone)

The Nature Conservancy
Illinois Field Office
79 W. Monroe St., Suite 708
Chicago, IL 60603
(312) 346-8166

Norris Woods

This stretch of inviting woodlands near St. Charles sprawls, wild and beautiful, over seventy-three acres of uneven terrain along the east bank of the Fox River. Within its depths is an old-growth stand of trees, dominated by red and white oaks and shagbark hickories, that is one of the least disturbed forests in the Chicago region. Beneath the outspread branches, soil untouched for centuries supports a diversity of woodland wildflowers. The Indian pipe and squawroot, colorless parasites of oak roots, are only two of several rare species that thrive in the deep litter of the forest floor.

Since this preserve is fairly new, wildlife surveys are still going on, but its value as a bird refuge is already established. The veery, a threatened species in Illinois, is known to breed here, and the blue-gray gnatcatcher, ovenbird, and hooded warbler are probable nesters.

On the level west bank of the Fox River, opposite Norris Woods, is forty-two-acre Ferson's Creek Marsh. The marsh, fed by pure spring waters, shelters the rare and unique northern fringed orchid and the small fringed gentian. Prothonotary and yellow-throated warblers nest in a forest of ash and silver maple trees, and the gnawing action of beaver is evident on many tree stumps. Although there is no public access to the marsh at the moment, it may be seen from IL 31, and a trails system is in the planning stage. Check with the St. Charles Park District or The Nature Conservancy, which was instrumental in saving both Ferson's Creek Marsh and Norris Woods, for an update on facilities.

Just south of Norris Woods is Pottawatomie Park, a city park bordering the Fox River where you can choose from a full range of recreational activities. There are picnic tables with stoves, a shelter, a refreshment stand, drinking water, restrooms, a children's playground, a nine-hole golf course, miniature golf, tennis courts, a softball diamond, and swimming pools. In addition, you may ride a miniature train through the park, take a five-mile cruise on the river aboard a paddle wheel riverboat, launch your own boat at a park ramp, go fishing in the summer and ice skating in the winter.

Norris Woods and Ferson's Creek Marsh are owned jointly by the city of St. Charles and the St. Charles Park District. The park district also owns Pottawatomie Park.

Hiking

Two trails, one along a sewer right-of-way and one along the Fox River, lead through Norris Woods for about two miles. Although the preserve includes bluffs with moderate to steep slopes, the trails have been developed over level terrain.

How to Get There: Norris Woods, Ferson's Creek Marsh, and Pottawatomie Park are located on the north side of St. Charles in east central Kane County. To reach Norris Woods from the intersection of IL 64 and IL 25 (here called Fifth Ave.) east of the Fox River in St. Charles, go north on IL 25 for approximately 1 mile to Marion Ave. (there's a church on the corner of IL 25 and Marion). Turn left (west) and proceed on Marion to N. Third St. Turn right (north) to preserve sign and entrance on the left (west). Park on Third St. To view Ferson's Creek Marsh from the road, find the intersection of IL 64 and IL 31 west of the Fox River in St. Charles, and go north on IL 31; the marsh will be on the right (east) side of the road just after you cross over Ferson's Creek. To reach Pottawatomie Park from the intersection of IL 64 and Second Ave. east of the Fox River in St. Charles, go north on Second Ave. to North Ave. Turn left (west) on North Ave. and proceed to park entrance. Parking on site.

Norris Woods open daily, year-round, during daylight hours. Free. Pottawatomie Park open daily, year-round; 8:00 A.M.–11:00 P.M., Memorial Day–Labor Day; daylight hours rest of year. Nominal entrance fee in summer.

For Additional Information:
St. Charles Park District
101 S. Second St.
St. Charles, IL 60174
(312) 584-1055—Information about Norris Woods, Ferson's Creek Marsh, Pottawatomie Park

The Nature Conservancy
Illinois Field Office
79 W. Monroe St., Suite 708
Chicago, IL 60603
(312) 346-8166—Information about Norris Woods, Ferson's Creek Marsh

North Branch Forest Preserve Division

This division, the most heavily used in the Cook County Forest Preserve District, edges the shoreline of the North Branch of the Chicago River as it twists its way south. Approximately half of the parklands lie within the city limits of Chicago on the far north side.

Lying on a flat basin that once was the bed of glacial Lake Chicago, this land has only a shallow layer of fertile topsoil that limits the types of flora found here. There are, however, some fine woodland groves to explore, especially in the northern half of the division, and an interesting stand of hackberry trees in the Edgebrook Woods area.

Cutting across the extreme southern end of the division in a northeast-southwest direction is the famous Indian Boundary Line. It marks the northern border of a twenty-mile-wide strip of land that extends from Lake Michigan to the town of Ottawa on the Illinois River, ceded to the whites by the Pottawatomi Indians in 1816.

Hiking, Bicycling, and Horseback Riding

An improved, multiuse trail for hikers, bicyclists, and horseback riders runs north from Oakton St. in the northern part of the division to join the trail system in the adjoining Skokie Division (described elsewhere). South of Oakton St. hikers will find several pathways that wander in all directions. The newest trail here is the North Branch Bicycle Trail. Still under construction, it will extend northward for 20 miles from Devon Ave., through both the North Branch and Skokie Divisions, to the Cook–Lake County line. At this writing, approximately twelve miles have been completed, including all of that portion in the North Branch Division. There are no horse rentals; an annual horse registration and rider's license are required.

Canoeing

All but a minute section of the North Branch of the Chicago River in this area is bounded on one or both sides by forest preserve lands, offering a pleasant canoe outing along wooded shorelines. You may put in at the Beckwith Road crossing at the division's northern boundary or at the Whealan swimming pool parking lot in the southern part of the division.

Swimming

The Whealan swimming pool is one of just three in the entire Cook County Forest Preserve District. It's usually very crowded, however. Located off Devon Road in the southern part of the division, it's open from 1:00 to 10:00 P.M. during warm summer months. Children under six are not admitted. There's a nominal admission fee, but children under twelve may swim free of charge from 2:30 to 4:30 P.M. each Monday, Wednesday, and Friday.

Picnicking

Because of this division's popularity, the forest preserve district offers many picnic areas here, and you're never far from the riverbank. Shelters are numerous, and some grills are available. Whatever spot you choose, you'll find parking space, drinking water, and toilet facilities close at hand. Groups of twenty-five or more must obtain a permit in advance by personally visiting the Permit Office, Room 230, County Building, 118 N. Clark St., Chicago.

Winter Sports

Most winter sports activities center around the popular toboggan slides just north of Devon Road near the swimming pool. You may bring your own toboggan or rent one; the slides are open daily 10:00 A.M.–10:00 P.M. when weather conditions permit. Near the slides are gentler slopes for sledding and an ice skating area; more sledding slopes are located at Indian Road Woods. Cross-country skiers follow the division's bicycle trail through the full length of the preserve, or the multiuse trail in the northernmost part of the division.

How to Get There: Located adjacent to Chicago's far north side near the town of Niles, part of the division is within Chicago's city limits. Parklands lie along the banks of the North Branch of the Chicago River between Beckwith Rd. (also called Church St. in places) on the north and Foster Ave. on the south. Since each division of the Cook County Forest Preserve District features several recreation areas and attractions, crisscrossed by many roads and in some instances disconnected, it's best to obtain division maps, directions for getting there, and other pertinent information from district or division headquarters before visiting one. To reach North Branch Division Headquarters from the intersection of Milwaukee Ave. (IL 21) and Oakton St. in Niles, go southeast on Milwaukee Ave. to Harts Rd. and turn left (northeast). Proceed on Harts Rd. to headquarters building on right (east) side of road just after you cross the river. Parking on site.

Preserve lands open daily, year-round, sunrise to sunset; free. Headquarters offices open Mon.–Fri., 8:30 A.M.–5:00 P.M., year-round; closed major holidays.

For Additional Information:
North Branch Division Headquarters
Cook County Forest Preserve District
6633 Harts Rd.
Niles, IL 60648
(312) 775-4060
(312) 775-4194

Conservation Department
General Headquarters
Cook County Forest Preserve District
536 N. Harlem Ave.
River Forest, IL 60305
(312) 261-8400—Chicago number
(312) 366-9420—Suburban number

Northwest Forest Preserve Division

See listing under Ned Brown Forest Preserve, p. 91.

Oakes Forest Preserve

See listing under Great Western Trail, p. 57.

Palos and Sag Valley Forest Preserve Divisions

These two adjoining divisions comprise the largest, most diversified holding in the Cook County Forest Preserve District. Located just southwest of Chicago in the hilliest, most scenic section of the county, the Palos and Sag Valley divisions sprawl over 10,000 acres of woodlands, meadows, lakes, ponds, sloughs, swamps, and small, twisting streams.

The Palos hills are a result of a great glacier that ended its southward march here. When the climate warmed and the glacier retreated, it left behind huge chunks of ice that had separated from the main tongue of the icefield. As these chunks melted down, the waters found their way into depressions in the land and formed the many small ponds and sloughs that exist here today.

One, Cranberry Slough, is the only quaking bog in Cook County. Located at the heart of a 372-acre state nature preserve, it is inhabited by beaver. This preserve is also notable for its sphagnum moss, the rare royal fern, a thicket of purple chokeberry, and, as the name of the slough implies, cranberry plants.

Three other state nature preserves lie within division boundaries. Black Partridge Woods is a varied eighty-acre tract that includes a meandering creek and several springs that flow year-round, river bluffs, and forested hillsides. This is the first place in the Chicago region that wildflowers bloom in the spring. Skunk cabbage and marsh marigold are particularly abundant.

In Paw Paw Woods, a magnificent, 105-acre forest, are three species rarely found in this area—pawpaws, which here reach the northernmost limits of their range in Illinois, shingle oaks, and one large chinquapin oak.

The Little Red Schoolhouse Nature Center in the Palos and Sag Valley Forest Preserve Divisions   *Bill Thomas*

The fourth preserve, Cap Sauers Holding, is the largest undeveloped tract of native landscape in the Cook County Forest Preserve District. Wild and isolated, teeming with wildlife, it includes 1,600 acres of rugged, hilly terrain blanketed with thickets of haws and crabs and dense growths of oaks and hickories. Several small streams flow intermittently through its depths, feeding adjacent wetlands, and one of the best defined eskers (glacial ridges) in Illinois is found within its boundaries. If you climb to the top of this ridge, you'll be rewarded with a spectacular overlook of the preserve.

Another dramatic view is available from atop the toboggan slides at Swallow Cliff Winter Sports Area. Although hordes of people descend upon this recreation area when the slides are in operation, it's relatively deserted during warm weather months.

Be prepared for a steep climb up a flight of stone steps, however.

Bird-watchers will enjoy the variety and abundance of birds found year-round at McGinnis, Saganashkee, and Longjohn sloughs, all maintained as wildlife sanctuaries by the forest preserve district. Huge numbers of waterfowl congregate at the first two each April, and many remain until the first fall freeze. In addition, whistling swans are sometimes seen in late November at McGinnis Slough, while peregrine falcons occasionally stop at Saganashkee. Longjohn Slough is noted for passerine migrants, herons, ducks, and swallows in both spring and fall.

Perched on a hill at the south end of Longjohn Slough is the Little Red Schoolhouse Nature Center, actually used as a school from the time it was built in 1886 until 1948. Its fascinating array of indoor and outdoor exhibits changes with the seasons.

One of the most unique natural features in the Sag Valley Division is also one of the least known. Located on the grounds of Camp Sagawau, an environmental education facility sponsored by the forest preserve district, is Sagawau Canyon, the only rock gorge in Cook County. It is just 1,100 feet long, 15 feet wide, and about 15 feet deep, carved by a tiny steam less than two miles in length, but it nurtures several species of ferns and wildflowers that are found nowhere else in Illinois. Since Camp Sagawau itself is not open to the general public, you should call the camp director at (312) 257-2045 for advance permission to visit the gorge and to learn its exact location.

Sagawau Canyon dates back to time primeval. A short distance to the north, in the Palos Division, one of the most somber moments in modern history is remembered. The original Argonne Laboratory for atomic research (now located in neighboring DuPage County and described elsewhere under Waterfall Glen), where the first atomic bomb was developed, stood here on forest preserve lands. You may walk to the site today along a peaceful trail bordered by hawthorns, crab apples, and wild prairie roses.

Hiking, Bicycling, and Horseback Riding

Some thirty-two miles of well-maintained trails are open to hikers, bicyclists, and horseback riders (no rentals; annual horse registration and rider's license required). They wind through nearly every part of both divisions and are laid out in loops, so that by the use of connecting trails or highways, a hike or ride of any length may be taken. Three marked nature trails circle through some three miles of woodland, marsh, and prairie at the Little Red Schoolhouse Nature Center. A trail that follows the northwestern bank of the Illinois and Michigan Canal for six miles in the Palos Division was established especially for bicyclists.

Boating and Fishing

Boating is allowed at designated areas in both Palos and Sag Valley divisions. At the largest body of water, 325-acre Saganashkee Slough in Palos Division, and at 160-acre Tampier Lake, you may rent a rowboat or bring your own. Rental rowboats only may be used on 55-acre Maple Lake in the Palos Division. Electric motors are permitted on all three. Since parts of Saganashkee and Tampier are wildlife refuges and closed to boating, be sure to observe all posted signs. Watercraft of all kinds, as well as electric and outboard motors, may follow the Des Plaines River, which lies just northwest of the main portion of the Palos Division. A small tract of forest preserve land on the northwest bank offers a free launch ramp on the river, but no rentals. The Illinois and Michigan Canal, which parallels the river, is open to canoes; put in at Willow Springs Road near the northwest corner of the Palos Division.

Forest preserve personnel claim that most of the best fishing waters in the Cook County Forest Preserve District are in these divisions. Elsewhere, only Busse Lake in the Northwest Division (described under Ned Brown Forest Preserve) is as good. Fishing is allowed at all aforementioned waters except the Illinois and Michigan Canal. In addition, shoreline fishing only is allowed at Belly Deep Slough, Bullfrog Lake, Joe's Pond, and Tuma Lake in Palos Division and at Horsetail Slough, McGinnis Slough, Papoose Lake, Sag Quarry East, and Sag Quarry West in Sag Valley Division. Bluegill are stocked in all division waters; other species found in one or more locations are northern pike, largemouth bass, sunfish, bullhead, channel cat, carp, goldfish, perch, rainbow trout, and crappie. The Des Plaines River yields all of the above except perch and rainbow trout.

Picnicking

Excellent picnic areas are located in many cool, scenic areas, with parking, drinking water, and toilet facilities close at hand. Most have grills, and several major areas also have shelters. Groups of twenty-five or more must obtain advanced permits in person from the Permit Office, Room 230, County Building, 118 N. Clark St., Chicago.

Winter Sports

The Swallow Cliff winter sports center in Sag Valley Division, open daily 10:00 A.M.–10:00 P.M. when weather conditions permit, includes six toboggan slides that are the highest and longest in the Chicago region, nearby slopes for children's sleds, and a warming shelter where a roaring fire and refreshments await you. You may rent toboggans here or bring your own and use the slides free of charge. Other hills in both divisions have slopes suitable for sledding. Cross-country skiers use the same slopes, as well as most of the developed trail system. Ice skaters and ice fishermen may use designated ponds when ice is judged safe.

How to Get There: The area is southwest of Chicago, near the western border of Cook County. Although Palos and Sag Valley are actually separate divisions, they do adjoin each other, and most people visit them both at the same time. Palos Division extends northward from the Calumet Sag Channel to I-294 at 79th St; Sag Valley sprawls southward from the channel to 143rd St. Most division lands are included in one large, connected tract, but a few areas are separate. Since each division of the Cook County Forest Preserve District features many recreation areas and attractions, crisscrossed by several roads and in some instances disconnected, it's best to obtain division maps, directions for getting there, and other pertinent information from district or division headquarters before visiting one. To reach the headquarters for the Palos and Sag Valley divisions from the village of Palos Heights, which lies just east of the two divisions, go to the intersection of IL 83 (Calumet Sag Rd.) and IL 43 (Harlem Ave.) on the northern side of Palos Heights. From that point, proceed west on IL 83 to its intersection with Willow Springs Rd. (104th Ave.) within the Sag Valley Division. To reach Sag Valley headquarters, turn left (south) on Willow Springs Rd. and go to McCarthy Rd. Turn right (west) and continue on McCarthy Rd. to headquarters building at southeast corner of McCarthy Rd. and Will-Cook Rd. To reach Palos Division headquarters from the intersection of IL 83 and Willow Springs Rd., go north on Willow Springs Rd., across the Calumet Sag Channel, to headquarters building on right (east) side of the road. To reach the Little Red Schoolhouse Nature Center, continue past the turnoff for the headquarters building a short distance to nature center on the left (west) side of Willow Springs Rd. Parking on site.

Preserve lands open daily, year-round, sunrise to sunset; free. Nature Center exhibit building open year-round, 9:00 A.M.–4:30 P.M., Mon.–Thurs.; 9:00 A.M.–5:00 P.M., Sat., Sun., and some holidays; grounds open daily, year-round, 8:00 A.M. to about half an hour before sunset; center closed Fridays, Thanksgiving, Christmas, New Year's Day. Free. Headquarters offices open Mon.–Fri., year-round, 8:30 A.M.–5:00 P.M.; closed major holidays.

For Additional Information:
Palos Division Headquarters
Cook County Forest Preserve District
9900 S. Willow Springs Rd. (104th Ave.)
Willow Springs, IL 60480
(312) 839-5617
(312) 839-5618

Sag Valley Headquarters
Cook County Forest Preserve District
12201 McCarthy Rd.
Palos Park, IL 60464
(312) 448-8532
(312) 448-8533

Little Red Schoolhouse Nature Center
P.O. Box 92
Willow Springs, IL 60480
(312) 839-6897

Conservation Department
General Headquarters
Cook County Forest Preserve District
536 N. Harlem Ave.
River Forest, IL 60305
(312) 261-8400—Chicago number
(312) 366-9420—Suburban number

Peacock Prairie

See listing under Woodworth Prairie Preserve, p. 136.

Pilcher Park

Pilcher Park, 327 acres of hills, meadows, dense woodlands, marshes, ponds, and streams was formerly a private arboretum.

More than 50 species of birds nest here, and some 118 species have been sighted, making this a prime bird-watching locale. In a section of the park known as Bird Haven are thickets crowded with crab apples and hawthorns that create excellent cover for small songbirds. The low areas support willows and maples and are dotted with marshes where woodcocks live. Covering the hills that form most of the parkland is an oak and maple forest favored by hawks, woodpeckers, flycatchers, thrushes, and, rarely, the long-eared owl. Hickory Creek, which flows through the park, attracts pied-billed grebes, great blue herons, sandpipers, and several kinds of ducks.

In early spring, before the trees leaf out, the floor of the forest is a vast flower garden. Mayapples, trilliums, wild ginger, trout lilies, toothworts, and many other flowers may be seen.

Although the woodland wildflowers have short lives, it is possible to view blossoming plants year-round in Pilcher Park. The Joliet Park District greenhouse, with its four rooms of trees, flowers, and cacti, is located in the eastern part of the park and offers seasonal shows.

Other special features include a flowing well, where you may taste the mineral water, and a small zoo housing such North American wildlife as foxes, owls, raccoons, and wolves. Adjacent to the zoo is a nature center, where you'll see small live animals (reptiles, fish, and birds), as well as natural history displays and nature films.

A former farm field near the nature center is gradually being restored to the prairie it once was. Over the years, it is hoped, the blazing star, compass plant, rattlesnake master, and other prairie plants that have been planted here will reestablish themselves. Regular visitors will have the opportunity to witness the transformation and learn about the ecology of a prairie in the process.

The park's environmental education program is outstanding. Besides participating in well-conceived wildflower walks, bird hikes, and pond studies, visitors may watch maple syrup being made each spring. Sap is collected from the sugar maple trees in plastic bags and boiled down to syrup in an evaporator hut. The process culminates with an annual pancake breakfast, after which bottled syrup may be purchased and taken home.

Hiking, Bicycling, and Nature Trails

Hiking trails wind through all portions of the park. Several of them form loops so that they may be easily combined. The entire system totals about four miles, and all trails begin at the nature center. One short trail leading through a sensory garden is blacktopped for the handicapped. Guided nature hikes are scheduled periodically. Bicyclists will find nearly five miles of trails beginning at a parking lot across the road from the nature center.

Picnicking

Two large picnic areas, one near the main entrance in the western part of the park and another at the opposite end, offer tables, drinking water, and stoves.

Winter Sports

Cross-country skiers may use some of the hiking trails when there is enough snow. Ask at the desk in the nature center for a special ski map. Tobogganing is permitted on some park hills, and ice skaters use the frozen surface of Hickory Creek.

How to Get There: Located on north side of US 30 in Joliet. Follow US 30 east from downtown Joliet to park entrance on left side of highway. Look for sign at entrance.

Open daily, year-round, during daylight hours. Nature center open 9:30 A.M.–4:30 P.M., Monday–Friday; 10:00 A.M.–4:30 P.M., Saturday and Sunday. Greenhouse open 9:00 A.M.–4:00 P.M. daily. Admission free.

For Additional Information:
Pilcher Park
c/o Joliet Park District
3998 W. Jefferson
Joliet, IL 60436
(815) 726-2207 (Pilcher Park)
(815) 727-4824 (Park District Office)

Plum Creek Nature Center

See listing under Goodenow Grove Forest Preserve, p. 54.

Pottawatomie Park

See listing under Norris Woods, p. 94.

Powers State Conservation Area

Straddling the Illinois–Indiana state line about three miles south of the Lake Michigan shoreline, virtually in the shadow of heavy industry, is one of the metropolitan area's finest fishing holes. Because of its proximity to greater Chicago, it is also one of the most popular.

Wolf Lake, separated into several sections by dikes built up during an old dredging project, is the focal point of a 580-acre Illinois parkland known as the William W. Powers State Conservation Area. Surprisingly, it is often quiet and peaceful here, particularly during the early morning hours. Low sand flats and marshes surround the lake, creating a haven for waterfowl, shorebirds, marsh dwellers, and songbirds. During each spring migration, from the last of April through the first part of May, Caspian terns pause here to rest. Shorebirds seen during both spring and fall migratory periods include sandpipers, common snipe, and white-rumped, buff-breasted, and piping plovers.

At the north end of Wolf Lake, you'll find an overlook that's part of the Calumet Forest Preserve Division (described elsewhere). There are no marked trails, but you may wander along the lakeshore, landscaped in some places, wooded in others, or walk atop the dikes that extend into the lake in both an east-west and a north-south direction. During warm-weather months, a concession stand near the main entrance offers refreshments and some fishing supplies.

Boating and Fishing

Much of the lake is open to boating; motors of ten hp or less are permitted. Just north of the main entrance is a two-lane launching ramp. Rental boats are available at the docks behind the park concession stand during warm-weather months, but you may bring your own at any time. You may also fish from the bank; about six miles of shoreline are open to anglers. Largemouth bass, northern pike, bluegill, redear sunfish, crappie, bullhead, carp, and yellow perch will test your abilities.

Picnicking

A pleasant picnic area with tables and stoves is shaded by willow and cottonwood trees; it's located just south of the main entrance. There's also a shelter, available on a first-come basis. Drinking water and restrooms are centrally located.

Winter Sports

Ice skating, ice fishing, and ice boating are permitted when the ice is thick enough.

How to Get There: Located in far southeastern Cook County. From downtown Chicago, take I-94 south to the Stony Island Ave./103rd St. Exit. Head east to Stony Island Ave., then turn south on Stony Island Ave. to 103rd St. Turn left (east) onto 103rd St., and proceed to Torrence Ave. Turn right (south) on Torrence, and continue to 106th St. Turn left (east) onto 106th St., go to Ave. O and turn right (south). The conservation area's main entrance is at Ave. O and 123rd St., on the left (east) side of Ave. O. Parking on site.

Open daily, year-round, 6:00 A.M.–sunset; closed Christmas Day and New Year's Day. Free.

For Additional Information:
Site Superintendent
William W. Powers Conservation Area
12800 Ave. O
Chicago, IL 60633
(312) 646-3270

Prairie Path

See Illinois Prairie Path listing, p. 70.

Pratt's Wayne Woods

Some of the finest marshlands in DuPage County are found at Pratt's Wayne Woods, a 1,281-acre expanse of meadow and forest. Lying at the edges of small, meandering streams and around the shores of a chain of lakes, the marshy areas lure sizable populations of shorebirds, amphibians, muskrats, and mink and, along with the preserve's other habitats, support a wealth of plant life. The Massasauga rattlesnake, DuPage County's only poisonous snake, is known to live here, but is rarely seen.

Pratt's Wayne Woods also features well-maintained facilities, including a model airplane field and sites for youth group and day camping, and a diversity of outdoor recreational opportunities.

Hiking, Bicycling, and Horseback Riding

Walks here are best described as light hikes. Although the trails are not difficult, some traverse the marsh and are quite soggy in spots. Also open to hikers, as well as bicycle riders, is the Illinois Prairie Path (described elsewhere), which runs along part of the preserve's western border. Horseback riders will find some bridle paths as well as an Olympic-caliber jump course. The latter is a cooperative venture of the forest preserve district, which owns the land, and the Wayne–DuPage Hunt Club, which maintains the course. Many equestrian competitions are held at Pratt's Wayne Woods. No rentals; annual registration is required.

Fishing

Fishing is among the best in the DuPage County Forest Preserve District. The largest lake is regularly stocked with largemouth and smallmouth bass, catfish, crappie, bluegill, bullhead, walleye, and northern pike. A sixteen-pound pike caught here set a district record.

Picnicking

Several picturesque picnic areas are scattered about the preserve. An entire area, as well as a shelter, may be reserved in advance for a nominal fee. Drinking water and toilets are provided.

Winter Sports

There are no marked trails for cross-country enthusiasts, but skiers are welcome to forge their own way over preserve lands. Ice fishermen and skaters use the lake when ice is at least three inches thick.

How to Get There: From the intersection of IL 64 (North Ave.) and IL 59 in West Chicago, go north on IL 59 to Army Trail Rd. Turn left (west) and proceed on Army Trail Rd. to Powis Rd. and turn right (north). The main entrance is on the left (west) side of Powis Rd., but the preserve borders both sides of this thoroughfare. Parking on site.

Open daily, year-round, from one hour after sunrise to one hour after sunset. Free.

For Additional Information:
DuPage County Forest Preserve District
P.O. Box 2339
Glen Ellyn, IL 60137
(312) 620-3800

Fullersburg Woods Nature Center
3609 Spring Rd.
Oak Brook, IL 60521
(312) 620-3843

Queen Anne Prairie—Eckert Cemetery

This tiny one-acre preserve is one of the few surviving remnants of the great tallgrass prairie that once covered more than half of Illinois, when the grass was belly deep on a horse. That vast expanse is now gone forever, but in such places as this you may marvel at the glory of the prairie that once was.

Plumed avens, prairie blazing star, rattlesnake master, purple prairie clover, prairie violet, and leadplant still appear on the landscape. More than fifty native Illinois prairie plants have been catalogued here, and the McHenry County Conservation District has erected a display board to assist plant identification and list approximate blooming times.

No development in any form exists on this preserve. It is for those who wish to see a genuine bit of prairie. An interpretive trail rims the cemetery, but you're asked not to enter the cemetery itself.

How to Get There: Located at 2335 N. Queen Anne Rd., northeast of Woodstock. From Woodstock, go northeast on IL 120 to Charles Rd. Turn left on Charles Rd. to Queen Anne Rd. and turn right. Prairie and cemetery are on left side of road, just north of intersection of Charles and Queen Anne Rds.

Open daily, year-round, 9:00 A.M. until dark. Free.

For Additional Information:
McHenry County Conservation District
6512 Harts Rd.
Ringwood, IL 60072
(815) 338-1405
(815) 678-4431

Raccoon Grove Forest Preserve

A lovely place in which to spend quiet moments, Raccoon Grove is perhaps most noted for its spring flowers. It lies atop approximately 150 acres of gently rolling hill country in eastern Will County and embraces the shores of Rock Creek. Covering most of the area is a forest dominated by oaks and hickories and interspersed with white ash and wild black cherry. Some sugar maples thrive in a narrow band on a park slope.

No noisy crowds here—this preserve is primarily for nature study.

Hiking

A trail system winds throughout the preserve. Guided nature hikes are featured in the spring and fall.

Picnicking

Both tables and shelters are available. Drinking water and restrooms are nearby.

How to Get There: From Monee, go south on IL 50 (Governors Hwy.) to Pauling Rd. and turn left (east). Proceed one-eighth mile on Pauling Rd. to preserve entrance on right. Parking on site.

Open daily, year-round; 8:00 A.M.–8:00 P.M., May–Oct.; 8:00 A.M.–5:00 P.M., Nov.–April. Free.

For Additional Information:
Plum Creek Nature Center
Goodenow Grove Nature Preserve
Box 241, R.R. 2
Beecher, IL 60401
(312) 946-2216

Forest Preserve District of Will County
US 52 and Cherry Hill Rd., R.R. 4
Joliet, IL 60433
(815) 727-8700

Reed–Turner Woodland

Within just thirty-two acres, this small tract of wilderness encompasses an amazing diversity of habitats. Its most outstanding scenic feature is a steep-walled ravine that has been carved by the south branch of Indian Creek. Over the past 10,000 years, the meandering stream has changed its course many times, and evidence of those changes is readily seen today. The north- and south-facing slopes present sharply contrasting environments. Dense oak and hickory woods with an understory of ironwood, black cherry, and various shrubs blanket the south-facing slope, while the cool, moist slope that faces north is lush with ferns, many uncommon to the Chicago area, and a mesic forest of red oak, basswood, and sugar maple. At the base of the ravine, the creek's narrow floodplain supports forests of bur oak and walnut ash.

Also lying within the preserve are a small alkaline meadow, a prairie restoration, a seepage fen, and portions of a man-made reservoir known as Reed Lake.

More than 225 species of plants thrive here, including, in the spring, great white trillium, baneberry, trout lily, wild columbine, and hyacinth. Later in the year, such flowers as the starry campion, yellow false foxglove, and locally rare fire pink cluster in small clearings. Woodpeckers, nuthatches, wood thrushes, and chipmunks reside in the woodlands, while herons and migratory waterfowl are often seen feeding in the lake.

When the first white settlers came to this region in 1837, they saw a forest much like the one seen here. The largest and least disturbed remnant of that original woodland is preserved here for posterity.

With the exception of the erosion-sensitive steeper ravine slopes, all major features of the preserve are touched by the well-maintained trail systems. A trail map guides visitors along the way.

How to Get There: Located in Lake County, one mile northwest of the village of Long Grove, on Old McHenry Rd. Access is by prior arrangement only; contact the preserve steward for permission to enter, as well as exact directions for reaching the site. Limited parking space is available on adjoining private property.

Open daily, year-round, from dawn to dusk. Free, but contributions to the Long Grove Park District or The Nature Conservancy are gratefully accepted.

For Additional Information:

Barbara Turner
Preserve Steward
Reed-Turner Woodland
Old McHenry Rd.
RFD 6, Box 213
Long Grove, IL 60047
(312) 438-7230

Long Grove Park District
Long Grove, IL 60047
(312) 438-8104

The Nature Conservancy
Illinois Field Office
79 W. Monroe St., Suite 708
Chicago, IL 60603
(312) 346-8166

Ryerson Conservation Area

Just seventeen miles from the northwest corner of Chicago, tucked away between the suburban communities of Lincolnshire and Riverwoods in Lake County, is an area containing the finest example of old-growth sugar maple forest in northeastern Illinois.

Of the conservation area's 550 acres, 279 are designated a nature preserve. Here, in the rich soils of the Des Plaines River floodplain, the trees grow tall and straight. The maples stand proudly alongside basswoods, swamp white oaks and slippery elms, bur oaks and walnut trees.

In spring and summer the asters, obedient plants, nodding trilliums, thistles, cardinal flowers, and purple-fringed gentians offer a parade of colors. But the great white trillium is the star of the show, growing in thick white masses.

Visitors may spot some unusual wildlife here. Three residents of the conservation area—the black-crowned night heron, the red-shouldered hawk, and the evasive Massasauga rattlesnake (also known as the swamp rattler and viper)—are endangered species in Illinois. Near the southern boundary, the Brewster's warbler has established its only known nesting site in the state. The extremely rare bald eagle and Swainson's hawk are occasionally seen near the river, and a stand of spruces at the north end of the preserve attracts finches and owls in the winter. Other interesting species found here are the red fox, white-tailed deer, and the blue-spotted salamander.

Complementing Ryerson's natural features are a nature center and library. An environmental education program known as Soaring Sights is conducted year-round for the general public, and offers activities such as night walks and maple sugar making. Special programs are also available for organized groups and school classes. Very nominal fees are charged (slightly higher for non-Lake County residents), and advance reservations are required.

In the northwestern part of the conservation area a working farm still operates as it did some forty years ago. Children are delighted with the chickens, geese, cows, pigs, horses, goats, and sheep that roam the barnyard. In the open fields, corn, oats, and wheat are grown as demonstration crops.

Because Ryerson Conservation Area is so unique, you will find stricter regulations here than at other forest preserves in Lake County. Nature is the chief attraction, and the preservation of the land is given prime consideration. There are no picnic facilities, no ballfields, no playgrounds. Fishing and swimming are not allowed. No motorized vehicles, bicycles, horses, or pets are permitted on preserve lands. Alcohol, radios, and taped music are taboo. Instead, this is a place for solitude and reflection.

Hiking

Nearly ten miles of trails branch out in various directions, leading through open meadows, beneath a canopy of huge trees, along the riverbank, and across farmland. It is possible to follow several loops or make one-way forays for any distance you choose to walk. A free trail map is available at the nature center.

Winter Sports

Six miles of trail may be used by cross-country skiers in snow season.

How to Get There: Located in southeastern Lake County, along the east bank of the Des Plaines River. From the intersection of I-94 and IL 22 (Half Day Rd.) in Lincolnshire, go west on IL 22 to Riverwoods Rd. and turn left (south). Proceed on Riverwoods Rd. to Ryerson Conservation Area on the right. Parking on site.

Preserve open daily, year-round, 9:00 A.M.–5:00 P.M. in summer; 9:00 A.M.–4:00 P.M. in winter. On Saturdays and Sundays during bird migration periods (usually the months of April, May, Sept., and Oct.), bird-watchers are allowed to enter the preserve at 6:30 A.M. Free admission at all times.

For Additional Information:
Lake County Forest Preserve District
2000 N. Milwaukee Ave.
Libertyville, IL 60048
(312) 367-6640

Edward L. Ryerson Conservation Area
3735 Riverwoods Rd.
Riverwoods, IL 60015
(312) 948-7750

Salt Creek Forest Preserve Division

A short distance west of central Chicago, the Salt Creek Division of the Cook County Forest Preserve District intermittently edges the banks of the Des Plaines River and its tributary, Salt Creek, near the point where their waters blend. It includes within its boundaries the Brookfield Zoo (described elsewhere) and the

Chicago Portage National Historic Site, a major factor in Chicago's metamorphosis from a trading post to a great city. Once one of the most important locations in North America, the Chicago Portage linked the waters of the Great Lakes with the Mississippi River. The most important east-west Indian trails merged here, and it was coveted equally by the Indians, French and British traders, and American pioneers.

In the division's westernmost section lies Salt Creek Woods, a 245-acre state nature preserve that encompasses some excellent wildlife habitat. Its ponds, marsh, oak woodlands, and the creek itself provide food and shelter for waterfowl and a thriving herd of deer.

Hiking, Bicycling, and Horseback Riding

Hikers will find many miles of trails along stream banks and through the nature preserve to follow. Most are footpaths, but there are developed trails in the Bemis Woods area in the westernmost portion of the division and in 425-acre Arie Crown Forest, the only tract of land in this division that does not border either Salt Creek or the Des Plaines River. One of the best systems of bicycle paths in the Cook County Forest Preserve District is in this division. It includes 3.2 miles of crisscrossing loops in Arie Crown Forest and a 6-mile-long segment that generally follows the banks of Salt Creek from Brookfield Woods to Bemis Woods South. Five miles of trails await equestrians. No rentals; annual horse registration and rider's license required.

Boating and Fishing

Watercraft and motors of all types ply the waters of the Des Plaines River. A free launch ramp is provided on the west bank of the river at Plank Road Meadow area.

The Des Plaines River yields such fish species as northern pike, largemouth bass, bluegill, channel cat, crappie, sunfish, bullhead, goldfish, and carp. Shoreline fishermen catch largemouth bass, bluegill, channel cat, bullhead, sunfish, and goldfish in Cermak Quarry and Catherine Mitchell Lagoon. Ida Lake is stocked with largemouth bass, bullhead, and bluegill.

Swimming

Cermak Swimming Pool, one of three in the Cook County Forest Preserve District, is located in the southeast portion of the division. Open daily, 1:00–10:00 P.M., during warm-weather months. Children under six are not admitted. There's a nominal admission fee, with special free times for children under twelve on Monday, Wednesday, and Friday from 2:30 to 4:30 P.M.

Picnicking

More than twenty picnic areas are located in open meadows, woodland clearings, or on stream banks. All have parking space, drinking water, and toilet facilities nearby; most have shelters and grills. Groups of twenty-five or more must obtain a permit in advance by personally visiting the Permit Office, Room 230, County Building, 118 N. Clark St., Chicago.

Winter Sports

Some toboggan slides and a warming shelter at Bemis Woods South are open daily 10:00 A.M.–10:00 P.M. when weather conditions permit. Cross-country skiers use the Salt Creek and Arie Crown bicycle trails, as well as the developed trails through Bemis Woods. The Bemis Woods and Westchester Woods areas, as well as an area adjoining the north parking lot of the Brookfield Zoo, have slopes for sledders. Surfaces on Ida Lake and Cermak Quarry are cleared for ice skaters.

How to Get There: Located directly west of midtown Chicago, near the suburb of Riverside. Division lands lie roughly between Roosevelt Rd. (IL 38) on the north and I-55 on the south. Since each division of the Cook County Forest Preserve District features several recreation areas and attractions, crisscrossed by many roads and in some instances unconnected, it's best to obtain division maps, directions for getting there, and other information from district or division headquarters before visiting one. To reach Salt Creek Division headquarters from the junction of 31st St. (also known as Logan Ave. in places) and Des Plaines Ave. in Riverside, go west on 31st St. Continue past Brookfield Zoo on the left (south) side of 31st St. to 17th Ave. and turn right (north). Proceed on 17th Ave. to headquarters building on right (east) side of the road just after you cross Salt Creek. Parking on site.

Preserve lands open daily, year-round, sunrise to sunset; free. Headquarters offices open Mon.–Fri., 8:30 A.M.–5:00 P.M., year-round; closed major holidays.

For Additional Information:
Salt Creek Division Headquarters
Cook County Forest Preserve District
17th Ave. at Salt Creek
North Riverside, IL 60546
(312) 485-8410
(312) 485-8411

Conservation Department
General Headquarters
Cook County Forest Preserve District
536 N. Harlem Ave.
River Forest, IL 60305
(312) 261-8400—Chicago number
(312) 366-9420—Suburban number

Shaw Woodlands and Prairies

This forty-three-acre preserve lying along the Skokie River in Lake Forest is one of the best areas in the Chicago region to see the rich black soil prairie upon which the state's agricultural economy was founded. Classified as a wet-mesic prairie, the Shaw site is recognized as the finest prairie ecosystem remaining in northeastern Illinois and as one of the top ten grasslands of its kind anywhere. Portions of it remain in their native state, thriving wild and undisturbed.

Visually, the prairie is at the peak of its beauty from May to September. Plants that today are quite rare in the region—northern dropseed grass, Indian paintbrush, and Indian plantain—grow here in abundance.

Wildlife that had been declining in the area is now returning, as meadowlark, colonial bob-o-link, and the reclusive smooth green snake, among others, establish homes in this small wilderness.

Leading through all parts of the preserve is a well-developed trail system that allows visitors to explore the various habitats found here. Besides the prairie sections, there are open meadows, ponds, and an oak forest. Numbered markers along the way, coordinated to a printed trail guide, identify such places of interest as an old hobo camp, animal tracking area, patches of moss, and a compost pile.

How to Get There: Located in Lake County, in the northern part of the village of Lake Forest, not far from the campus of Lake Forest College. The site, owned jointly by the Illinois chapter of The Nature Conservancy and the Lake Forest Open Lands Association, is open by permission only. To obtain a permit for parking and to enter the preserve, and for exact directions to the site, contact the latter.

Open daily, year-round, during daylight hours. No entrance fee, but a donation is appreciated.

For Additional Information:

Lake Forest Open Lands Association
P.O. Box 941
Lake Forest, IL 60045
(312) 234-0565

The Nature Conservancy
Illinois Field Office
79 W. Monroe St., Suite 708
Chicago, IL 60603
(312) 346-8166

Shoe Factory Road Nature Preserve

See listing under Crabtree Nature Center, p. 36.

Silver Springs State Park

Silver Springs State Park, containing 1,314 acres, was once an experimental farm owned and operated by the *Chicago Tribune*. In 1969, the state of Illinois acquired most of the land and began developing it into a state park.

The picturesque site, with its tranquil woodland setting, was named after a small, bubbling pool of clear water that's rimmed by beds of watercress. Even in the coldest weather, the pool never freezes, maintaining a temperature of forty degrees and offering a constant source of water for wildlife.

The Fox River snakes through the park, and there are several small man-made lakes located near its south shoreline. Although a devastating tornado tore through the park in 1974, causing much damage, there are still fine forests of red and white oak, hickory, ash, sycamore, maple, and beech here. The combination of woods and water attracts a multitude of songbirds, as well as pheasant and migratory waterfowl. Deer are often seen in a wildlife viewing area east of Loon Lake, and mink and muskrat remain active all year long in the marshes. In the blooming season, the land is studded with wildflowers.

Hiking and Horseback Riding

A 2^1/$_2$-mile-long trail winds along the river, through wooded areas overlooking the lakes, into a special wildlife viewing area, and past Silver Springs. Along the way, you'll see a small beaver pond. A 6-mile equestrian trail is available, but you'll have to bring your own horse. During hunting season, this trail is closed.

Boating and Fishing

Boats are permitted on the Fox River. There is no horsepower limit, but small motors are recommended because the river is shallow here. The Fox is probably the most traveled canoe route in Illinois. There's a canoe landing in the park, and a nearby canoe rental concession is usually open on weekends and holidays from April to October. You may want to canoe the entire distance from Yorkville to the Illinois River; it's a lovely thirty-mile stretch that combines wooded shores, rocky bluffs, and rippled waters in country that's frequented by wildlife.

Channel catfish, largemouth and smallmouth bass, bluegill, and crappie are present in two park lakes. All of these species, plus bullhead, carp, sunfish, pike, sauger, and sucker thrive in the Fox River. Bank fishing only is permitted in the lakes; fishing from both banks and boats is allowed in the river.

Picnicking

Areas at the park entrance and along the river are set aside for picnicking. They offer tables, charcoal grills, drinking water, and restrooms. A shelter is available near the main entrance.

Winter Sports

A 5^1/$_2$-mile-long cross-country trail has sections for beginning, intermediate, and expert skiers; a warming house is located at the office. Ice fishing is permitted on all park lakes, and there are special areas for ice skating and tobogganing.

How to Get There: Located in northwestern Kendall County. From Yorkville, head west on Fox Rd., which ends in the park.

Open daily, 7:00 A.M.–10:00 P.M., year-round. Admission free.

For Additional Information:
Site Superintendent
Silver Springs State Park
R.R. 1, Box 318
Yorkville, IL 60560
(312) 553-6297

Skokie Forest Preserve Division

Once this land was hauntingly beautiful, a vast marsh pulsating with life. Native grasses, sedges, and swamp flowers grew among twisting channels of water, creating a sanctuary for muskrats, mink, ducks, wading and shore birds, yellow-headed and red-winged blackbirds, marsh wrens, martins, swallows, and turtles.

The Cook County Forest Preserve District, realizing the ecological value of this wondrous wetland along the Skokie River, made plans early in the century to purchase and preserve it. Unfortunately, before the entire property could be acquired, the marsh was mutilated by drainage ditches that lowered the water level, promoting the proliferation of rank vegetation and uncontrollable peat fires.

The forest preserve district went ahead with its purchase plans, however, and the seven lagoons you see there today were constructed to reclaim the marsh, provide flood, fire, and mosquito control, and establish a recreation area for the general public.

In addition to the lagoons, the islands strewn about their 190-acre surface, and narrow ribbons of land along both shorelines, this division includes the forested banks of the Skokie River south of the lagoons and a separate tract of parkland bordering two forks of the North Branch of the Chicago River. All three streams merge within the preserve to form the North Branch of the Chicago River, which flows southward through another holding of the Cook County Forest Preserve District, the North Branch Division (described elsewhere).

Between the Cook–Lake County line and Dundee Road, the lagoons and most of the surrounding land are managed as the Chicago Botanic Garden (described elsewhere). One lovely eighty-acre recreation area in the northeast corner, known as Turnbull Woods, lies partially in and partially out of the garden. When this land was purchased by the forest preserve district in 1917, it was described thus: "In rugged natural beauty and splendid growth of timber, no woodland acquired by the Board equals the Turnbull grant." Today, it remains rich in native plants and is especially noted for the white trillium that flourish here in early spring. The fifteen acres included in the garden are also resplendent with ferns, rhododendrons, and evergreens, placed there by the Chicago Horticultural Society.

At the extreme southern end of the division lies Harms Woods, containing some fine old trees.

In the winter, when the ice is thick on Lake Michigan, water birds come to the open waters of the lagoons to feed. One of the best places from which to watch them is the Dundee Road bridge just east of Edens Expressway (I-94). Many shore and water birds also congregate here during spring and fall migrations. Just west of the lagoons, between Tower and Willow roads, you can see almost all of the warblers and vireos found in the Chicago area during migratory periods, and yellow-crowned night herons have nested here since 1972.

Hiking, Bicycling, and Horseback Riding

There are numerous trails and footpaths covering several miles, including those in the botanic garden, for hikers to enjoy. One multiuse trail lies along both banks of the Skokie River in the southern part of the division, then merges east of the stream and follows the shoreline before crossing over to the west side of the lagoons; another wanders through preserve lands west of the Middle Fork of the Chicago River. Together, they offer more than seventeen miles of trails that may be used by hikers, bicyclists, and horseback riders. There are no horse rentals; an annual horse registration and rider's license are required. The twenty-mile-long North Branch bicycle trail, currently under construction, will provide a continuous path through all of this division and most of the adjoining North Branch Division just to the south. At present, the trail has been totally completed in the North Branch Division and in approximately half of this division.

Boating and Fishing

More people come to this division to canoe than for any other reason. Since it's possible to make a round trip in these waters, there's no need to arrange any shuttle service. A complete circuit around the connecting channels is about six miles and is a very scenic trip. Dinghy sailboats and rowboats are also allowed here, but no motors of any kind are permitted. There are no rentals, but you'll find a free launch ramp on the west bank of the lagoons just southeast of the intersection of Edens Expressway (I-94) and Tower Road. Since the lagoons are interconnected, they may all be reached from this ramp.

One of the prime reasons these lagoons were constructed was to provide good fishing waters. Unfortunately, due to heavy pollution, fishing has not been good here. Efforts are underway to improve water quality, but much depends on budget allocations. Rough fish are currently the main catch, but there are also some crappie, bluegill, and largemouth bass.

Picnicking

Picnic areas are serene and scenic. Several have grills and shelters, with parking, drinking water, and toilet facilities near all of them. Groups of twenty-five or more must obtain a permit in advance by personally visiting the Permit Office, Room 230, County Building, 118 N. Clark St., Chicago.

Winter Sports

Cross-country skiing is the only designated winter sport. The flatness of the terrain makes it ideal for beginners.

How to Get There: Located near Northfield in the northeastern corner of Cook County between the Cook–Lake County line on the north and Beckwith Rd. (also known as Church St. in places) on the south. The North Branch Division of the Cook County Forest Preserve District adjoins the Skokie Division at its southern boundary. Since each division of the Cook County Forest Preserve District features several recreation areas and attractions, crisscrossed by many roads and in some instances disconnected, it's best to obtain division maps, directions for getting there, and other pertinent information from district or division headquarters before visiting one. To reach Skokie Division headquarters from the junction of Willow and Wagner roads in Northfield, go east on Willow Rd. Just after you cross Edens Expwy. (I-94), look for the headquarters entrance road on the left (north) side of Willow Rd. Parking on site.

Preserve lands open daily, year-round, sunrise to sunset; free. Headquarters offices open Mon.–Fri., 8:30 A.M.–5:00 P.M., year-round; closed major holidays.

For Additional Information:
Skokie Division Headquarters
Cook County Forest Preserve District
Willow Rd. and Edens Expwy.
Northfield, IL 60093
(312) 446-5652
(312) 446-5676

Conservation Department
General Headquarters
Cook County Forest Preserve District
536 N. Harlem Ave.
River Forest, IL 60305
(312) 261-8400—Chicago number
(312) 366-9420—Suburban number

Spring Lake Nature Preserve

See listing under Crabtree Nature Center, p. 36.

Thorn Creek Forest Preserve Division

Most of the Thorn Creek Division of the Cook County Forest Preserve District, located just a few miles south of Chicago, borders the meandering stream for which it is named. Despite the fact that it lies in the midst of a highly developed area, this lovely green sanctuary offers some outstanding natural features.

Three areas within its boundaries are so unique that they have been dedicated as state nature preserves. Several acres of blueberries and colonies of rare plants thrive in the 120-acre Jurgensen Woods Nature Preserve, which borders a tributary of Thorn Creek called North Creek. There also are some interesting specimens of sour gum and sassafras trees, a stately pine grove, and a fine woodland of towering hardwoods to explore.

Situated adjacent to Jurgensen Woods is the 440-acre Thornton–Lansing Road Nature Preserve, a blending of oak forest, marshland, and prairie. It, too, is notable for its sour gum and sassafras trees, southern species that here reach the northern limit of their range in Illinois. Other unusual flora growing among the more than 110 species found in this preserve are sweet fern, lupine, butterfly weed, and several types of orchids.

The smallest of the three nature preserves, seventy-acre Sand Ridge Prairie, is a sea of wildflowers from spring through fall. Composed of low sand dunes alternating with marshy swales, it supports native vegetation associated with wet and dry prairies—little bluestem, bluejoint grass, fringed and closed gentians, prairie dock, and blazing stars. A view from above is fascinating here—seen from an airplane, the dunes appear as ridge after ridge paralleling Lake Michigan, looking as if a giant had raked his outstretched fingers through a colossal sand pile. The ridges were formed by wave action some 15,000 years ago, when ancient Lake Chicago, sixty feet higher than its descendant, Lake Michigan, covered this land.

Not far away, the Sand Ridge Nature Center provides a glimpse at the area's geological and historical past. Reconstructed log cabins, vegetable gardens, and split-rail fences nestle in a clearing behind the nature center, and such nineteenth-century crafts as spinning, weaving, and candle-making are often demonstrated here. A 500-foot-long Braille Trail and three longer trails emphasize the natural history of the surrounding region.

Elsewhere in Thorn Creek Division, more visible reminders of geological history may be viewed by traveling along Thornton–Lansing Rd. and Glenwood–Dyer Rd. These thoroughfares follow the crests of sand dunes left behind by a receding Lake Chicago. And although it lies just outside preserve lands, you might want to take a look at awesome Thornton Quarry, largest in the Chicago area. In our primeval past, some 400 million years ago, the quarry was a massive coral reef, and the fossilized remains of thousands of creatures, preserved through hundreds of centuries in the Niagara limestone, are still imbedded in its rock face.

Noteworthy botanical specimens in Thorn Creek Division, other than those in the three nature preserves, include the bur oaks in Steger Woods, the huge white oaks in Schubert's Woods, and the Ohio buckeye trees that grow along Thorn Creek between Western Ave. and Glenwood Rd.

Hiking, Bicycling, and Horseback Riding

Many miles of hiking trails lead throughout every part of Thorn Creek Division, including paths that follow Thorn Creek itself. Nearly nine miles of developed trails in the southern part of Thorn Creek Division are also suitable for bicyclists, while in the northern section some five miles of hiking trails are shared by equestrians (no rentals; annual horse registration and rider's license required). Three trails at the Sand Ridge Nature Center vary in length. Redwing Trail, a 1/2-mile-long loop, leads through an oak forest beyond the pioneer cabins to a cattail marsh. One-mile-long Dogwood Trail passes a diminutive grassland aptly named Pee-wee Prairie and a large prairie restoration project, crosses a marsh via a boardwalk, and skirts a vernal pond. Lost Beach Trail, a walk of 2 miles, winds through dense woodlands, past two small ponds and remnants of prairie, to a small sand dune. The Braille Trail just behind the nature center's exhibit building accommodates the visually handicapped.

Fishing

Available for shoreline fishing only, thirty-five-acre Wampum Lake is stocked with largemouth and smallmouth bass, bluegill, sunfish, channel catfish, and bullhead.

Swimming

Green Lake Swimming Pool, one of only three pools in the entire Cook County Forest Preserve District, is located in this division. Open daily, 1:00–10:00 P.M., during warm-weather months. Children under six are not admitted. There's a nominal admission fee, with special free times for children under twelve on Monday, Wednesday, and Friday from 2:30–4:00 P.M.

Picnicking

Many picnic areas and shelters are scattered throughout division lands. Tables and drinking water are provided at all picnic spots; major areas also have some grills and shelters. Groups of twenty-five or more must obtain advanced permits in person from the Permit Office, Room 230, County Building, 118 N. Clark St., Chicago.

Winter Sports

Sledding is permitted at Indian Hill. More than ten miles of trails are open to cross-country skiers, and Wampum Lake is used by ice skaters and ice fishermen.

How to Get There: Located in southeastern Cook County between

154th St. on the north and Steger Rd. along the Cook–Will County line on the south. The major part of this division is a long, narrow belt of green that borders Thorn and North creeks, but there are also a few unconnected parcels of parkland. Since each division of the Cook County Forest Preserve District features many recreation areas and attractions, crisscrossed by many streets, it's best to obtain a division map, directions for getting there, and other pertinent information from division or district headquarters before visiting one. To reach Thorn Creek Division headquarters from the nearby village of Lansing, go west on Thornton–Lansing Rd. Just after crossing over Calumet Expwy., Thornton–Lansing Rd. enters Thorn Creek Division. Look for signs identifying the headquarters building on the right (north) side of the road. Sand Ridge Nature Center, which lies near the village of South Holland, is also a good information source. To reach it, proceed east from South Holland on US 6 (159th St.) to Paxton Ave. and turn left (north); the center is on the right (east) side of Paxton Ave. Parking on site.

Preserve lands open daily, year-round, sunrise to sunset; free. Headquarters offices open Mon.–Fri., year-round, 8:30 A.M.–5:00 P.M.; closed major holidays. Nature center open year-round; trails open daily, 8:30 A.M.–5:00 P.M.; exhibit room open Mon.–Thurs., 9:00 A.M.–4:30 P.M.; Sat., Sun., and holidays, 9:00 A.M.–5:00 P.M.; closed Friday, Thanksgiving, Christmas, and New Year's Day; free.

For Additional Information:

Thorn Creek Division Headquarters
Cook County Forest Preserve District
Thornton-Lansing Rd.
Lansing, IL 60438
(312) 474-1221
(312) 474-1227

Sand Ridge Nature Center
R.R. 1, Box 72
South Holland, IL 60473
(312) 868-0606

Conservation Department
General Headquarters
Cook County Forest Preserve District
536 N. Harlem Ave.
River Forest, IL 60305
(312) 261-8400—Chicago number
(312) 366-9400—Suburban number

Thorn Creek Nature Preserve

Park Forest is a most unusual town in the Chicago area. Built after World War II as the country's first planned community, it has twice been voted an "All-American City." Part of its uniqueness is its successful coexistence with nature, and Thorn Creek Nature Preserve is one of the most beautiful examples of the city's green spaces that are so treasured by residents. Although it's located within the boundaries of Park Forest and the adjacent village of Park Forest South, the 808-acre parkland includes 500 acres that have been assigned wilderness status by the Illinois Nature Preserves Commission.

The diverse terrain encompasses the headwaters of Thorn Creek, glacial potholes, ponds, a small remnant of prairie, springs, and a forest dominated by white and red oak trees that date back more than 100 years. A mix of level uplands, steep ravines, and creek bottom supports more than 120 species of trees, shrubs, and flowers. Among the rich herbaceous flora found in the wilderness area are such unusual wildflowers as the yellow trout lily, spotted coral-root orchid, and Schreber's aster.

A thriving herd of white-tailed deer shares the woodland with foxes, raccoons, opossums, chipmunks, muskrats, rabbits, squirrels, and a resident population of some fifty species of birds. During migration periods, eighty more avian species pause to rest here.

A nature center on the west side of the woods is housed in a charming white wood church that's more than a century old. The displays depict the flora and fauna of the preserve, and there's a logbook that catalogs the most recent bird and wildflower sightings.

Hiking and Nature Trails

There are two loop trails through the woods for the hiker to follow. A half-mile nature trail begins near the nature center. Approximately midway around it, a 1¼-mile trail branches off across Thorn Creek. Be sure to pick up a free interpretive brochure at the nature center before starting your walk. It not only identifies plant species along the way, but describes their roles in the succession of the forest and its understory and often explains their practical uses. The fruit of the wild black cherry tree, for instance, was once used to flavor rum and whiskey, and the bark is used today to make cough syrup. Rose hips, rich in Vitamin C, are obtained from the multiflora rosebush. And, although it is not compatible with a human population, poison ivy is a source of food for muskrats, rabbits, and many types of birds. Guided hikes may be arranged in advance.

How to Get There: Located immediately south of the Will–Cook County line within the villages of Park Forest and Park Forest South in eastern Will County. From the intersection of US 30 (Lincoln Hwy.) and Orchard Dr. near the north end of Park Forest, head south on Orchard Dr. until it deadends at Monee Rd. Turn right and proceed to nature center on right side of Monee Rd. Look for signs just before reaching the nature center. Limited parking on site.

Grounds open daily, year-round, 8:00 A.M.–8:00 P.M., May–Oct.; 8:00 A.M.–5:00 P.M., Nov.–April. Nature center open Thurs.–Sun., year-round, noon–4:00 P.M.; closed Thanksgiving, Christmas, and New Year's Day. Other hours may be arranged with naturalist. Free.

For Additional Information:
Thorn Creek Nature Preserve
247 Monee Rd.
(Mailing Address: 200 Forest Blvd.)
Park Forest, IL 60466
(312) 747-6320

Will County Forest Preserve District
US 52 and Cherry Hill Rd., R.R. 4
Joliet, IL 60433
(815) 727-8700

Timber Ridge Forest Preserve

At present, Timber Ridge is 611 acres of wilderness used mostly by hikers and fishermen. It encompasses a diversity of habitats that supports many types of wildlife. The West Branch of the DuPage River is joined by smaller tributaries as it weaves its way past wooded banks and marshlands. In the southern part of the preserve is a small lake that is home to many aquatic creatures.

There are no facilities here. The southern boundary of Timber Ridge Preserve is formed by Geneva Road. Just south of this road is another tract of land owned by the forest preserve district. Called Winfield Mounds, it is totally undeveloped and offers visitors an additional 337 acres to explore.

Hiking and Bicycling

Hiking trails that range from easy to fairly rugged allow you to explore each habitat of the preserve's environment. Slicing through the heart of the preserve is a section of the Illinois Prairie Path for hikers and bicyclists (described elsewhere).

Fishing

Anglers catch largemouth and smallmouth bass, crappie, sunfish, carp, goldfish, bluegill, and bullhead in the DuPage River.

Winter Sports

Timber Ridge offers solitude for cross-country skiing—you'll have to break your own trail, though. Ice fishing and skating are permitted when the ice is at least three inches thick.

How to Get There: Located in west central DuPage County. From the intersection of IL 59 and Geneva Rd. in West Chicago, go east on Geneva Rd. for about 2 miles to preserve on left (north) side of the road; or continue east to the intersection of Geneva and County Farm roads, turn left (north) on County Farm Rd., and proceed to another section of Timber Ridge on the left (west) side of County Farm Rd. Parking is along Geneva Rd. or County Farm Rd.

Open daily, year-round, from one hour after sunrise to one hour after sunset. Free.

For Additional Information:
DuPage County Forest Preserve District
P.O. Box 2339
Glen Ellyn, IL 60137
(312) 620-3800

Fullersburg Woods Nature Center
3609 Spring Rd.
Oak Brook, IL 60521
(312) 620-3843

Tinley Creek Forest Preserve Division

This division of the Cook County Forest Preserve District lies southwest of Chicago atop the Tinley moraine, a high ridge of land running in a southeast-northwest direction that was formed by the last great glacial incursion. Most of the recreation facilities here are in the northern third of the division, leaving lots of open space to the south where you may forge your way through woods and meadows on your own.

During spring and fall migration periods, various species of waterfowl and shorebirds, some quite rare in these parts, may be observed feeding and resting in the marsh areas north of Vollmer Road, the division's southern boundary.

Yankee Woods and St. Mihiel Preserve in the division's midsection are especially worth visiting, for their wildflower and foliage displays, in the spring and fall. Also in these two areas, you'll see small fragments of native prairie that contain rare species of plant and insect life.

The central and southern portions of Tinley Creek Division boast numerous reforestation projects, planted in the late 1960s as part of the forest preserve district's efforts to reestablish examples of the native woodlands that thrived here 200 years ago. In Tinley Creek Woods in the northern part of the division, however, a few huge oaks still survive from the region's original primeval forest.

While the streams of Tinley Creek themselves are not particularly impressive, they do flow through some deep, picturesque ravines and gullies, and nearby Carlson Springs is one of the few large springs in Cook County that still flows.

Meadows and woodland clearings in many locations throughout the division are dotted with blackberry, dewberry, and raspberry patches that are heavy with ripe fruit in July, and in autumn the woodland floors yield an abundance of mushrooms.

For an unusual view of the Chicago skyline, some twenty miles to the northeast, visit a scenic overlook near the northeast corner of the intersection of Oak Park Avenue and 159th Street in the central part of the division.

Hiking, Bicycling, and Horseback Riding

Approximately 3¼ miles of improved trails in the northern and central sections are used by hikers, bicyclists, and horseback riders (no rentals; annual horse registration and rider's license required). Elsewhere, many interesting walks may be taken by following footpaths or striking out cross-country.

Boating and Fishing

Sailboats skim the surface of Turtlehead Lake, the only boating area in this division. There are no rentals. Turtlehead Lake is also open to fishermen, as are Midlothian Reservoir and Ham Bone Lake. Largemouth bass, bluegill, sunfish, bullhead, and crappie test the skills of shoreline fishermen.

Picnicking

Picnic areas have been established in every section of Tinley Creek Division, although those in the southern third are especially for families. Groups who might prefer shelters will find several of those in the central and northern sections. All areas have nearby parking, drinking water, toilet facilities, and tables; most have grills. Groups of twenty-five or more must apply for an advance permit in person at the Permit Office, Room 230, County Building, 118 N. Clark St., Chicago.

Winter Sports

Cross-country skiers may follow improved trails or strike out on their own. Some areas have slopes that are suitable for both skiers and sledders. Ice skating is permitted on Ham Bone Lake.

How to Get There: Located east of the village of Orland Park, between 131st St. on the north and Vollmer Rd. on the south, in southwestern Cook County. Since each division of the Cook County Forest Preserve District features several recreation areas and attractions, crisscrossed by many roads and in some instances disconnected, it's best to obtain division maps, directions for getting there, and other pertinent information from division or district headquarters before visiting one. To reach Tinley Creek Division Headquarters from Orland Park, go east on 143rd St. to Harlem Ave. (IL 43) and turn left (north). The headquarters building is on the right (east) side of the road soon after you turn. Parking on site.

Preserve lands open daily, year-round, sunrise to sunset; free. Headquarters offices open Mon.–Fri., year-round, 8:30 A.M.–5:00 P.M.; closed major holidays.

For Additional Information:
Tinley Creek Division Headquarters
Cook County Forest Preserve District
13800 S. Harlem Ave.
Orland Park, IL 60462
(312) 385-7650
(312) 385-7654

Conservation Department
General Headquarters
Cook County Forest Preserve District
536 N. Harlem Ave.
River Forest, IL 60305
(312) 261-8400—Chicago number
(312) 366-9420—Suburban number

Trout Park

Along the high bluffs of the meandering Fox River in Kane County lies Trout Park, a thirty-four-acre natural area known also as the Elgin Botanical Garden. The small park is noted as one of the last havens for the plant and animal life of the oak grove savanna region in the morainic hills of northeastern Illinois. Most easily identified by a forest floor of dense prairie grass spread beneath mighty oak trees, these savannas were common during the days preceding the arrival of the European man and were an integral part of the character of the tallgrass prairie.

The cliffs in the park follow the eastern shoreline of the Fox River, one of the most beautiful streams in the Chicago area. Composed of glacial drift, these cliffs are dotted with numerous springs and seeps that spill down the slopes into the river. These water sources, which flow to some degree year-round, are responsible for the preserve's mesic vegetation—a mixture of plants that grow in habitats neither extremely wet nor extremely dry. In the damp areas, growing abundantly, are arbor vitae trees that are older than our nation. These evergreens are rarely found in this part of the country, and the stand in Trout Park is believed to be the southernmost natural occurrence. Other trees in and near the seepage areas include black ash, green ash, and black willow. Sprawling over the steep slopes are witch hazel, basswood, white ash, and red oak, while atop the bluffs, the forest changes to a mix of white oak, wild black cherry, white ash, bur oak, and northern red oak.

Numerous rare plants thrive here. Among them are six species of orchids, the fringed gentian, bottle gentian, purple avens, bloodroot, and hemlock parsley, which is found nowhere else in the Prairie State. Plants growing in the seepage areas include skunk cabbage, marsh marigold, great angelica, starry false Solomon's seal, swamp goldenrod, and bittersweet nightshade. The higher and drier ground is a fertile site for the dogtooth violet, wake-robin, wild ginger, and white snakeroot. Because of the extensive variety of plants found here, including more than sixty species of grass, this preserve is noted as one of the richest botanical areas in northern Illinois.

Many resident insects are also unusual. They include seven

species of caddis flies that have adopted Trout Park as their only home in Illinois, a rare mayfly, two rare stoneflies, and two rare butterflies (the swamp metalmark and Harris's checkerspot).

Two tracts in the park, covering a combined total of twenty-six acres, have been designated a state nature preserve. Once Trout Park contained nearly sixty acres, including a unique ravine filled with the most diverse mix of vegetation in the area. Now that ravine and the plants it harbored are gone, ravaged by a superhighway (I-90) that slices through its heart.

Near the springs and seeps flowing from the bluffs are some interesting tufa rock formations. The underground water that emerges here is so laden with calcium carbonate that much of this mineral is deposited on the hillsides during the process of evaporation. Sometimes soft and crumbly, sometimes hard, the tufa rock thus created gradually builds itself up, including other rocks and mosses and debris within its mass.

Goshawks can be sighted most winters, and the majestic snow and blue geese sometimes fly over the Fox River in late November and December. From December to May, several types of owls gather in the densest parts of the woods. Squirrels and raccoons scurry busily about, and groundhogs come to nibble on the young shoots of great angelica.

Although most of the park is set aside as a preserve, such facilities as a playground, tennis courts, and ballfields are also offered.

Hiking and Nature Trails

Well-blazed trails wind throughout the park, but they are not for casual walkers. They climb up wooded slopes and steep bluffs, but the scenic overlooks are well worth the effort required. A printed guide is available for the Trout Park Woods Nature Trail, which loops through the mature forest for about half a mile.

Canoeing

The Fox River is an outstanding canoe stream. Visitors will find several access points along the river from which a canoe may be launched. Bring your own, or rent one in the area.

Picnicking

Several tables and a shelter are provided beneath a canopy of tall trees.

How to Get There: Located in northeast corner of Elgin. From center of Elgin, go north on Dundee Ave. to Congdon Ave. Turn left on Congdon and go to Duncan Ave. Turn right on Duncan and proceed to park, which borders Duncan on both sides of the road. When you reach Trout Park Blvd., which crosses Duncan, you may turn either left or right into the park. Parking on site.

Open daily, year-round, from dawn to dusk. Free.

For Additional Information:
Parks and Recreation Department
City of Elgin
150 Dexter Ct.
Elgin, IL 60120
(312) 695-6500

Van Patten Woods Forest Preserve

See listing under Des Plaines River Trail, p. 41.

Veterans Acres Park

The 140 rolling acres contained within this city park provide a playground for both observers of nature and those seeking more active recreation in the outdoors. Approximately one-half of the site, a mix of woodland and hillside prairie, flourishes in its natural state. Although the prairie is dominated by Indian grass, there are some excellent growths of little bluestem atop the hills, as well as patches of big bluestem and side-oats grama. All grow free and wild, undisturbed by man. Gorgeous prairie wildflowers are scattered among the grasses.

Since winter is also an active time here, the park and most of its facilities are open year-round.

Hiking

Several miles of trails wind through woods and prairie. The terrain varies from flat to gently rolling and is quite scenic. Most trails are loops, with secondary trails leading from them and intersecting them. A nature trail of about half a mile, especially suited for youngsters who may not be up to a longer walk, loops through the developed portion of the park. In addition to passing beneath tall trees and past a small plot of prairie, it skirts the edge of a pond. Organized running events are scheduled on a regular basis when weather permits.

Fishing

Catfish, bass, and bluegill await anglers in the park pond.

Picnicking

A shaded picnic area is situated at the edge of a wooded grove near the pond. Restrooms and drinking water are close at hand, and a ballfield is within sight.

Winter Sports

Cross-country skiers will find five miles of trails that lead through every part of the park. The terrain is hilly in places, but the trail is not difficult. Skiers may warm themselves in the park's headquarters building. Ski races are held on a regular basis. The frozen surface of the pond is used by ice skaters, and a special hill is set aside for tobogganers.

How to Get There: Located in the community of Crystal Lake in southeastern McHenry County. From the intersection of US 14 (Northwest Hwy.) and IL 31 just east of Crystal Lake, go north on IL 31 to IL 176 (Terra Cotta Ave.) and turn left (west). Proceed on IL 176 to park on right side of road at intersection of IL 176 and Walkup Ave. Parking on site on the north side of IL 176 or east side of Walkup Ave.

Open daily, year-round, 9:00 A.M.–dusk. Free.

For Additional Information:
Crystal Lake Park District
300 Lake Shore Dr.
Crystal Lake, IL 60014
(815) 459-0680

Volo Bog State Natural Area

Approximately 12,000 years ago, the last great glacier receded from northeastern Illinois and left behind a rare natural treasure. Volo Bog is the sole remaining open-water bog in the state, and through a miracle of survival, it is the only one in Illinois where all stages of the natural succession of a bog may be seen. Its significance was nationally recognized in 1974, when the United States Department of the Interior declared it a national natural landmark.

The vast lake created here by glacial meltwater has, through the intervening years, gradually filled in and become a bog. Today that original lake has shrunk in size until it is barely more than a large, oval-shaped pond, and it too is destined someday to die. Like a tightening noose, the unstable mat of sphagnum moss that encircles the open water is slowly advancing inward. The sphagnum firms up as other plants take root and establish themselves in it, and it eventually can support the weight of a person. A stamp of the foot, however, may still send tremors forty feet away.

Beyond the scrubby rim of the pond grows a well-developed tamarack forest. The tamarack, a conifer that sheds its needles in winter, is rare in Illinois and is listed as a threatened species in the state. In the fall, its needles turn a glorious gold and light up the landscape.

Volo Bog is also the haunt of the cinnamon fern, the insectivorous pitcher plant, the sundew, the rose pogonia, and ragged fringed orchids, and it is the only place in Illinois where the superb wild calla, an enchanting water lily, still survives.

Among the animals that reside here permanently are painted

turtles, frogs, muskrats, mink, weasels, voles, a variety of snakes, and the predators they attract—red-tailed hawks, owls, foxes. Swamp sparrows, cardinals, and red-winged blackbirds nest in the bog, while green and great blue herons visit frequently.

Many special programs, guided walks, and other activities are scheduled by the staff of the visitor center. To protect the fragile soils and plant life of Volo Bog, the site is managed primarily for nature study and such passive recreation as walking, birdwatching, and photography. No picnicking, pets, horses, bicycles, or cross-country skiing are allowed.

Two other bogs, Brandenburg and Pistakee, lie within this natural area. Although they are not accessible to the public at present, they may be in the future.

Nature Trail

A half-mile interpretive trail that begins at the parking lot follows a path strewn with wood chips to a floating boardwalk. You may walk here at any time by yourself, or go along on regularly scheduled guided excursions. A very informative trail brochure is available. Visitors must remain on the trail at all times, and they are encouraged to bring field guides, binoculars, and cameras.

How to Get There: Volo Bog and the visitor center are located in west central Lake County, although part of the natural area reaches westward into McHenry County. From the intersection of US 12/IL 59 and IL 120 in the town of Volo, go north on US 12/IL 59 to Sullivan Lake Rd. and turn left. Proceed on Sullivan Lake Rd. about 1 1/2 miles to Brandenburg Rd., the first street on the right. Turn right and follow Brandenburg Rd. a short distance to the preserve parking lot on the right. Look for a sign at the entrance. Follow the trail, which begins at the parking lot, to the visitor center.

Natural area open daily, 8:00 A.M.–6:00 P.M., June 1–Aug. 31; 8:30 A.M.–4:30 P.M., Sept. 1–May 31. Visitor center open 9:00 A.M.–noon and 1:00–4:00 P.M., Wed.–Sun., June–Aug.; weekends and holidays only, Sept. 1–May 31. All facilities closed Christmas and New Year's Day. Free.

For Additional Information:
Volo Bog State Natural Area
28478 W. Brandenburg Rd.
Ingleside, IL 60041
(815) 344-1294

Wadsworth Prairie

See listing under Des Plaines River Trail, p. 41.

Waterfall Glen Forest Preserve

The largest forest preserve in DuPage County, Waterfall Glen is also one of the most beautiful. Located on 2,434 acres in the Des Plaines River Valley, the rugged preserve encompasses old pine plantations, oak woodlands, forested ravines, fern-draped bluffs, patches of marsh, meadows, and several waterfalls. Sawmill Creek winds through the eastern part of Waterfall Glen, eventually finding its way to the Des Plaines River, which touches the southern boundary of the preserve.

Because the sprawling terrain is so wild and varied, plant and animal life are both diverse and abundant. Bird-watching in particular is excellent here.

Public facilities include drinking water and toilets. Young people may attend an Outdoor Education Camp that offers several environmental study programs and group camping.

A circular preserve, Waterfall Glen completely surrounds Argonne National Laboratory, established in 1942 as part of the Manhattan atomic bomb project. Today, the University of Chicago operates it as an environmental and energy research institution. A wide range of scientific activities includes the study of pollution in the Great Lakes and the atmosphere, a search for new ways to use high-sulfur coal in an environmentally acceptable manner, and methods of transforming abandoned strip mines into productive land. Guided tours are offered at 9:00 A.M. and 1:30 P.M. each Saturday to persons over sixteen years of age. Because of the lab's vast scope, the 3 1/2-hour tours may be tailored to meet the needs of each group. Participants can schedule tours for their own groups or join small groups already scheduled, but reservations are required and must be made at least two weeks in advance.

Hiking and Horseback Riding

Hikers and horseback riders use a ten-mile-long marked trail that encircles the preserve. No horse rentals; annual registration is required. Walking is strenuous and might more accurately be described as wilderness backpacking. A permanently marked course has been established to help visitors learn the art of orienteering (finding your way with a map and compass). Compasses are available, and groups can be accommodated if they make advance reservations.

Fishing

Preserve streams yield sunfish, bullhead, bluegill, largemouth and smallmouth bass, goldfish, and carp.

Winter Sports

Six miles of scenic marked trails lead cross-country skiers through the northwestern quadrant of the preserve. Fishermen cut holes in river ice that is at least three inches thick.

How to Get There: Located in the southeastern corner of DuPage County. From the intersection of I-55 and Cass Ave., just southeast of Darien, proceed south on Cass Ave. to the preserve entrance on the right (west) side of the road. Parking on site.

Open daily, year-round, from one hour after sunrise to one hour after sunset. Free.

For Additional Information:
DuPage County Forest Preserve District
P.O. Box 2339
Glen Ellyn, IL 60137
(312) 620-3800

Fullersburg Woods Nature Center
3609 Spring Rd.
Oak Brook, IL 60521
(312) 620-3843

Public Relations Department
Argonne National Laboratory
9700 S. Cass Ave.
Argonne, IL 60439
(312) 972-2773

West Chicago Prairie

Few natural areas in northeastern Illinois recapture the feeling of the land's original prairie wilderness like West Chicago Prairie. Located in an industrial park in the village of West Chicago, this 154-acre stretch of prairie, marsh, and savanna is one of the largest preserved prairies in the state.

It was slated for development until the mid-1970s, when West Chicago's mayor, The Nature Conservancy, and the DuPage County Forest Preserve District joined forces to prevent its destruction. Without their combined intervention, Illinois would have lost, in this single parcel, one-eighth of its remaining mesic/wet-mesic prairie.

From spring through autumn, the beauty of the prairie literally takes your breath away. Some 350 plant species, more than forty percent of all species native to DuPage County, thrive here. Golden Alexanders, prairie milkweed, prairie dock, prairie blazing star, and sky blue aster grow alongside species rare in the region—tall green milkweed, cream false indigo, Indian plantain, and the federally endangered white lady's slipper orchid.

The Massasauga rattlesnake, poisonous but nonaggressive, and Blanding's turtle, both rare species, breed here, as do the long-billed wren, swamp sparrow, meadowlark, and bob-o-link. Occasionally, the state-endangered marsh hawk is seen foraging in low sweeps over the preserve, and deer and raccoons live here year-round. The plains garter and declining green snakes find an abundance of small mammals to feed on.

Trails created in the past by trespassers and by power-line development lead through the area's major features. Because the area is so fragile, the DuPage County Forest Preserve District requests visitors to obtain permission from their office before entering the preserve. The district plans to dedicate this site as a state nature preserve and to develop interpretive facilities and improved trails.

How to Get There: Located in west central DuPage County in the village of West Chicago. Exact directions will be given when you obtain permission to visit there.

Open daily, year-round, during daylight hours. Free.

For Additional Information:
DuPage County Forest Preserve District
P.O. Box 2339
Glen Ellyn, IL 60137
(312) 620-3800

West DuPage Woods Forest Preserve

The West Branch of the DuPage River snakes its way through the midst of this parkland. Also contained within the preserve's 470 acres are forest, marsh, fen, and a large pond—a variety of ecosystems that support many species of plant and animal life.

Although West DuPage Woods is well developed and offers several activities for visitors, including camping for youth groups, the natural features have been scrupulously protected. Elsen's Hill Winter Sports Area in the southeastern portion of the preserve lures many fans of cold-weather outings.

Hiking and Horseback Riding

Elsen's Hill Trail on the south side of the DuPage River loops through woods, meadow, and marsh for two miles. A one-mile-long loop trail near the western edge of the preserve, on the opposite side of the river, passes primarily through open meadow; patches of marsh may be observed along the way. The terrain of the preserve includes a few steep hills. Both trails are also open to equestrians. No rentals; annual registration is required.

Fishing

A record catch of a seventeen-pound carp was taken from the river here. You'll also find catfish, bullhead, goldfish, bluegill, crappie, largemouth and smallmouth bass, and sunfish.

Picnicking

Several picnic areas with drinking water and toilets are available and may be reserved in advance for a nominal fee.

Winter Sports

This is one of the best areas in DuPage County for winter sports. The two hiking/bridle trails are both open to cross-country skiers. A few steep hills are challenging to experts, while the scenic terrain is a delight for everyone. A small pond near Elsen's Hill is open to ice skaters. Fishermen cut holes in the ice to pursue their sport. Elsen's Hill offers both sled and toboggan runs.

How to Get There: Located in west central DuPage County. There are two entrances. From the intersection of IL 59 and IL 38 in the southeastern part of the village of West Chicago, proceed north on IL 59 to entrance on the right (east) side of the road. Or, from the same intersection, proceed east on IL 38 (Roosevelt Rd.) to Gary's Mill Rd., turn left (northeast) and continue on Gary's Mill Rd. to entrance near Elsen's Hill on left (north) side of the road. Parking at both entrances on site.

Open daily, year-round, from one hour after sunrise to one hour after sunset. In the winter, when weather conditions are right, Elsen's Hill is open until 10:00 P.M. for nighttime sledding on Friday, Saturday, Sunday, holidays, and during Christmas vacations. The area is well lit and well patrolled by park rangers on these late evenings.

For Additional Information:
DuPage County Forest Preserve District
P.O. Box 2339
Glen Ellyn, IL 60137
(312) 620-3800

Fullersburg Woods Nature Center
3609 Spring Rd.
Oak Brook, IL 60521
(312) 620-3843

Willowbrook Wildlife Haven

In central DuPage County, a tiny oasis called Willowbrook Wildlife Haven serves as both hospital and orphanage for an assortment of wild creatures, providing a lifeline for injured and homeless animals that is unique in the Chicago region. Residents have included a three-legged opossum, the victim of a steel leg-hold trap; a raccoon blinded by dogs; a sparrow hawk waiting for his broken wing to mend; a duck suffering from botulism, contracted from a stagnant pond; and a wounded sandhill crane that had been illegally shot by a hunter. Willowbrook's staff cares for more than 2,000 patients annually.

Occupying forty-three wooded acres, this unique sanctuary

has been a rehabilitation center for native wildlife since 1958, and thousands of creatures have been cared for since that time. It is a place that graphically illustrates some of the dangers faced by urban wildlife, and as such it offers an excellent learning experience for children. Some birds and animals can eventually be returned to the wild, but many will never be able to fend for themselves again.

Although area veterinarians and other professionals provide medical care, much of the staff is made up of students and young people who volunteer their services, and additional volunteers are always welcome. Some of the patients come from other forest preserves, but DuPage County residents are urged to bring disabled animals and birds to the clinic as well.

Willowbrook is also one of the area's top tourist attractions, accommodating more than 50,000 visitors of all ages each year. They come primarily, of course, to watch the staff tend to injured and infant wildlife and to see live exhibits that feature such animals as woodchucks, skunks, eagles, coyotes, red foxes, and great horned owls. But they come, too, to wander along sun-dappled paths leading through the quiet forest that surrounds the buildings and to enjoy a picnic lunch. Drinking water and restrooms are available.

How to Get There: Located in south Glen Ellyn. From the intersection of IL 53 and IL 38 (Roosevelt Rd.) in Glen Ellyn, head west on IL 38 to Park Blvd. and turn left (south). Proceed south on Park Blvd. to Willowbrook on the left (east) side of the road. Parking on site.

Open daily, year-round, except Thanksgiving, Christmas, and New Year's Day; hours are 9:00 A.M.–5:00 P.M. daily, but may be extended during summer months. Free.

For Additional Information:
Willowbrook Wildlife Haven
525 S. Park Blvd.
Glen Ellyn, IL 60137
(312) 620-3845

DuPage County Forest Preserve District
P.O. Box 2339
Glen Ellyn, IL 60137
(312) 620-3800

Winfield Mounds

See listing under Timber Ridge Forest Preserve, p. 123.

Wolf Lake

See listing under Powers State Conservation Area, p. 105.

Woodworth Prairie Preserve

The James Woodworth Prairie Preserve, a tiny patch of tallgrass prairie just north of Chicago known to some as Peacock Prairie, is one of the finest examples of original Illinois landscape found anywhere. Administered by the University of Illinois at Chicago Circle, the preserve contains only about 5 1/3 acres, but is so extraordinary that it inspired private citizens, local government agencies, the federal government, and the university to join forces and fight for its survival.

Between three and four of the preserve's acres exist in a virgin state. The field appears much as it probably did 1,000 years ago—only its surroundings have changed. By concentrating on its natural beauty, you will be able to forget that this tiny preserve is actually surrounded on all sides by housing developments and fast-food restaurants.

The preserve, once part of a vast estate owned by the Peacock family, is a sliver of its former self. What remains, however, is even more precious because of its diminished size, and the prairie is managed accordingly. A short, narrow trail provides the only access to the virgin tract, and visitors are urged not to leave this path.

Since the face of the prairie changes often, you will appreciate it more fully if you visit here at different times during the months the center is open. Approximately 130 plant species have established themselves in the rich black soil—among the plants you may see are the white and purple prairie clover, closed gentian, Turk's-cap lily, cup lily, nodding ladies' tresses, prairie dock, big bluestem grass, and rattlesnake master.

Near the entrance is a small interpretive center where you may learn something about the natural history of the area and pick up a trail booklet. A display garden of prairie plants around the outside of the center will further increase your awareness of prairie ecology before you enter the virgin section at the rear of the building.

How to Get There: Located in Cook County between Niles and Glenview. From the intersection of IL 62 and Milwaukee Ave. (IL 21) in Niles, go north on Milwaukee Ave. past the Golf Mill Shopping Center and Greenwood Ave. The preserve lies on the right (east) side of Milwaukee Ave. about half a mile north of the shopping center and a quarter-mile north of the Greenwood Ave. intersection. A sign identifies the preserve, but you'll have to watch for it carefully. Turn right onto the driveway and proceed to a small parking lot behind the interpretive center.

Center and preserve open 10:00 A.M.–3:00 P.M., June 1 through mid-Sept.; closed Independence Day and Labor Day. Grounds open all year. Free.

For Additional Information:
Director
James Woodworth Prairie Preserve
c/o Department of Biological Sciences
University of Illinois at Chicago Circle
Box 4348
Chicago, IL 60680
(312) 996-8673—Director's Office, year-round
(312) 965-3488—Interpretive Center, June 1 through mid-Sept.

Part 3

Bill Thomas

Natural Attractions in
Wisconsin

Bong State Recreation Area

This vast outdoor playground offers relatively few improved facilities, but has more than 4,500 acres of wilderness to roam in a part of Wisconsin where parks rarely cover more than 300 acres at most.

Although much of the land is open to seasonal hunting, one section is managed as a wildlife refuge and several other areas are set aside for family recreation. Nearly thirty waterfowl blinds may be used by photographers during no-hunting periods.

The lakes, potholes, prairie, marsh, and woodlands are astir with wildlife. Pheasants, squirrels, rabbits, muskrats, beavers, owls, hawks, and, each spring and fall, a bevy of waterfowl find in this place a safe retreat from the encroachment of civilization.

A nature center, open during summer months, offers several special programs on a regular basis.

Hiking, Bicycling, and Horseback Riding

The relatively large size of the area accommodates trails several miles long. Most are secluded loop trails with cutoffs that permit shorter jaunts. Twelve miles of established trails, as well as a mile-long nature trail through the wildlife refuge, await hikers. Naturalists lead regularly scheduled hikes from spring through fall; special hikes and other programs may be arranged during the rest of the year by contacting the office. Ten miles of pathways are provided for bicyclists, and equestrians will find eleven miles of horse trails (no rentals).

Fishing

The small lakes and potholes sprinkled about the recreation area are stocked primarily with largemouth bass and bluegill; bank fishing only.

Swimming

Visitors will find a swimming beach at the west end of a lake near the area's main entrance. Change houses are provided.

Picnicking

Picnic areas with tables and grills are found in nearly every part of the park. Drinking water and restrooms are near each of them, and several shelters are available.

Winter Sports

Wisconsin winters are quite cold, but that doesn't stop hardy cross-country skiers and snowshoers from following six miles of established trails and forging across open terrain on their own. Ice skating and ice fishing are permitted in designated areas. To add to the enjoyment of it all, there are feeding stations where, if you're patient, you can observe resident wildlife.

How to Get There: Located in northwestern Kenosha County, southeast of Burlington. From Burlington, follow WI 142 east for about 7 miles to park entrance on the right (south) side of the road. Parking on site.

Park open daily, year-round, 6:00 A.M.–11:00 P.M.; nominal vehicle admission fee is slightly more for out-of-state residents. Office open year-round, Mon.–Fri., 7:45 A.M.–4:30 P.M.; weekend and hunting season hours vary.

For Additional Information:
Bong State Recreation Area
State Rd. 142
Kansasville, WI 53139
(414) 878-4416

Public Information Officer
Wisconsin Department of Natural Resources
Southeast District Headquarters
P.O. Box 13248
Milwaukee, WI 53213
(414) 257-6543

Hawthorn Hollow

Although this beautiful sanctuary covers just forty acres, it seems much larger because there is such a variety of habitats.

Pike Creek twists lazily through the gentle hills in the western part of the sanctuary for three-quarters of a mile. To the west of it lie nine acres of prairie, four of which are virgin. The stream valley and its bordering bluffs support an eighteen-acre woodland, including a fine natural stand of hawthorns. Toward the south end, east of the creek, is a small swamp traversed by a spring-fed brook.

More than 200 species of wildflowers, some of them quite rare, have been identified in the woods and on the prairie, and bird-watchers claim that Hawthorn Hollow is home to more birds than any other place in this part of the state.

In the eastern part of the preserve, enclosed by the circular entrance road, is a thirteen-acre arboretum of some 600 trees. Species to be seen include both natives and such exotics as the ginkgo, yellowwood, magnolia, and plane tree. South of the driveway are fifty French hybrid lilacs.

Hawthorn Hollow was for years the private retreat of two sisters, Margaret and Ruth Teuscher of Racine, who eventually made their home here. In 1967, they deeded their land to the Hyslop Foundation to be preserved as a nature sanctuary. The residence the sisters built still stands, adjacent to a formal garden and a nature center.

Also found on the grounds are three historical buildings from the immediate area that were moved here to save them from destruction—two schoolhouses, one built in 1847, the other in

1906, and an old town hall, constructed in 1859 and still containing its original furnishings.

Hawthorn Hollow is beautiful in every season, but in May and October, it is spectacular. From mid-May to early June, more than 300 ornamental crab apple and other flowering trees burst into glorious bloom. In October, those same trees blaze with brilliant fruits and glowing leaves.

Two miles of nature trails loop and intersect through the woods, prairie, and arboretum.

Picnicking

No picnicking is permitted at Hawthorn Hollow, but Petrifying Springs County Park (described elsewhere), located nearby on the opposite side of Green Bay Road, has excellent picnic facilities.

How to Get There: Located north of Kenosha in Kenosha County. From the intersection of WI 50 and Green Bay Rd. (WI 31) just west of Kenosha, go north on Green Bay Rd. about 8 miles to sanctuary entrance on left (west) side of the highway. Parking on site.

Open Mon.–Fri., during daylight hours, from spring to fall. Opening and closing dates depend upon the weather; generally open mid-April to mid-Nov. Guided tours for small groups are available; advance reservations necessary. The sanctuary is also open to the general public on Sat. in season if arrangements are made in advance. Free.

For Additional Information:

Director
Hawthorn Hollow
880 Green Bay Rd.
Kenosha, WI 53142
(414) 552-8196

Hyslop Foundation
Herman G. Gundlach, Treasurer
625-57th St., Suite 612
Kenosha, WI 53140
(No phone)

The Nature Conservancy, Wisconsin Field Office

See listing under The Nature Conservancy, Illinois Field Office, p. 90.

Petrifying Springs County Park

Petrifying Springs offers many opportunities for recreation in each season of the year, but it is most noted among nature lovers for the beauty of its mature hardwood forest.

Found in three separate areas of the 270-acre park, the woods are composed primarily of oak and maple trees, interspersed with white ash, hop hornbeam, black cherry, and basswood. Their flaming colors in the fall make this one of southeast Wisconsin's most popular destinations.

In spring, visitors wander through a landscape bright with

blossoms. More than fifty species of wildflowers and many flowering shrubs grow throughout the forest and along the banks of Pike Creek, which meanders picturesquely through the park.

During winter months, the park becomes an all-white world, offering quiet walks and winter sports.

The cool, green parkland is also a perfect place to spend the warm, lazy days of summer. It's rarely too hot, though, to prevent the youngsters from enjoying a game of softball on the park diamond or to keep dad away from the eighteen-hole golf course.

Hiking and Horseback Riding

Several miles of hiking and bridle trails wind through the woods and along Pike Creek. A license is required for equestrians; no rentals.

Picnicking

Picnic areas and shelters are located in several sections of the park. Refreshments may be purchased at a concession stand, and there are playgrounds for young children.

Winter Sports

The park lures many sledders and cross-country skiers, and an outdoor rink is provided for ice skaters.

How to Get There: Located in Kenosha County, north of Kenosha and adjacent to Parkside University. From the intersection of WI 50 and Green Bay Rd. (WI 31) just west of Kenosha, go north on Green Bay Rd. to park entrance on right (east) side of road, just before you reach the Kenosha–Racine County line. Parking on site.

Open daily, year-round, sunrise–10:00 P.M. Nominal vehicle admission fee.

For Additional Information:
Kenosha County Park System
761 Green Bay Rd.
Kenosha, WI 53140
(414) 552-8500

Part 4

United States Department of the Interior, National Park Service Photo

Natural Attractions in
Indiana

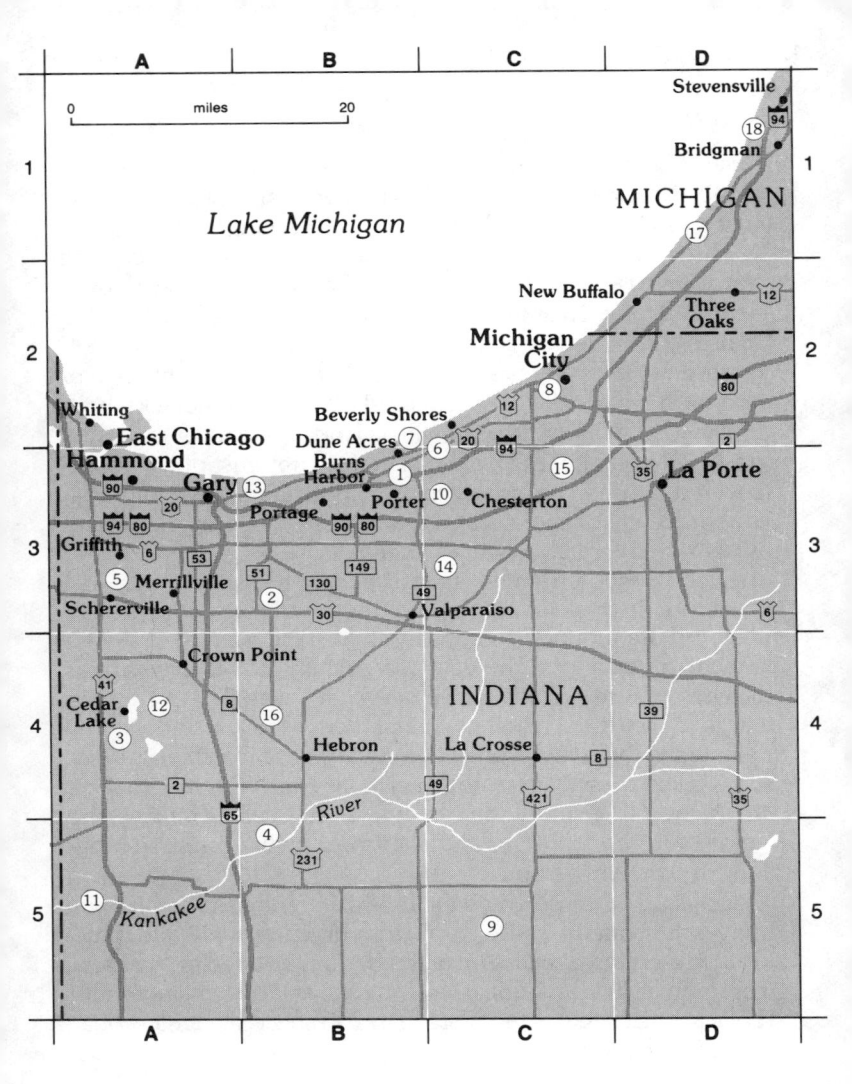

INDIANA–MICHIGAN

1. Cowles Bog **B–3**
2. Deep River County Park **A/B–4**
3. German Methodist Cemetery Prairie **A–4/5**
4. Grand Kankakee Marsh County Park **B–5**
5. Hoosier Prairie **A–3**
6. Indiana Dunes National Lakeshore **C–3**
7. Indiana Dunes State Park **B–3**
8. International Friendship Gardens **C–2**
9. Jasper–Pulaski State Fish and Wildlife Area **C–5**
10. Langeluttig Swamp **C–3**
11. LaSalle State Fish and Wildlife Area **A–5**
12. Lemon Lake County Park **A–4**
13. Miller Woods **B–3**
14. Moraine Nature Preserve **C–3**
15. Pinhook Bog **C–3**
16. Stoney Run County Park **B–4**
17. Robinson Preserve **D–1**
18. Warren Dunes State Park **D–1**

Cowles Bog

Cowles Bog, tucked away amid the great sand dunes of Indiana Dunes National Lakeshore, is so unique in the Chicago region that it has been declared a national natural landmark.

Three distinct habitats—bog, marsh, and an area undergoing transition to a swamp—lie within the boundaries of the fifty-six-acre landmark. Near the wet heart of the bog area float quaking mats of moss that are centuries old. A ten-acre "island" of high ground contains a grove of white cedars that is the only one of its type in Indiana. These cedars and a group of tamaracks, both thriving so far from others of their kind, are part of an as yet unsolved botanical puzzle. The five-foot upthrust of the cedar-covered mound has also been an intriguing mystery, although it has recently been theorized that it was pushed up by ground water under terrific pressure beneath it.

Even in modern times, several people have reportedly lost their way as they forged through the marshy forest of cattails that ring the mound. It's easy to understand why—the cattails grow to a height of eight feet. Occasionally, you'll come across patches of rare orchids and other wildflowers that are throwbacks to a past era when the marsh was a sedge meadow.

Entering the swamp forest that encircles the marsh at its outer edge is like passing into another climatic zone. The hummocky, moss-covered ground, the red maples and yellow birches, the goldthread, bunchberry, and starflower plants commonly belong in the North Woods.

Cowles Bog is also noted for its birdlife. Within its depths, you may see Canada geese, mallards, green-winged and blue-winged teals, great blue and green herons, hooded mergansers, common gallinules, killdeer, black terns, and belted kingfishers. They are just a few of the more than 265 species that have been recorded in the dunes area.

Hiking

At present, this place may be visited only with a guide—check at the Indiana Dunes National Lakeshore Visitor Center to find out when free ranger-led tours are scheduled. Generally, the hikes are conducted on weekends and last from three to five hours each. You'll be walking a distance of three to six miles, so be sure to wear sturdy shoes. Also, bring insect repellent, drinking water, and, for the longer hikes, a lunch.

How to Get There: Located in north central Porter County near the Lake Michigan shoreline and just south of the community of Dune Acres. Check at the visitor center for exact directions when you sign up for a nature hike.

Visitor center open daily, year-round; 8:00 A.M.–6:00 P.M., Memorial Day–Labor Day; 8:00 A.M.–5:00 P.M., rest of year. Free.

For Additional Information:
Superintendent
Indiana Dunes National Lakeshore
1100 N. Mineral Springs Rd.
Porter, IN 46304
(219) 926-7561

Deep River County Park

Although it is located in one of the most heavily industrialized regions in the world, the Deep River corridor is surprisingly primitive along most of its twenty-two-mile length. Dense woodlands reach outward from stream banks for at least twenty miles in both directions, offering only occasional glimpses of residential areas and pastureland.

Bordering both sides of the river for approximately four miles, Deep River County Park covers some 900 acres of both forest and prairie. It offers a fine array of recreational facilities, some outstanding natural features, an historic grist mill, and an Indian mound.

In the northwest corner of the park, a thirty-nine-acre forest blankets the steep slopes along Deep River. It is a wild place, made up of oaks, hickories, and wildflowers, and inhabited by many deer. Managed as a natural area, it preserves one of the finest tracts of woodland in Lake County.

The focal point of all nature-oriented activities in the county park system is the Deep River Nature Center, located at the extreme southern end of the park. Among its exhibits are live amphibians and reptiles, weather instruments, a working beehive, and an 8,000-year-old mastodon skull unearthed near the park. Staff naturalists conduct many special workshops, interpretive programs, and nature walks in this and other parks throughout the county.

On the riverbank just east of the nature center stands John Wood's Old Mill, the first industrial site in Lake County. Its significance was recognized in 1975 when it was placed on the National Register of Historic Places. Built in 1838, rebuilt in 1876, it is operated today as a living history exhibit. Visitors may watch corn being ground daily and purchase the cornmeal. A country store in the mill sells locally produced crafts items, and such craftsmen as a weaver, potter, and woodworker are on hand from 1:00 to 5:00 P.M. each Sunday the mill is open to demonstrate their various skills. Nearby, in a small cemetery overlooking the river, are the graves of the Wood family and other early settlers of this area.

Such special events as a quilting bee and the Wood's Mill Faire are held in the park each summer, and group hayrides are offered from spring through fall to those making reservations with the park department's main office at least two weeks in advance.

Hiking and Horseback Riding

Six miles of connecting trails lead along the riverbank and through the nature preserve. A special bridle trail has also been established; no rentals. Ask for a trail map at the nature center.

Canoeing

With your own canoe, it is possible to paddle northward from the park's canoe launch to Lake Michigan. Your route will follow the Deep and Little Calumet rivers and Burns Ditch. Be sure to inquire about portages along the way before you start out.

Two-person canoes may be rented in the park for a $2^1/_2$-mile trip on Deep River within park boundaries. Rental fee includes transportation from the terminus of the canoe trail back to your starting point. The nature center staff begins accepting reservations about March 1 for a season that runs from April 1 to mid-June, at which time the river level is usually too low to permit canoeing. Reservations should always be made at least one week in advance.

Picnicking

Picnic areas and shelters offer a panoramic view of the Old Mill and an open meadow. For a nominal fee, shelters may be reserved through the main office of the parks department. Food concessions in the park are open during summer months.

Winter Sports

A cross-country ski trail parallels the west bank of Deep River for approximately $2^1/_2$ miles; lessons and rental equipment are available.

How to Get There: Located in east central Lake County, northeast of Merrillville. From the intersection of I-65 and US 30 (81st Ave.) in Merrillville, head east on US 30 to Randolph St. Turn left (north) onto Randolph and proceed to Old US 330 (also known as Old Lincoln Hwy.). Turn right (east) onto Old US 330 and proceed to park entrance near nature center on left (north) side of the road just before Old US 330 crosses Deep River. Parking on site.

Park open daily, year-round, 7:00 A.M.–dusk and in evenings for special programs; free. Nature center open daily, 9:00 A.M.–5:00 P.M., May–Oct.; and weekends, 9:00 A.M.–4:00 P.M., Nov.–April; closed some holidays; nominal admission fee. Old Mill open 9:00 A.M.–5:00 P.M. daily, May–Oct.; free.

For Additional Information:
Deep River Nature Center
Deep River County Park
Rt. 2, Old US 330
Deep River (Hobart), IN 46342
(219) 769-9030

Superintendent
Lake County Parks and Recreation Department
2293 N. Main St.
Crown Point, IN 46307
(219) 738-2020, Ext. 391

German Methodist Cemetery Prairie

Tiny German Methodist Cemetery Prairie is one of the smallest prairie preserves in the nation. Containing just one acre, this silt loam tract is located at the rear of German Methodist Cemetery southwest of Crown Point.

During the middle of the nineteenth century, early settlers in

Rare species of prairie grasses and flowers thrive in tiny German Methodist Cemetery Prairie   *Bill Thomas*

this area set aside three acres of land to be used as a cemetery. The front two-thirds of the tract were utilized for that purpose, but the one-third in the rear was never needed. Thus it remained untouched.

In terms of ecological diversity, this acre is one of the richest in the Hoosier State—more than eighty rare and vanishing species thrive in the fertile black soil. The dominant grass is prairie dropseed, an indicator of virgin prairie. Also found growing here are big bluestem grass, Indian grass, prairie dock, shooting star, prairie gentian, bird's-foot violet, prairie lily, stiff aster, and cream wild indigo.

A high chain link fence has been erected around the prairie to protect the fragile plant life yet still permit observation. Visitors are asked to treat the adjacent cemetery with respect.

How to Get There: Located in Lake County. From intersection of US 41 and 141st St. in Cedar Lake, go south one mile to cemetery on left. At this writing, there are no signs identifying either prairie preserve or cemetery, so watch carefully.

Open daily, year-round, during daylight hours. Free.

For Additional Information:
The Nature Conservancy
Indiana Field Office
4200 N. Michigan Rd.
Indianapolis, IN 46208
(317) 923-7547

Grand Kankakee Marsh County Park

The Grand Kankakee Marsh once covered more than half a million acres in northwest Indiana alone. Today it exists only in a few remnant patches along the Kankakee River in the Hoosier State and Illinois. This 940-acre linear park along the river's north bank preserves one of the best examples of that vast, glorious landscape.

Acquired in the mid-1970s as a cooperative project of The Nature Conservancy and the Lake County Parks and Recreation Department, the tract is Indiana's first county-owned wildlife area. The great blue heron, great horned owl, wood thrush, red-shouldered hawk, wood duck, mallard, and Canada goose are just a few of the species that make this an excellent bird-watching area. Although other forms of wildlife in the park—white-tailed deer, red fox, raccoon, muskrat, eastern chipmunk, fox squirrel—are typical for the region, they are present here in exceptional abundance.

Nature photographers are lured to this park by the opportunity to photograph a diversity of wild creatures in their natural habitat. Several photography blinds are available for their use, and the park is rarely crowded.

Late in September, a two-day Outdoor Rendezvous is held for outdoorsmen of all ages. Dog trial demonstrations, duck calling contests, bow and arrow demonstrations, and orienteering races are just a few of the scheduled activities.

Hiking

The only land access to this park is on foot. Trails wander along the riverside, through the woods, and to the waterfowl resting areas.

Canoeing and Fishing

A canoe trip is the ideal way to explore the marshlands. You may rent canoes from the park's livery every weekend from July through October. Reservations should be made in advance through the park department's main office.

The Kankakee River yields walleye, northern pike, and panfish. Panfish and northern pike are also found in the side ditches, along with largemouth bass and crappie. No fishing during fall hunting seasons.

Pickicking

A picnic shelter is located near the visitor center; for a nominal fee, it may be reserved in advance.

Winter Sports

Cross-country skiers may follow existing trails or forge their own; lessons and rental equipment are available.

How to Get There: Located along the north bank of the Kankakee River in southeastern Lake County, not far southeast of Lowell. From Lowell, go east on IN 2 (181st Ave.) to Range Line Rd. Turn right (south) and proceed on Range Line Rd. (also called Clay St. in places) into park. Parking on site.

Park open daily, 7:00 A.M.–dusk, Jan.–Sept.; due to hunting restrictions, admittance from Oct. to Dec. is by permit only. Free.

For Additional Information:
Superintendent
Lake County Parks and Recreation Dept.
2293 N. Main St.
Crown Point, IN 46307
(219) 738-2020, Ext. 391

Deep River Nature Center
Deep River County Park
Rt. 2, Old US 330
Deep River (Hobart), IN 46342
(219) 769-9030

Grand Kankakee Marsh County Park
Range Line Rd.
Hebron, IN 46341
(219) 696-9951

Hoosier Prairie

Here, on the doorstep of the heavily industrialized Gary–Hammond region, lies a 304-acre wilderness similar to the landscape that greeted the area's first white settlers. Hoosier Prairie is the largest intact remnant of grassland in Indiana.

A description of Hoosier Prairie in an 1834 survey reveals that the character of the land has changed little since then. Among its diverse habitats are rounded sand rises covered with large black oak trees, spaced far enough apart to permit a lush understory of sun-loving prairie vegetation. More oaks and willows grow in shrubby thickets adjacent to patches of wet prairies and cattail marshes.

Over 300 species of native plants, some 40 of which are believed to be rare or uncommon in the Hoosier State, have been identified here.

The prairie grasses, some growing to a height of twelve feet, shelter many types of prairie mammals. Masked and short-tailed shrews, deer mice, green snakes, meadow jumping mice, Franklin's ground squirrels, and white-tailed deer, crowded out elsewhere, find refuge here and flourish.

Since fire is necessary to prevent woody vegetation from dominating prairie plants, the grassland is occasionally burned over, but the resilient prairie quickly springs to life once more. It is green again about three weeks after a spring burn and is in full bloom in two months. The rebirth of the prairie is fascinating to watch.

Hoosier Prairie lies within the acquisition boundaries of Indiana Dunes National Lakeshore but is removed from the main body of the park by several miles. Originally acquired by The Nature Conservancy in 1976, it is now owned and maintained by the state of Indiana as a nature preserve. Its unique natural features have also resulted in its designation as a national natural landmark.

Hiking

The most fragile areas of the preserve are scrupulously protected, but a self-guiding trail approximately two miles long winds through the central park of the preserve and allows the hiker to view several types of habitat. Insect repellent will make your visit here more of a pleasure.

How to Get There: Located in northwestern Lake County, west of the community of Griffith. From the intersection of Main St. (53rd Ave.) and Broad St. (IN 73) in Griffith, head west on Main St. Look for a small parking lot and sign on the left (south) side of Main St., just before you reach Kennedy Ave. The trail into Hoosier Prairie begins at the parking lot.

Open daily, year-round, during daylight hours; free.

For Additional Information:
Division of Nature Preserves
Indiana Department of Natural Resources
601 State Office Bldg.
Indianapolis, IN 46204
(317) 232-4052

Indiana Field Office
The Nature Conservancy
4200 N. Michigan St.
Indianapolis, IN 46208
(317) 923-7547

Superintendent
Indiana Dunes National Lakeshore
1100 N. Mineral Springs Rd.
Porter, IN 46304
(219) 926-7561

Indiana Dunes National Lakeshore

Extending around the southern end of Lake Michigan is the striking Indiana Dunes National Lakeshore. Formally established in 1972, it was our nation's first urban national park. Not only is it a premier waterfront playground, but it is one of America's great natural landmarks.

Poet Carl Sandburg described the dunes thus: "The Indiana Dunes are to the Midwest what the Grand Canyon is to Arizona and Yosemite is to California. They constitute a signature of time and eternity. Once lost, the loss would be irrevocable."

This is a land of wonder and mystery, with pockets of pristine beauty. Within the park's boundaries are high sand dunes, grass-tussocked hills, patches of prairie, lush wetlands, and cool forests flecked with sunlight.

Unlike most national parks, Indiana Dunes is a patchwork of several scattered units that surrenders here and there, in marked contrast, to steel mills, an industrial port, and small villages. When a national lakeshore was first authorized in 1966, it consisted of about 6,000 acres. It has grown since then, by bits and pieces, to more than 12,000 acres, and additional land will be acquired as funds become available.

Located between the metropolitan areas of Gary on the west and Michigan City on the east, the park sweeps along the water's edge for $13^{1}/_{2}$ miles and inland nearly 2 miles, while several disjointed parcels of park property lie a few miles south of the main parklands.

Because the climatic zones of north and south meet and mingle here, creating a diversity of habitats, an amazing variety of flora and fauna is found in the relatively small area of the park. More than 1,000 species of flowering plants and ferns, 75 kinds of trees, and 26 members of the orchid family thrive in a mix of environments, while some 300 species of birds and 30 types of land mammals live or visit here. Visitors may see plants and wildlife native to the frozen tundra of the North, the deep South, the Great Plains of mid-America, and the deserts of the Southwest. Flourishing side by side are such diverse plants as prickly pear cactus, Southern dogwood, orchids, Arctic bearberry, sphagnum moss, sundew and pitcher plants. Wooded areas contain tamarack bogs and ancient oak trees, while arrowhead, pickerel weed, and smartweed grow amid colorful algae.

Among the many bird sightings considered rare in this part of the country are the Carolina wren, the orchard oriole, the yellow-crowned night heron, Cooper's hawk, the king rail, the osprey, and the bald eagle.

The six-lined lizard swiftly weaves a crooked trail on the surface of the sand, while digger wasps tunnel into the cool sand below. Although rare, the poisonous Massasauga rattler inhabits the climax forest of beech and maple. The red fox, otter, and coyote are also becoming rare, but are occasionally spotted. Other mammals who find sanctuary here include the white-tailed deer, Illinois skunk, thirteen-lined ground squirrel, pocket gopher, and woodchuck. For summertime visitors, however, the most abundant species of wildlife is likely to be the mosquito, and a strong insect repellent is recommended.

Among the special features of Indiana Dunes is Mt. Baldy; classified as a living dune, it reaches a height of 180 feet and moves inland at a rate of about $4^1/_2$ feet each year. The Bailly Homestead, dating to 1822, and the Chellberg Farm, built in the late 1880s, offer a glimpse at the period in time when this land underwent transition from wilderness to settlement. Miller Woods, Cowles Bog, and Pinhook Bog are of such exceptional interest to naturalists that they are described separately elsewhere in this book. Two other areas, Hoosier Prairie and Indiana Dunes State Park, although owned by the state of Indiana, are an integral part of the dunes landscape and should not be missed during a visit here (see their listings).

This is a place to be enjoyed in all seasons, with organized activities and special events offered throughout the year. In early March, volunteers demonstrate how to make maple syrup at a Maple Sugar Festival. Perhaps the major event of the year is the Duneland Folk Festival, held each July; it features crafts workshops, historical displays, and folk music. In January, rangers teach winter survival and conduct cross-country ski clinics. Each week, in every season, there are ranger-led hikes and programs that focus on such themes as edible wild plants, nature photography, and dune ecology.

Hiking, Bicycling, and Horseback Riding
More than twenty-five miles of little-used foot trails meander

through the swales and around the bogs and ponds between the dunes, along the Little Calumet River, into the forests, and over the dunes. Nearly all trails are easy walking and range in length from one-half mile to $3^{1}/_{2}$ miles. Visitors may also walk along the beach, or follow the 0.7-mile loop nature trail at the visitor center.

The Calumet Trail, 9.2 miles long, is Indiana's first long-distance trail built exclusively for hiking and bicycling; many people also use it for jogging.

The only horse trail, also used by hikers, is a $3^{1}/_{2}$-mile loop called Ly-co-ki-we Trail; bring your own horse.

Guided nature hikes are conducted periodically by park service naturalists; check with the visitor center for a schedule.

Swimming

There are four beaches with parking—West Beach, Kemil Road, Central Avenue, and Mt. Baldy. Lifeguards work West Beach and Kemil Road during the summer. West Beach has showers, bathrooms, and concessions; the others have portable toilets (no water). A nominal parking fee is charged at West Beach during the summer; it's extremely popular, so get there early.

Camping

There is year-round camping at Indiana Dunes State Park, not far from the National Lakeshore Visitor Center, and at numerous commercial campgrounds in the area. Although the United States Congress has approved a National Lakeshore campground, it has not been built as of this writing. Check with the visitor center for the latest details.

Picnicking

Picnicking is a delight at Indiana Dunes. There are a few established picnic areas, but you may want to spread your tablecloth on the beach where you can watch the waves come in as you eat.

Winter Sports

Cross-country skiing and snowshoeing are favorite ways to view the winter landscape. The visitor center issues a brochure that describes the trails open for these sports, and rangers often conduct ski clinics.

How to Get There: The best place to start your visit here is at the National Lakeshore Visitor Center, where an excellent staff will provide you with a map of the area and direct you to the various units. From Gary, go east on US 12 to IN 49 and continue east on US 12 for 3 miles to Kemil Rd. Turn right on Kemil to the visitor center; there are many signs to guide you.

Park open daily, year-round; hours vary from area to area and are subject to change. Visitor center open daily, year-round, 8:00 A.M.–

6:00 P.M., Memorial Day–Labor Day; 8:00 A.M.–5:00 P.M., rest of year. The only fee in the park is a nominal parking fee at West Beach from Memorial Day through Labor Day; everything else is free.

For Additional Information:
Superintendent
Indiana Dunes National Lakeshore
1100 N. Mineral Springs Rd.
Porter, IN 46304
(219) 926-7561

Indiana Dunes State Park

The Indiana Dunes area is known as the "Birthplace of American Ecology," thanks to the arrival just before the turn of the century of Professor Henry C. Cowles of the University of Chicago, who began the pioneering studies that gave rise to the science of plant ecology on this continent. Here, he proclaimed, was a botanical gold mine where one could witness a succession of plant life that elsewhere might take hundreds of years to evolve.

The rich diversity of flora found here then and now is due to a historical blending of climatic zones that resulted in an unusual mix of plant species. The prickly pear cactus usually associated with the southwest desert grows on the warm, sunlit sands, and the flowering dogwood so common in the South blooms each spring in some of the forested areas. In shady spots that are often subjected to frigid north winds, lichens, mosses, and bearberry of the Arctic tundra thrive in abundance along with some beautiful stands of northern pines.

The fauna, too, are varied—nearly every wild animal and bird native to the Midwest is found in the dunes area. Offering isolation, food, and cover, the region attracts such birds as snow geese from the Arctic Circle, warblers and plovers from South America, and little blue herons, Carolina wrens, and Louisiana waterthrushes from the deep South.

Spotted occasionally, but becoming rarer with the passing of time, are the otter, coyote, fox, and the area's only poisonous snake, the Massasauga rattler. Many species, including the Bonaparte weasel, rufescent woodchuck, Rafinesque's bat, Mississippi Valley mink, and Bachman's shrew, reach their geographic limits here.

Established in 1925, Indiana Dunes State Park is a delightful 2,182-acre mix of rolling sand dunes, marshes thick with tallgrasses, and verdant forests. A white sand beach rambles along the Lake Michigan shoreline for approximately three miles. When conditions are just right, the drifting sands emit a low, humming sound that resembles the drawing of a bow over the strings of a bass viol.

Here and there in the dunes are huge blowouts, great bowlike crevices scooped out over the years by blowing winds. A starkly beautiful tree graveyard of white pines, some seventy feet tall, now stands naked against the sky after lying beneath the restless sands for years.

Spectacular views of the surrounding terrain and Lake Michigan are available from atop the park's highest dune, 192-foot-tall Mt. Tom, and from a 40-foot-high lookout tower.

With the exception of a strip of beach along the lakeshore, the eastern two-thirds of the park has been set aside as the largest state nature preserve in Indiana. Its 1,530 acres harbor the largest variety of trees in the Midwest.

Although the combination of natural phenomena and fine recreational facilities may attract as many as 22,000 visitors a day, especially on holiday weekends in the summer, there are always serene corners in the park in which to get away from it all.

Hiking and Bicycling

An excellent trail system for hikers wanders through the woods, across the marsh, along the Lake Michigan shoreline, and over the tops of the three highest dunes; a park naturalist conducts guided hikes in the summer. Each of the eight trails is identified on the park map as easy, moderate, or rugged. They vary in length from 1/8 mile to 5 1/2 miles and cover a total of 16 1/2 miles, but several of them crisscross, allowing you to alter your route if you so choose. The 9.2-mile-long Calumet Trail, which adjoins the park's southern boundary, is the state's first long-distance trail built exclusively for bicycling and hiking. It also passes through the Indiana Dunes National Lakeshore. Indiana's only youth hostel, which features dormitory-style overnight accommodations at a low cost for hikers and bicyclists, is located approximately three miles southwest of the state park at the intersection of County Road 100 W and US 20; for information, phone (219) 926-1528 or inquire at the state park or national lakeshore visitor center.

Camping

The campground lies alongside tiny Dune Creek in a low, wooded area that provides complete seclusion from other park visitors. Facilities include modern restrooms, some electrical hookups, a dump station, and a children's playground. Open year-round; some of the more than 300 sites may be reserved from Memorial Day to Labor Day; and since this is a very popular campground, reservations are advised. A youth group tenting area is available by reservation only the year-round. Wood, ice, picnic supplies, and groceries are available during summer months.

Swimming

A free swimming beach is open from Memorial Day through Labor Day weekend; swimming permitted only when lifeguards are on duty, generally from 11:00 A.M. to 7:00 P.M. on weekends and noon to 6:00 P.M. weekdays. The two-story brick pavilion that houses the bathhouse, refreshment services, and souvenir stands was designed by Frank Lloyd Wright.

Picnicking

Several scattered picnic areas offer tables, grills, drinking water, toilet facilities, playground equipment, playfields, and five shelters.

Winter Sports

Three trails in the park, as well as the Calumet Trail, are open to cross-country skiers. You may bring your own equipment, or rent poles, skis, and boots in the park for a nominal fee. Skiing is usually permitted from 9:00 A.M. to 4:00 P.M.

How to Get There: Located along the shore of Lake Michigan in Porter County, midway between Gary on the west and Michigan City on the east. From the intersection of I-65 and I-94 in Gary, go east on I-94 to IN 49. Head north on IN 49, which leads into the park. Parking on site.

Park open daily, year-round, during daylight hours; nominal vehicle entrance fee. Visitor center open 9:00 A.M.–5:00 P.M. daily, Memorial Day–Labor Day; 9:00 A.M.–4:00 P.M., rest of year; closed Thanksgiving, Christmas, New Year's Day.

For Additional Information:
Superintendent
Indiana Dunes State Park
1600 North, 25 East
Chesterton, IN 46304
(219) 926-4520

Indiana Department of Natural Resources
Division of State Park
616 State Office Bldg.
Indianapolis, IN 46204
(317) 232-4124
(800) 622-4931—In Indiana Only

International Friendship Gardens

Lying along Trail Creek in the midst of the Indiana dune country are the beautiful International Friendship Gardens, dedicated to friendship, unity, and understanding among the nations of the world. They regularly draw garden and nature lovers from the four corners of the earth.

Established in 1935, the gardens are a charming blend of modern and traditional horticulture. The extensive plantings, which include flowers, shrubs, and trees collected from all over the globe, are arranged as they would be in the homelands of various nations. Among the countries represented here are Canada, Poland, Australia, France, Greece, Scotland, Switzerland, England, Sweden, Germany, Norway, Holland, Lithuania, China, Italy, and Turkey. Trail Creek and Willow Creek meander through the gardens, and several pools of clear water reflect the tranquil beauty around them.

Two collections here are particularly notable. For two to three weeks each May, an array of brilliantly hued tulips bloom profusely. Holland donated some 200,000 tulip bulbs for a single planting, and thousands more are added annually. Later, around June 15, myriads of roses appear.

The thirty-five acres of gardens are surrounded by a cool green forest, some sixty-five acres left wild and undeveloped. Visitors are welcome to wander through the woods.

It would be difficult to imagine a lovelier setting for an outdoor wedding than these gardens, evidenced by the fact that couples come here from many parts of the world to exchange their vows. And if you choose to visit the gardens on a night when one of the many operatic, choral, or orchestral productions is being presented, you will find the combination of blossoms, music, and starlight irresistible.

How to Get There: From downtown Michigan City, go east on US 12 to Liberty Trail and turn right. Follow Liberty Trail to garden sign and entrance on left side of road. Parking on site.

Open daily, 9:00 A.M. until dark (later on concert nights), year-round. An admission fee is charged.

For Additional Information:
International Friendship Gardens
Michigan City, IN 46360
(219) 874-3664

Jasper–Pulaski State Fish and Wildlife Area

Each spring and autumn, Jasper–Pulaski presents one of nature's most magnificent pageants. It is then that thousands of greater sandhill cranes pause here to rest before proceeding to their winter homes in Florida or their summer nesting areas in Michigan, Minnesota, and Canada. This refuge is believed to be the only place east of the Mississippi River where this species of crane stops en masse during migration.

Generally, the spring influx begins in late February, achieves its maximum number the last two weeks in March, and is gone by mid-April. The fall migrants start to arrive during the first half of September, reach and maintain their peak population throughout November, and are gone by mid-December. Dur-

Elk can be seen at Jasper–Pulaski State Fish and Wildlife Area   *Bill Thomas*

ing their tenure, the cranes may best be observed in early morning and early evening; and you are likely to see them in their greatest concentration in the autumn.

The huge birds stand nearly four feet tall, have a wingspan of more than six feet, and are known as much for their clarion calls as for their impressive appearance.

Every day at dawn, when the marsh is still shrouded in mist, the fluted voices of up to 13,000 cranes blend in a chorus that has echoed across this land for eleven million years. Ancestors of these sandhills sang for prehistoric man, making this species' pedigree one of the oldest on this continent.

Although the cranes are Jasper–Pulaski's main attraction, there is other wildlife on the preserve's 8,000 acres. A walk through the marsh on almost any day of the year will enable one to see Canada geese, and deer may often be seen along refuge roads and trails in early morning or at dusk. Wood ducks, mallards, redheads, teals, and canvasbacks, like the cranes, rest here during migration; and quail and woodcock live here year-round. You can also visit some game pens where pheasant are reared as stock for other wildlife areas in Indiana. Nearby, wapiti elk, American bison, and white-tailed deer roam fenced-in pastures.

Two observation towers are provided, one overlooking the sandhill crane and Canada geese feeding area, the other offering a view of the marsh complex. Visitors must obtain a free permit to gain access to them, however.

Seasonal activities at Jasper–Pulaski include mushroom hunting, berry picking, and nut gathering.

Located in the northwest portion of the refuge is the 480-acre Tefft Savanna Nature Preserve. Its high, oak-covered dunes are interspersed with low-lying patches of wet prairie. Many of the plants that thrive here are extremely rare in the Midwest.

You may learn more about the entire area by visiting some natural history and wildlife exhibits maintained in one of the service buildings. The staff naturalist will be happy to answer any questions you might have.

Fishing

The only areas open to fishing are the display pond near the headquarters building (for children under sixteen only) and certain upper parts of Ryan Ditch. Bass, bluegill, and catfish are stocked in these waters. Ditch fishing requires a special permit.

Camping

A fine shaded campground with more than fifty sites, drinking water, and a modern restroom is provided near the headquarters building; no hookups and no showers. All sites have tables; some have grills and camper pads. The nominal fee is reduced even more between Labor Day and Memorial Day weekend.

Picnicking

Two picnic areas and three shelters lie near the main parking area. Restrooms and playground equipment are nearby.

How to Get There: Located in portions of Jasper, Starke, and Pulaski counties. From the town of Medaryville in northwestern Pulaski County, go north on US 421 to IN 143, which meets US 421 on the left (west) side of the road, and turn left. Proceed on IN 143 to County Rd. and turn right (north). The area's headquarters building is on the right (east) side of County Rd. just after you turn. Look for signs. Parking on site.

Refuge open daily, year-round at all times; free. Office open 7:00 A.M.–3:30 P.M., Mon.–Fri.; may be open earlier, later, or on weekends seasonally.

For Additional Information:
Manager
Jasper–Pulaski State Fish and Wildlife Area
R.R. 1, Box 166
Medaryville, IN 47959
(219) 843-4841

Indiana Department of Natural Resources
Fish and Wildlife Division
607 State Office Bldg.
Indianapolis, IN 46204
(317) 232-4080

Tefft Savanna Nature Preserve
c/o Division of Nature Preserves
601 State Office Building
Indianapolis, IN 46204
(317) 232-4052

Langeluttig Swamp

Although it covers just ten acres, this "pocket preserve" is a prized addition to Indiana's Wetland Conservation Area Program. It lies on the floodplain of the Little Calumet River and is part of a more extensive swamp habitat that is home to an amazing amount of wildlife.

Because the Little Calumet empties into Lake Michigan, it is a spawning ground for lake fish. The dense vegetation found on the preserve, which is a composite of second-growth upland woods and marshy river bottoms, provides food, shelter, and nesting areas for many types of birds, especially aquatic species. No matter when you visit this area, you will likely see ducks, herons, and many shorebirds. Fur-bearing animals, such as beaver, mink, and muskrat, come here seeking haven from trappers on adjoining lands, and raccoons, foxes, and opossums wander about at night.

Once this was a seasonal swamp, but since the construction of I-94 half a mile to the north blocked drainage outlets, the swamp generally remains wet year-round.

Langeluttig Swamp was originally purchased by The Nature Conservancy, but was transferred a few years ago to the Fish and Wildlife Division of the Indiana Department of Natural Resources. Since the only practical land access is across private property, you must make an appointment to visit here, and once here, you'll have to forge your own way because there are no established trails. This area will appeal to visitors wishing to experience the swamp in its natural and wild setting.

Fishing

Several species of trout and salmon spawn in the Little Calumet River, which is one of the only two Indiana rivers that flow into Lake Michigan. The fishing is generally excellent in the spring and fall.

How to Get There: Located in northeastern Porter County along the Little Calumet River, just southeast of the intersection of I-94 and IN 49, and just northeast of Chesterton. Exact directions will be given when you contact the Indiana Department of Natural Resources for an appointment to visit here.

Open daily, year-round, during daylight hours; free.

For Additional Information:

Indiana Department of Natural Resources
Fish and Wildlife Division
607 State Office Bldg.
Indianapolis, IN 46204
(317) 232-4080

Indiana Field Office
The Nature Conservancy
4200 N. Michigan St.
Indianapolis, IN 46208
(317) 923-7547

LaSalle State Fish and Wildlife Area

This area bears the name of the French explorer who in 1679 became the first white man to travel the Kankakee River. Then the river snaked its way through a million-acre marsh that teemed with wildlife. Today, it is an arrow-straight ditch, the result of channelization, and the rich, productive wetland that adjoined it has been reduced to little more than a thousand acres. A small remnant of that legendary marsh is preserved within this 3,640-acre refuge.

The Kankakee River flows through the heart of the area, flooding 1,000 acres of river bottoms along the way and creating a habitat attractive to migrating waterfowl.

Although the refuge is used by Canada geese and several species of ducks, including mallards, black ducks, blue- and green-winged teals, widgeons, pintails, ringnecks, buffleheads, gadwalls, shovelers, and mergansers, the colorful male wood duck is the star attraction. The flamboyant drakes, along with the drabber colored hens, begin to arrive from their southern wintering grounds in early March, selecting suitable tree cavities or man-made boxes in which to nest. They stay throughout the summer and into the fall, raising their young, then start heading south in late September. By the end of November, the exodus is complete.

The refuge also hosts large numbers of prothonotary warblers and some impressive flocks of lesser golden plovers in the spring. White-tailed deer, raccoons, mink, muskrats, beavers, rabbits, quail, and pheasants live year-round in the woodlands and marsh and along the bayous just off the river.

Visitors may obtain a free permit to hunt mushrooms and wild berries in season.

Hiking

Although no extensive trail system exists at LaSalle, visitors may hike along several miles of roads that penetrate the areas. Be sure to avoid restricted areas during hunting season. A map is available at the headquarters building.

Boating and Fishing

Rowboats and canoes are used on the Kankakee River; only electric trolling motors are permitted. Two free launching ramps are available, one on the river's south bank near LaSalle's western boundary, which abuts the Indiana–Illinois state line, and another on a bayou south of the river near the refuge's eastern border. Boaters who enter Illinois will find a different Kankakee River. Never channelized west of the state line, the Kankakee there reverts to its natural state, a twisting, winding stream that is home to a spectacular array of wildlife.

The Kankakee River yields northern pike, walleye, smallmouth bass, largemouth bass, crappie, and catfish. Its waters are purer in Illinois and have produced state record catches of the first three.

Camping

Nearly fifty primitive sites are available in a campground in the east central portion of the refuge. Pit toilets and drinking water are available; a boat launch ramp is nearby. The nominal fee is reduced even more between Labor Day and Memorial Day weekend.

Picnicking

Just east of the campground, a quiet, shaded picnic area lies near the shore of a bayou. A launch ramp is located just across the road.

Winter Sports

Cold-weather activities include ice fishing, ice skating, and cross-country skiing.

How to Get There: Located along both banks of the Kankakee River, just southwest of the community of Schneider. This part of the Kankakee River forms the boundary line between Lake County to the north and Newton County to the south; the fish and wildlife area is bounded on the west by the Indiana–Illinois state line. From Schneider, go south on US 41, across the Kankakee River, to IN 10. Turn right (west) onto IN 10 and proceed to LaSalle's main entrance on the right (north) side of the road. Parking on site.

Refuge open at all times; free. Office open 7:00 A.M.–3:30 P.M., Mon.–Fri., year-round; may be open earlier, later, or on weekends seasonally.

For Additional Information:
Manager
LaSalle State Fish and Wildlife Area
R.R. 1, Box 80
Lake Village, IN 46349
(219) 992-3019

Indiana Department of Natural Resources
Fish and Wildlife Division
607 State Office Bldg.
Indianapolis, IN 46204
(317) 232-4080

Lemon Lake County Park

This 280-acre parkland, with its mix of active recreation facilities and secluded woodlands, offers something for the entire family. Although no portion of it has been specifically set aside as a nature preserve, every effort is made to protect all flora and fauna.

Most facilities have been constructed in the western half of the park, and include softball diamonds, archery, soccer, and football fields; volleyball courts, lighted tennis and basketball courts, and large, open meadows for free play, as well as an arts and crafts center.

In the southwestern corner and the eastern half of the park, there are wild stretches to explore. The wetlands, wooded groves with trees higher than a ten-story building, an arboretum, and two lakes shelter a variety of wildlife, and such wildflowers as yellow adder's tongue, violets, and cinquefoil grow in random profusion. There's a delightful children's playground between the two lakes, complete with its own covered bridge and treehouses.

Group hayrides are available from spring through fall; make reservations at least two weeks in advance by phoning the main office. Each May, the parks department sponsors a Craft Carnival; the snow season is highlighted by a fun-for-all-ages Winter Carnival, usually held in late January.

Hiking

Several miles of easy-to-walk trails wind through the forested areas of the park. The 3/4-mile-long Touchstone Trail provides a wide, smooth surface for blind and handicapped visitors; it encircles the wooded shoreline of Lemon Lake North, entering natural wooded areas along the way. A physical fitness trail is very popular with joggers.

Boating and Fishing

Paddleboats may be rented on Lake Lemon. Fishing from the shoreline for bass, bluegill, and catfish is a popular sport.

Picnicking

Picnic areas with shelters are located in the forest and near the recreation facilities. For a nominal fee, shelters may be reserved in advance. Food concessions operate during summer months.

Winter Sports

Winter sports include cross-country skiing and sledding. Lessons and rental equipment are available for skiers, and inner tubes may be rented at Lemon Lake's sledding hill. An outdoor ice skating rink opens at dawn and is lighted for night skating until 9:00 P.M. A warming shelter with a fireplace provides a cozy retreat from the cold weather.

How to Get There: Located in central Lake County southwest of Crown Point. From Crown Point, take IL 55 (Old Jackson Hwy.) south to 133rd Ave. (Cedar Lake Rd.) and turn right (west). Proceed on 133rd Ave. to Lemon Lake Park on the right (north) side of the road at 6322 W. 133rd Ave. Parking on site.

Open daily, year-round; 7:00 A.M.–11:00 P.M., Memorial Day to Labor Day; 7:00 A.M.–dusk, rest of year (except lighted sports areas). Nominal vehicle admission fee.

For Additional Information:
Superintendent
Lake County Parks and Recreation Dept.
2293 N. Main St.
Crown Point, IN 46307
(219) 738-2020, Ext. 391

Deep River Nature Center
Deep River County Park
Rt. 2, Old US 330
Deep River (Hobart), IN 46342
(219) 769-9030

Marquette Park

See listing under Miller Woods, below.

Miller Woods

You may be astonished that this 435-acre oasis could exist in the heart of Gary, better known nationwide for its industry and pollution. Yet Miller Woods, a cool, green sanctuary favored by nature lovers for nearly a century, has miraculously survived.

Formally designated a savanna, the woodland represents an ecosystem that used to be quite common throughout the Midwest, but has now nearly vanished from the region. The tract, kept wild first by neglect and then by controversy over how it should be used, was in private ownership until 1980. Then U.S. Steel, which had originally purchased part of the area as a possible extension site in the early 1900s, donated 214 acres to Indiana Dunes National Lakeshore, and soon thereafter Congress authorized the purchase of another 221 acres from various owners.

The grasses, sedges, and bracken fern grow so thickly on the ground that they prevent other taller vegetation from gaining a foothold, while the trees, black oaks scattered at random, are spaced fairly far apart, resulting in the openness that is characteristic of savannas. There are wildflowers here, too—blazing stars, bird's-foot violets, false dandelions, and myriads of others that dot the landscape. Rose gentians and blue-flowered Kalm's lobelias rim the long, narrow ponds.

Lying between Miller Woods and the Lake Michigan shoreline are some high sand ridges anchored by marram grass, trailing grapevines, rows of cottonwood trees, and a variety of wildflowers. They make up one of the most complex foredune systems in the national lakeshore.

More dunes are present in Marquette Park, a 240-acre property of the Gary Parks and Recreation Department that's nestled in the midst of national parklands just east of Miller Woods. It also offers a picturesque lagoon, manicured lawns, formal flower beds, lighted tennis courts, a picnic area, concession stands, and an excellent swimming beach on Lake Michigan.

Hiking

A trail approximately two miles long leads across the foredune system, then dips into the woodland. Ranger-guided tours are scheduled periodically throughout the spring and summer; check at the national lakeshore visitor center for details.

How to Get There: Located in northeastern Lake County, in the eastern part of Gary. From the convergence of US 12, US 20, I-65, and I-90 in Gary, go east on US 12 (Dune's Hwy.) to Lake St. Turn left (north) and proceed on Lake St. until it ends at the Lake St. Beach parking lot in Marquette Park. Miller Woods may be entered only on foot, and the trail leads west from this parking lot.

Miller Woods open daily, year-round, during daylight hours; free. Marquette Park open daily, year-round, 9:00 A.M.–10:30 P.M.; a nominal vehicle admission fee, slightly higher for nonresidents, is charged at the beach parking lot during peak use periods.

For Additional Information:

Superindendent
Indiana Dunes National Lakeshore
1100 N. Mineral Springs Rd.
Porter, IN 46304
(219) 926-7561

Property Manager
Gary Parks and Recreation Dept.
300 Jackson St., Box 507
Gary, IN 46402
(219) 944-6571

Moraine Nature Preserve

This beautiful preserve contains some of the most diversified terrain in Indiana's nature preserve system. A fine example of the many land forms associated with the Valparaiso glacial moraine, which extends for several hundred miles through Wisconsin, Illinois, Michigan, and Indiana, Moraine Nature Preserve contains some 300 acres of rolling ridges, steep sidehills, muck pockets, and potholes.

The muddy flats of shallow Carlson Pond are covered with spatterdock, rice cutgrass, and water smartweed, creating an area attractive to wild ducks and great blue herons. Except for a few grassy fields, the ridges and slopes are entirely wooded.

An ongoing botanical inventory has thus far included 155 plant species, many of which are unusual flowers. Wild ginger, large-flowered and prairie trillium, false and true Solomon's seal, ginseng, wild sarsaparilla, and several kinds of violets grow in shady spots. In old fields, you'll see nodding ladies' tresses and green-carpeted beds of club moss. Lady fern and Indian cucumber root grow in the moist soil that borders one of the preserve's swamps. Christmas, broad beech, and grape ferns, as well as ebony spleenwort, are common.

Sometimes called the Womer Tract in honor of the couple who donated the original and major portion of this tract to The Nature Conservancy, Moraine Preserve is currently owned and managed by the Indiana Department of Natural Resources. The Womers retain a house on the property and must be contacted for permission to enter preserve lands.

Hiking

Many well-maintained trails provide access to the various land forms; some are steep.

How to Get There: Located in northeastern Porter County, a few miles south of Chesterton. From the intersection of I-90 and IN 49 in Chesterton, head south on IN 49 to 750 N Rd. Turn left (east) on 750 N, and proceed approximately one-half mile to Moraine Preserve. The preserve extends both north and south of this road. Parking on site.

Open daily, year-round, during daylight hours; free, but permission to enter must first be obtained from John or Mary Louise Womer.

For Additional Information:

Mr. and Mrs. John Womer
Preserve Stewards
240 E-750 N Rd.
Valparaiso, IN 46383
(219) 464-4941

Indiana Field Office
The Nature Conservancy
4200 N. Michigan St.
Indianapolis, IN 46208
(317) 923-7547

Division of Nature Preserves
Indiana Department of Natural Resources
601 State Office Bldg.
Indianapolis, IN 46204
(317) 232-4052

The Nature Conservancy, Indiana Field Office

See listing under The Nature Conservancy, Illinois Field Office, p. 90.

Pinhook Bog

Pinhook Bog is one of the most unique wetlands in Indiana, a pristine area born of the Ice Age. Although it is administered as part of the Indiana Dunes National Lakeshore, it lies by itself approximately eight miles south of Michigan City, some distance from the main segment of the national parkland.

The bog, a national natural landmark, lies within a bowl-shaped depression believed to be a glacial kettle hole. To understand the description "quaking bog," step lightly on the floating mat of sphagnum moss that covers most of the watery surface and watch its gentle undulations. In places, the mat is overgrown with leatherleaf, bog rosemary, blueberries, and chokeberry, and the huckleberries grow to the size of grapes. The hills that rim the wetland are blanketed with tamarack, white pines, red maples, and ash trees.

Among the array of rare plants that grow here are the carnivorous pitcher plants and sundews. Both capture and feed on insects, and it's sometimes possible to watch the process.

Some visitors swear that mosquitoes make up the greatest percentage of wildlife here, but if you should suffer a few bites, it may be of some comfort to know that you encountered one of two species that are extremely rare in Indiana.

Hiking

At present, you may enter this fragile ecosystem only on a guided walking tour. Check at the Indiana Dunes National Lakeshore Visitor Center to find out when hikes are scheduled. Each hike is limited to thirty participants, and advance reservations are necessary. Hikes last about three hours, and you'll cover about two miles. Be sure to bring some insect repellent.

How to Get There: Located in northwest LaPorte County, about four miles south of Waterford and just north of I-80/I-90 (East-West Toll Road). The visitor center will provide more exact directions when you make your reservation.

Visitor center open daily, year-round, 8:00 A.M.–6:00 P.M., Memorial Day–Labor Day; 8:00 A.M.–5:00 P.M., rest of year. Free.

For Additional Information:
Superintendent
Indiana Dunes National Lakeshore
1100 N. Mineral Springs Rd.
Porter, IN 46304
(219) 926-7561

Stoney Run County Park

Stoney Run Park is a prime area in which to observe the natural order of the world. Although there's a Timberform playground for young children, most of the other facilities here have been engineered by nature.

The park is a combination of cool, dense woodlands, meadows, and small ponds. In the spring and summer, the park blooms with mayapple, spring beauty, and cardinal flowers. Autumn is a quieter time, but visually it is the most spectacular.

You may also want to drop in at the Lake County Parks and Recreation Department's tree nursery located in the northernmost portion of Stoney Run. From spring through fall, you can sample the old-fashioned fun of a hayride; phone the main office at least two weeks in advance for a reservation.

Three annual events can be enjoyed by the entire family. The Stoney Run Fitness Fun and a Camping Exposition are held in June; a Bluegrass Festival is scheduled for August.

Hiking and Horseback Riding

Several miles of footpaths loop through the forest in the eastern half of Stoney Run; a shorter woodland loop serves as a physical fitness trail. You may also make your way at random through the more secluded forest in the western portion of the park. Equestrians follow a bridle path that skirts the entire perimeter of the park and passes through its most remote areas; no rentals.

Fishing

Two ponds offer catches of perch, bluegill, and catfish. Bramlett's Pond in the northeastern corner of the park is surrounded by woods; the other, a recently constructed pond in the southeastern part of the park, lies in an open meadow near the picnic area. Only cane poles may be used in the latter.

Camping

A primitive tent camping area, located in a secluded part of the park near the edge of the forest, is available year-round. Reservations for both individuals and groups may be made by phoning the main office.

Picnicking

Shelters and picnic tables with grills are situated in the southeastern part of the park. Shelters may be reserved in advance for a nominal fee; otherwise, they are available free on a first-come, first-serve basis.

Winter Sports

Cross-country ski trails, as well as lessons and rental equipment, are available. A small lake near the park's southeastern corner is used by ice skaters. Chilled participants can warm fingers and toes before a blazing fire.

How to Get There: Located in eastern Lake County, southeast of

Crown Point, near the Lake–Porter County line. From Crown Point, head southeast on US 231/IN 8 (Joliet St.), through Leroy, to 145th Ave. Turn left (east) and proceed on 145th Ave. until it ends at Union St. Turn left (north) to 142nd Ave., then right (east) on 142nd Ave. to park entrance on left (north) side of the road. Parking on site.

Open daily, year-round, 7:00 A.M.–dusk; nominal vehicle entrance fee.

For Additional Information:

Superintendent
Lake County Parks and Recreation Dept.
2293 N. Main St.
Crown Point, IN 46307
(219) 738-2020, Ext. 391

Deep River Nature Center
Deep River County Park
Rt. 2, Old US 330
Deep River (Hobart), IN 46342
(219) 769-9030

Part 5

Bill Thomas

Natural Attractions in Michigan

Grand Mere Nature Study Area

See listing under Warren Dunes State Park, p. 177.

The Nature Conservancy, Michigan Field Office

See listing under The Nature Conservancy, Illinois Field Office, p. 90.

Robinson Preserve

Visitors to The Nature Conservancy's Robinson Preserve will find a blending of gently undulating dunes, a deeply incised stream valley, deciduous woodlands, and flat sand barrens. Because the eighty-acre area is compact, easily accessible, and never crowded, yet very diverse, it constitutes a marvelous outdoor laboratory for nature study.

The least disturbed section of the preserve is a thirty-acre climax forest of oaks and hickories that harbors such rare wildflowers as the showy orchis and closed gentian. A deep, stream-cut ravine draped with luxurious ferns and trailing arbutus wanders through the forest.

Old apple orchards are still found on once-cultivated ground in another part of this sanctuary, but much of that land has reverted to a young forest of red maple, sassafras, black cherry, and big-tooth aspen.

Wildlife takes refuge here—red foxes, opossums, and raccoons make this preserve their permanent home, and birdwatchers may spot yellow-billed cuckoos, indigo buntings, crested flycatchers, scarlet tanagers, great gray owls, woodcocks, and red-tailed hawks.

While Michigan is noted for its proliferation of mushrooms, one mushroom expert remarked that he had seen more mushrooms at this preserve than at any other area in the state.

A single trail leading south from the entrance through the preserve's midsection offers a pleasant round-trip walk of about one mile. You'll find a shelter at trail's end where you may rest and observe the surrounding terrain, or simply enjoy the silence. Before visiting here, request permission to enter from the preserve steward.

How to Get There: Located in southwestern Berrien County, a few miles northeast of New Buffalo. From the intersection of I-94 and US 12 just northeast of New Buffalo, go west on US 12 to Red Arrow Hwy. Turn right (north) onto Red Arrow Hwy. and proceed to East Rd. in Lakeside. Turn right (east) onto East Rd. and continue for about 1 1/2 miles to preserve on the left (north) side of the road. A sign marks the entrance. Limited parking near entrance.

Open daily, year-round, during daylight hours; free.

For Additional Information:

Stan Showalter
Preserve Steward
Lakeside Rd.
Lakeside, MI 49116
(616) 469-3906

Michigan Field Office
The Nature Conservancy
531 N. Clippert St.
Lansing, MI 48912
(517) 332-1741

Warren Dunes State Park

Warren Dunes, the southernmost of all Michigan state parks, is a lakeside playground rich in natural diversity. Each year, well over a million visitors come here to enjoy the expansive white sand beach that stretches along the Lake Michigan shoreline for nearly two miles, containing tall, spectacular dunes and isolated pockets of wilderness.

This land was saved for posterity by a single man, Edward K. Warren of Three Oaks, who began purchasing this acreage in 1879 because he felt it would be invaluable as a place of recreation for future generations. Some 1,500 acres in two separate tracts were acquired and eventually turned over to the state of Michigan for use as a public park.

Approximately 1,200 acres are adjacent to Lake Michigan. All of the park's recreational facilities are here, as well as untouched areas that have been shaped only by the elements. Nestled in the dunes and forests behind the beach is a 488-acre nature study area that visitors may enter only on foot. Here the active, shifting dunes of modern times provide a vivid contrast to older fossil dunes now stabilized by the forests that cloak their ridges. Several blowouts, great bowl-like depressions scooped out by the wind, invade the wooded hills.

Approximately five miles to the south lies the park's second tract, a 312-acre natural area known as Warren Woods. A trail winds through a quiet hardwood forest, part of which has never known an axe or chain saw. In this virgin woodland, the last known one of its type in Michigan that has escaped logging, there are sycamores, beeches, and maples that tower to a height of 125 feet and have diameters of nearly 5 feet. Their leafed-out branches form a canopy so dense that sunlight rarely penetrates it, permitting only a sparse understory to survive. Flowing through the rolling terrain, cutting deeply into the land, is the Galien River, whose narrow, moist floodplain supports a greater variety of vegetation than the upland forest. There you will see such species as swamp white oak, basswood, pawpaws, spicebush, and redbuds, in addition to the trees mentioned previously.

A recent addition to the park is situated about three miles north of the dunes area. Known as the Grand Mere Nature Study Area, it sprawls over some 1,200 acres of wild and beautiful land that edges Lake Michigan. The ancient dunes that rise behind the beach are forested with mature oak, beech, sugar maple, and, on north-facing slopes, hemlock. Inland, beyond the dunes, a string of three lakes and a cranberry bog born of different geological ages illustrate various stages of vegetational succession. The many plant communities, representing the entire range from aquatic to terrestrial, contain several relict species that are extremely rare in southern Michigan. One of the area's access routes, Wishart Road, has been proposed for designation as southwest Michigan's only scenic road.

Since all park units are on the direct route of bird migrations in the spring and also, to a lesser extent, in the fall, they lure many bird-watchers. Grand Mere, considered the best all-round birding area in Berrien County, is used by hawks, veery, and prairie and Canada warblers. The Louisiana waterthrush and Acadian flycatcher have been seen at Warren Woods, and the hooded warbler is known to nest there. Although Warren Dunes receives far more public use than the other two, especially on warm summer days, it still harbors numerous ducks, gulls, and shorebirds.

Another sight at Warren Dunes also draws a lot of attention to the skies. Hang gliders from all over the globe find that the prevailing winds from the lake and the 200-foot vertical drop afforded by Tower Hill create ideal conditions in which to practice their sport. Flights of more than an hour's duration have been recorded.

Hiking

Several miles of trails at Warren Dunes lead through the dunes and forests and along the beach. An unimproved trail winds through Warren Woods; most of it is very easy to walk, but you will have some up-and-down climbing to do if you want to descend to the river and its floodplain. There is no real trail system at Grand Mere Nature Study Area, but you can follow dirt and gravel roads and some unimproved footpaths.

Camping

Two campgrounds at Warren Dunes feature nearly 200 sites that can accommodate either recreational vehicles or tents. Facilities at both include electricity and modern restrooms with hot showers and flush toilets (in winter, only chemical toilets are available). These campgrounds often operate at capacity on spring and summer weekends and on holidays; advance reservations may be made from May to Sept. Fees are reduced during winter months. A year-round tent campground for organized youth groups can accommodate up to 150 people, but it's available only on a first-come, first-serve basis.

Swimming

An excellent swimming beach in a beautiful setting is the single most popular feature of Warren Dunes. Bathhouses, modern toilet facilities, and concession stands are open from approximately mid-April to mid-Oct.

Picnicking

Several quiet picnic areas behind the dunes are available for both families and groups. Tables and grills are provided at each site; drinking water, restrooms, concession stands, and a children's playground are nearby.

Winter Sports

Snow-covered hills attract many sledders and tobogganers. Cross-country skiers and snowshoers follow established trails or forge their own.

How to Get There: Located in southwest Berrien County. Warren Dunes State Park lies just southwest of Bridgman. From the intersection of I-94 and Red Arrow Hwy. in Bridgman, go south on Red Arrow Hwy. to park entrance on right (west) side of the road. Look for signs. Parking on site. To reach Warren Woods, continue south on Red Arrow Hwy. past entrance road to Warren Dunes, until you reach Warren Woods Rd. Turn left (east) onto Warren Woods Rd. and proceed approximately 2½ miles to Warren Woods on the right (south) side of the road. There's a sign next to the trailhead. Park at side of road. To reach Grand Mere Nature Study Area from Bridgman, go north on I-94 to the Stevensville exit. Head west from this exit to the first intersection. If you continue across this intersection, you will be on Grand Mere Rd., which runs through the northern part of the preserve. Or you may turn left (south) onto Thornton Rd. at this intersection and continue south to Willow Rd. Turn right (west) onto Willow and proceed to Wishart Rd., where another turn to the right (north) will lead you into the southern half of Grand Mere. Park at side of road. Since both Warren Woods and Grand Mere are a little difficult to locate because of poorly marked roads, you may want to double-check your directions with the staff at Warren Dunes before starting out.

Warren Dunes is open daily, year-round, 8:00 A.M.–10:00 P.M.; a nominal vehicle admission fee is slightly higher for out-of-state residents. Warren Woods and Grand Mere are open daily, year-round, dawn to dusk; free.

For Additional Information:

Superintendent
Warren Dunes State Park
Rt. 1
Sawyer, MI 49125
(616) 426-4013

Michigan Department of Natural Resources
Parks and Recreation Division
Stephen T. Mason Bldg.
Box 30028
Lansing, MI 48909
(517) 373-1220

Warren Woods

See listing under Warren Dunes State Park, p. 177.

Index

Altorf (or Langham) Island, 75
Animals. *See* Endangered species: animals; Wildlife sanctuaries; Zoos; *and specific types*
Aquariums, 14–15, 76
Arbor Lake, 88
Arbor vitae, 126
Arboretums, 78–80, 87–89, 141, 167
Archery, 12, 13, 167
Argonne National Laboratory, 100, 131
Arie Crown Forest, 112
Asphodel, false, 24
Axehead Lake, 72, 73

Bailly Homestead, 156
Bald eagle, 42, 68, 156
Basketball courts, 5, 7, 9, 10, 12, 13
Bees and beehives, 39, 149
Begonia, 30
Belmont Prairie, 20
Bemis Woods, 112, 113
Berkeley Prairie, 2–21
Betz, Robert, 52
Bicycle paths
  Great Western Trail, 57–59
  Illinois and Michigan Canal State Trail, 65–67
  Illinois Prairie Path, 70–71
Bicycle paths (Chicago), 4, 7, 8, 10, 12, 13–14
Bicycle paths (Illinois), 39, 72, 74, 76, 83, 85, 92, 96, 100, 104, 106, 112, 117, 120, 123, 125
Bicycle paths (Indiana), 157, 159
Bicycle paths (Wisconsin), 140
Bird-watching areas (Chicago), 8, 9, 12
Bird-watching areas (Illinois), 22, 24, 25, 28, 32, 35, 42, 44, 56, 59, 62, 67–68, 75–76, 78, 80, 82, 85, 88, 93, 94, 100, 103, 105, 109, 115, 117, 122, 124, 130, 131
Bird-watching areas (Indiana), 148, 152, 156, 158, 164

Bird-watching areas (Michigan), 176, 178
Birds. *See* Bird-watching areas; Migratory birds; Waterfowl; *and specific types*
Bitterns, 28, 93
Black Partridge Woods, 98
Blackbirds
  red-winged, 28, 116, 130
  yellow-headed, 28, 116
Blackwell Recreational Preserve, 21–23
Blind, attractions for, 7, 119, 120, 167
Blueberry, 119
Bluebird, 25, 75–76
Bluff Spring Fen, 24
Boating
  on Busse Lake, 92
  in Chain O'Lakes area, 32
  on Chicago River, North Branch, 96
  on Des Plaines River, 40, 43, 72, 101, 112
  on DuPage River, 23
  on Fox River, 46, 53, 86, 115, 127
  on Illinois and Michigan Canal, 65, 66, 83, 101
  on Kankakee River, 43, 76, 153, 166
  on Lake Defiance, 86
  on Lake Michigan, 8, 9, 10, 12–13
  on Lemon Lake, 167
  on Little Calumet River, 28, 150
  on Nippersink Creek, 53–54
  on North Shore Channel, 79
  on Powderhorn Lake, 28
  on Saganashkee Slough, 101
  on Silver Lake, 23
  on Skokie River and lagoons, 117
  on Tampier Lake, 101
  on Turtlehead Lake, 125
  on Wolf Lake, 105
  See also Canoeing
Bob-o-link, 22, 25, 114, 132

181

Index

Bogs, 32, 52, 84–85, 98, 129–30, 148–49, 156, 171, 178. *See also* Marshlands
Bong State Recreation Area, 140–41
Bonsai, 34
Botanic Garden, Chicago, 33–34
Botanical gardens, 6–7, 12, 33–34, 46, 103
Braidwood Dunes and Savanna, 24–25
Braille Trail, 119, 120
Brandenberg Bog, 130
Bridle paths. *See* Horseback riding
Brookfield Zoo, 25–27
Brown (Ned) Forest Preserve, 37, 91–93
Bryant, William Cullen, xvii
Buckingham Fountain, 8
Buffalo, 48
Buffalo Rock State Park, 65, 66
Burnham, Michael H., Sr., xv
Busse Forest, 91
Busse Lake, 91

Cactus, 7, 34
  prickly pear, 67, 156, 158
Calumet Forest Preserve Division, 27–29
Calumet River, 28–29
Camp Pine Woods, 39
Campsites (Illinois), 23, 33, 43, 55, 59, 63, 64, 66, 69, 70, 77, 106, 131, 133
Campsites (Indiana), 157, 159, 163, 166, 172
Campsites (Michigan), 178
Canada geese, 36, 85, 148, 152, 162, 165
Canals, 65–66, 82, 83
Canoeing
  on Busse Lake, 92
  in Chain O'Lakes area, 32
  on Chicago River, North Branch, 96
  on Deep and Little Calumet rivers, 150
  on Des Plaines River, 40, 43, 72
  on Fox River, 46, 53, 86, 115, 127
  on Illinois and Michigan Canal, 65, 66, 83, 101
  on Kankakee River, 43, 76, 153, 166
  on Nippersink Creek, 53–54
  on North Shore Channel, 79
  on Powderhorn Lake, 28
  on Silver Lake, 23
  on Skokie River and lagoons, 117
Cantigny, 30
Cap Sauers Holding, 99
Carlson Pond, 169
Carlson Springs, 124
Cary Prairie, 31
Center for Natural Landscaping, 60
Cermak Swimming Pool, 112
Chain O'Lakes State Park, 31–33
Channahon State Park, 65, 66
Chellberg Farm, 156
Chess, 12
Chicago Academy of Sciences, 4
Chicago Botanic Garden, 33–34, 116
Chicago Historical Society museum, 12
Chicago Horticultural Society, 33, 116
Chicago Peace Rose, 30
Chicago Portage National Historic Site, 112
Chicago Regional Planning Association, xvi
Chicago River, North Branch, 21, 79, 96, 116
Chicago Zoological Park. *See* Brookfield Zoo
Children
  Discovery Den for, at Goodenow Grove Forest Preserve, 55
  farm animals for, 11, 110–11
  nature trail for, 128
  playgrounds for, 4, 9, 10, 95, 127, 167, 171–72
  zoo for, 11
Chokeberry, 25
Chrysanthemum, 10
Churchill Woods Forest Preserve, 35–36
Cinquefoil, 24, 167
Compass plant, 74, 103
Conservatories. *See* Botanical gardens
Coot, 58, 80, 93
Cowles, Henry C., 158
Cowles Bog, 148–49
Coyote, 56, 76, 135, 156, 158
Crabtree Nature Center, 36–38
Craft demonstrations, 51, 62, 149, 156, 167
Cranberry, 98, 178
Cranberry Slough, 98
Crane, Sandhill, 9, 78, 161–62

Dan Ryan Woods, 28
Dawn redwood, 30

Day lily, 78
Dead River, 67, 68
Deep River, 149, 150
Deep River County Park, 149–51
Deer, 22, 58, 112, 115, 162
  fallow, 78
  Father David's, 27
  white-tailed, 25, 32, 33, 36, 43, 48, 56, 62, 78, 82, 85, 110, 122, 152, 154, 156, 163, 165
Deer Grove Forest Preserve, 37
Des Plaines Forest Preserve Division, 38–41
Des Plaines Game Farm, 43
Des Plaines River, 38, 40, 41, 42, 43, 71–72, 77–78, 80, 82–83, 101, 111–12, 131
Des Plaines River Trail, 41–42
Des Plaines State Conservation Area, 42–44
Dickcissel, 25
Dog training and field trials, 59, 153
Dogwood, 12, 58, 74, 85, 156, 158
Dole Wildlife Sanctuary, 44–45
Douglas Park, 4–5
Ducks, 8, 9, 33, 39, 43, 58, 76, 85, 100, 103, 164, 165, 170. *See also* Mallard
Duneland Folk Festival, 156
Dunes (Illinois), 24–25, 60, 68, 74, 75, 119
Dunes (Indiana), 148, 155, 158–59, 169
Dunes (Michigan), 176, 177–78
DuPage River, East Branch, 59
DuPage River, West Branch, 22, 23, 123, 133

Eagle, bald, 42, 68, 156
Eckert Cemetery, 107, 108
Eggers Grove, 28
Elgin Botanical Garden (Trout Park), 126–28
Elk, 91
Elsen's Hill Winter Sports Area, 133
Endangered species
  animals, 11, 26–27, 67, 100
  birds, 93, 94, 110
  plants, 20, 24, 25, 67, 80, 132
  trees, 129
Energy sources, alternative, 79
Environmental education centers. *See* Nature centers
Eskers, 99
Evanston Environmental Association, 79

Fabyan, Col. George, 45
Fabyan Forest Preserve, 45–46
Falcon, peregrine, 68, 100
Farm animals, 11, 110–11
Fens, 24, 44, 80, 84, 93, 109, 133
Fermilab Prairie, 46, 48–49
Ferns, 6, 12, 33, 34, 109, 116, 170, 176
  cinnamon, 129
  royal, 98
Ferson's Creek Marsh, 94, 95
Field Museum of Natural History, 5–6
Films, 4, 6, 22
First Division Museum, 30
Fish. *See* Aquariums; Fishing
Fish hatchery, 32
Fishing (Chicago), 13, 14
Fishing (Illinois), 23, 28, 32–33, 35, 41–42, 43, 54, 59, 64, 66, 69, 72, 77, 83, 86, 92, 105, 107, 112, 115, 120, 123, 125, 128, 131, 133
Fishing (Indiana), 153, 163, 164, 166, 167, 172
Fishing (Wisconsin), 140
Fishing, on ice, 23, 29, 33, 35, 40, 44, 46, 59, 73, 77, 92, 102, 106, 107, 115, 120, 123, 131–32, 134, 140, 166
Flower show, 7
Flowers. *See* Gardens; Prairie plants; Wildflowers; *and specific types*
Footpaths. *See* Hiking trails
Forest Preserves, xv–xvi, 21, 25, 33, 36, 38, 48, 54, 59, 71, 77, 81, 82, 83, 91–92, 96, 98, 108, 111, 116, 118, 123, 124, 131, 133
  of Northeastern Illinois, 47–48
Fossil hunting, 119
Fountain, 8
Fox River, 31, 45, 46, 53, 64, 84, 86, 94–95, 115–16, 126–27
Fringed gentian, 67, 93, 94, 110, 119, 126
Fringed orchid, 94, 129
Fringed puccoon, 24
Fullersburg Woods Nature Preserve, 50–51

Galapagos tortoise, 26
Galien River, 177
Gardens (Chicago)
  Douglas Park, 4
  Garfield Park, 6–7
  Grant Park, 7, 8

Gardens (Chicago) *(cont'd)*
  Jackson Park, 10
  Lincoln Park, 12
  Marquette Park, 13
Gardens (Illinois)
  Brookfield Zoo, 27
  Cantigny, 30
  Chicago Botanic Garden, 33–34
  Des Plaines Forest Preserve Division, 39
  at Fabyan Forest Preserve, 45
  at Fermilab Prairie, 46
  at Grosse Point Lighthouse Park, 60
  at The Grove, 62
  at Morton Arboretum, 88
Gardens (Indiana)
  International Friendship, 160–61
Garfield Park, 6–7
Gebhard Woods State Park, 65, 66
Geese, 33, 36, 43
  blue, 45–46, 127
  Canada, 36, 85, 148, 152, 162, 165
  snow, 45–46, 127
Gensburg-Markham Prairie, 51–52
Gentians, 56
  bottle, 126
  closed, 119, 136, 176
  downy, 37
  fringed, 67, 93, 94, 110, 119, 126
  prairie, 152
  rose, 169
  yellow, 20
German Methodist Cemetery Prairie, 151–52
Gingko, 60, 141
Glacial Park, 53–54
Golf, 10, 12, 14, 95, 143
Goodenow Grove Forest Preserve, 54–55
Goose Lake Prairie State Park, 56–57
Goshawk, 46, 127
Grand Calumet River, 28–29
Grand Kankakee Marsh County Park, 152–53
Grand Mere Nature Study Area, 177–78
Grant Creek Prairie, 43
Grant Park, 7–8
Grass Lake, 32
Grasses. *See* Prairie
Great Western Trail, 57–59
Grebes, 28
  pied-billed, 28, 57, 103
Green Lake Swimming Pool, 120

Greene Valley Forest Preserve, 59–60
Grosse Point Lighthouse Park, 60–61
Grove, The, 61–63
Guided walks (Illinois), 21, 30, 32, 34, 38, 39–40, 42, 55, 57, 58, 59, 60, 62, 63, 64, 69, 76, 78, 80, 81, 83, 84, 85, 88–89, 100, 104, 108, 114, 122, 127, 128, 130, 136
Guided walks (Indiana), 148, 154, 156–57, 159, 169, 171
Guided walks (Wisconsin), 142
Gulls, 8, 12

Hackberry tree, 96
Hairy-nosed wombat, 27
Ham Bone Lake, 125
Handicapped
  nature trail for, 32
  trails for, 76, 104, 167
  See also Blind, attractions for
Hang gliding, 178
Harms Woods, 117
Harrison-Benwell Conservation Site, 63–64
Hawks, 22, 60, 76, 80, 103, 140, 178
  Cooper's, 156
  goshawk, 46, 127
  marsh, 132–33
  red-shouldered, 110, 152
  red-tailed, 62, 82, 130, 176
  sparrow, 82
  Swainson's, 42, 110
Hawthorn Hollow, 141–42
Hayrides, 149–50, 167, 172
Heart-leaved plantain, 83
Hemlock parsley, 126
Herb gardens, 13, 39
Heritage Nature Trail, 83
Herons, 22, 100, 109, 164
  black-crowned night, 28, 93, 110
  great blue, 58, 64, 85, 103, 130, 148, 152, 170
  green, 9, 80, 85, 130, 148
  yellow-crowned night, 117, 156
Hickory, 32, 58, 63, 75, 85, 108, 109, 115, 149
  shagbark, 94
Hickory Creek, 103
Hickory Grove, 64–65
Hiking trails, xv
  Illinois and Michigan Canal State Trail, 65–67
  Illinois Prairie Path, 70–71
  See also Guided walks

Hiking trails (Illinois), 20, 21, 22, 24, 25, 28, 32, 35, 37, 39, 41–42, 43, 44, 51, 52, 53, 55, 57–58, 59, 68–69, 72, 74, 76, 78, 83, 84, 85, 89, 92, 93, 95, 96, 100, 104, 106, 108, 109, 111, 112, 114, 115, 117, 120, 122, 123, 125, 127, 128, 131, 133
Hiking trails (Indiana), 150, 153, 156–57, 159, 165–66, 167, 169, 170, 172
Hiking trails (Michigan), 176, 178
Hiking trails (Wisconsin), 140, 143
Historic sites
  Bailly Homestead, 156
  Cantigny, 30
  Chain O'Lakes area, 32
  Chellberg Farm, 156
  Chicago Portage, 112
  Fabyan estate, 45
  Grove, The, 61–63
  at Hawthorn Hollow, 141–42
  John Wood's Old Mill, 149
  See also Indian artifacts and history; Pioneer buildings and artifacts
Homewood dunes, 74
Hoosier Prairie, 154–55
Horseback riding (Chicago), 10, 12
Horseback riding (Illinois), 22, 32, 35, 39, 41–42, 44, 51, 53, 59, 64, 72, 96, 100, 106–07, 112, 115, 117, 120, 125, 131, 133
Horseback riding (Indiana), 150, 157, 172
Horseback riding (Wisconsin), 140, 143
Horseshoe pits, 7, 13
Huckleberry, 25
Hummingbird, 68, 76
Hunting, 140
Hyacinth, 10, 109
Hyslop Foundation, 141

I&M Canal. *See* Illinois and Michigan Canal
Ice boating, 106
Ice fishing. *See* Fishing, on ice
Ice skating (Chicago), 9, 10, 13, 14
Ice skating (Illinois), 23, 29, 33, 35, 40, 46, 73, 92, 97, 102, 104, 106, 107, 113, 115, 120, 123, 125, 129, 134
Ice skating (Indiana), 166, 168, 172
Ice skating (Wisconsin), 140, 143
Illinois and Michigan Canal, 65–66, 82, 83, 101

Illinois and Michigan Canal State Trail, 65–67
Illinois Audubon Society, 44
Illinois Beach State Park, 67–70
Illinois Prairie Path, 22, 35, 70–71, 106
Illinois Trees Nature Trail, 89
Illinois Waterway Visitor Center, 66
Indian artifacts and history, 38–39, 48, 56, 65, 71–72, 76, 149
Indian Boundary Forest Preserve Division, 71–74
Indian Boundary Park, 8–9
Indian Creek, 109
Indiana Dunes National Lakeshore, 148, 154, 155–58
Indiana Dunes State Park, 158–60
International Friendship Gardens, 160–61
Izaak Walton Preserve, 74–75

Jackson Park, 9–11
Japanese gardens, 10, 30, 34, 45
Jasper-Pulaski State Fish and Wildlife Area, 161–64
Jogging. *See* Running trails
Joliet Park District greenhouse, 103
Jurgensen Woods Nature Preserve, 119

Kames, 53
Kankakee mallow (*Iliamna remota*), 75
Kankakee River, 25, 42, 43, 75–76, 77, 152, 153, 165, 166
Kankakee River State Park, 75–77
Keepataw Forest Preserve, 77–78
Kennicott family, 61–62
Kingbird, western, 68

Ladd Arboretum, 78–80
Lady's slipper, 20
Lake Avenue Woods, 39
Lake Chicago, xvi, 52, 68, 74, 96, 119
Lake Defiance, 84–85, 86
Lake Michigan shoreline
  Grand Mere Nature Study Area on, 176–77
  Grant Park on, 8
  Illinois Beach State Park on, 67–70
  Indiana Dunes National Lakeshore on, 155–58
  Indiana Dunes State Park on, 158–59
  Jackson Park on, 9–10
  Lincoln Park on, 11–13

Index

Lake Michigan Shoreline (cont'd)
  Warren Dunes State Park on, 177–78
Langeluttig Swamp, 164–65
LaSalle County Historical Museum, 65–66
LaSalle State Fish and Wildlife Area, 165–67
Latrium, 74
Leatherleaf Bog, 85
Lemon Lake County Park, 167–68
Lighthouse Nature Center, 60
Lilac, 12, 88, 141
Lincoln Park, 11–13
Little Calumet River, 28–29, 150, 157, 164
Little Red Schoolhouse Nature Center, 100
Lockport Prairie, 80–81
Lotus, 32
Lyle C. Thomas Park and Landing (formerly Spring Grove Park Landing), 53–54
Lyons Prairie, 64

Mallard, 9, 85, 148, 152, 162, 165
Mammoth, woolly, 22, 50
Maple Grove Forest Preserve, 81–82
Maple syrup and sugar production, 39, 104, 110, 156
Maple trees, 38, 60, 74, 81, 91, 94, 103, 108, 109, 110, 115, 142, 148, 171
Maritime museum, 60
Marquette Park (Chicago), 13–14
Marquette Park (Gary), 169
Marshlands (Illinois), 22, 28, 35, 37, 42, 43, 53, 54, 56, 58, 63, 68, 84–85, 93–94, 98, 105, 106, 116, 119, 123, 132, 133
Marshlands (Indiana), 165
Marshlands. *See also* Bogs
Massasauga rattlesnake, 106, 110, 132, 156, 158
McCormick, Robert R., 30
McCormick (Robert R.) Museum, 30
McHenry Dam State Park. *See* Moraine Hills State Park
McKinley Woods Forest Preserve, 82–83
Meadowlark, 22, 25, 76, 132
Messenger Woods Forest Preserve, 83–84
Midlothian Reservoir, 125
Midway Plaisance, 10

Migratory birds, 8, 9, 28, 32, 36, 42, 43, 59, 60, 64, 88, 100, 105, 109, 115, 117, 122, 124, 161–62, 165, 178
Miller Woods, 168–69
Milliken Lake, 42, 43
Model airplane field, 106
Moraine Hills State Park, 84–86
Moraine Nature Preserve, 169–70
Morton, Joy, 87
Morton Arboretum, 87–89
Morton Grove Prairie, 89–90
Mt. Baldy, 156
Mt. Hoy, 22
Mt. Tom, 159
Murray Prairie, 57–58
Museum of Science and Industry, 10
Museums
  Chicago Academy of Sciences, 4, 12
  Chicago Historical Society, 12
  Crabtree Nature Center, 36
  at Des Plaines Forest Preserve Division, 39
  Field Museum of Natural History, 5–6
  First Division, 30
  at Grosse Point Lighthouse Park, 60
  Kennicott house, 62
  LaSalle County Historical, 65–66
  Old Graue, 50–51
  Robert R. McCormick, 30
  of Science and Industry, 10
  Trailside, 72
Muskrat, 22, 64, 78, 93, 106, 115, 116, 122, 130, 140, 152, 164, 165

Narcissus, 10
Native Americans. *See* Indian artifacts and history
Nature centers, 34, 36, 38–39, 50, 54–55, 62, 85, 103, 110, 119, 122, 136, 140, 149. *See also* Museums
Nature conservancy, xvi, 24, 46, 52, 90–91, 132, 152, 154, 164, 170, 176
Nature trails. *See* Guided walks; Hiking trails
Ned Brown Forest Preserve, 37, 91–93
Nelson Lake Marsh, 93–94
Nippersink Canoe Base, 54
Nippersink Trail, 53

Norris Woods, 94–95
North Branch Forest Preserve Division, 96–98
North Shore Channel, 79

Oak, 21, 32, 35, 58, 63, 81, 84, 85, 91, 98, 99, 103, 108, 109, 114, 124, 142, 149, 156, 176
  black, 24–25, 60, 85, 154, 168
  bur, 48, 68, 74, 110, 119–20, 126
  northern red, 126
  red, 81, 94, 109, 115, 122, 126
  swamp white, 110
  white, 69, 94, 115, 120, 122, 126
Oakes (Leroy) Forest Preserve, 57
Okapi, 27
Old Graue Mill and Museum, 50–51
Olmsted, Frederick Law, 10
Orchids, 12, 34, 119, 126, 148, 156, 176
  grass pink, 52
  nodding ladies' tresses, 80
  northern fringed, 94
  ragged fringed, 129
  spotted coral-root, 122
  tubercled, 25
  white lady's slipper, 132
Orienteering, 131, 153
Owls, 22, 28, 42, 76, 110, 127, 130, 140
  great barred, 82
  great gray, 176
  great horned, 32, 45, 62, 65, 135, 152
  long-eared, 88, 103
  saw-whet, 32, 88

Paddle wheel boat, 95
Palm trees, 7, 12
Palos and Sag Valley Forest Preserve Divisions, 98–103
Park Forest, Ill., 121
Paul H. Douglas Nature Sanctuary, 9
Paw Paw Woods, 98
Peacock Prairie (Woodworth Prairie Preserve), 136–37
Peat bogs and deposits, 32, 53, 85
Peattie, Donald Culross: *Prairie Grove, A*, 62
Peregrine falcon, 68, 100
Petrifying Springs County Park, 142–43
Pheasant, 43, 56, 115, 140, 162–63, 165

Photography blinds, 140, 152
Picnic sites (Chicago), 12
Picnic sites (Illinois), 29, 30, 33, 37, 40, 42, 43, 46, 51, 54, 55, 57, 58, 61, 63, 64, 66, 69, 73, 74, 77, 79, 83, 84, 86, 90, 92, 94, 97, 101, 104, 105, 107, 108, 112–13, 115, 117–18, 120, 125, 127, 128, 135
Picnic sites (Indiana), 150, 153, 157, 160, 163, 166, 167, 169, 172
Picnic sites (Michigan), 179
Picnic sites (Wisconsin), 140, 143
Pike Creek, 141, 143
Pike Marsh, 85
Pilcher Park, 103–04
Pinhook Bog, 171
Pioneer buildings and artifacts, 22, 38, 39, 50–51, 56, 62
Pistakee Bog, 130
Pitcher plant, 85, 129, 156, 171
Playgrounds, 4, 9, 10, 95, 127, 167, 171–72
Plovers, 105, 158, 165
Plum Creek, 54
Plum Creek Nature Center, 54–55
Potholes, glacial, 56, 122
Pottawatomie Park, 94–95
Powderhorn Lake, 28, 29
Powers (William W.) State Conservation Area, 28, 105–06
Prairie, xvi
  Belmont, 20
  Berkeley, 20–21
  Blackwell Recreational Preserve, 22
  Bluff Spring Fen, 24
  Braidwood Dunes and Savanna, 25
  Cary, 31
  at Chicago Botanic Garden, 34
  at Churchill Woods Forest Preserve, 35
  at Crabtree Nature Center, 36–37
  at Deep River County Park, 149
  at Des Plaines Forest Preserve Division, 38–39
  at Dole Wildlife Sanctuary, 44
  Fermilab, 46, 48–49
  Gensburg-Markham, 51–52
  German Methodist Cemetery, 151–52
  Goose Lake, 56–57
  Grant Creek, 43
  at Hawthorn Hollow, 141
  at Hickory Grove, 64

Prairie (cont'd)
  Hoosier, 154–55
  at Izaak Walton Preserve, 74
  at Ladd Arboretum, 79
  Lockport, 80–81
  Lyons, 64
  at Morton Arboretum, 88
  Morton Grove, 89–90
  Murray, 57–58
  at Pilcher Park, 103–04
  Queen Anne, 107–08
  at Reed-Turner Woodland, 109
  Sand Ridge, 119
  Shaw Woodlands and Prairies, 113–14
  at Veterans Acres Park, 128
  Wadsworth, 42
  West Chicago, 132–33
  Woodworth, 136–37
  at Yankee Woods and St. Mihiel Preserve, 124
Prairie clover, 80, 107, 136
Prairie plants, 20, 24, 25, 34, 37, 43, 48, 52, 56, 70, 80, 89–90, 107–08, 114, 119, 124, 128, 136, 154
Prairie Trail, 89
Prairie violet, 24, 107
Pratt's Wayne Woods, 106–07
Prickly pear cactus, 67, 156, 158
Przewalski's horse, 26

Quail, 52, 56, 76, 162, 165
Quaking bog, 98, 148, 171
Queen Anne Prairie, 107–08

Raccoon Grove Forest Preserve, 108–09
Railroads
  miniature, 95
  narrow-gauge, 27
Rattlesnake, Massasauga, 106, 110, 132, 156, 158
Rattlesnake master, 31, 37, 56, 103, 107, 136
Redfield, Louise: *American Acres*, 62
Redfield Cultural Center, 62
Reed Lake, 109
Reed-Turner Woodland, 109–10
Rhododendron, 33, 116
River Trail Nature Center, 38
Robinson Preserve, 176–77
Rock Creek, 75–77
Rock garden, 12
Rose gardens, 13, 30, 161
Running trails and tracks, 4, 12

Ryerson Conservation Area, 110–11

Sag Valley Forest Preserve Division, 98–103
Saganashkee Slough, 101
Sagawau Canyon, 100
St. Joseph Creek, 81
St. Mihiel Preserve, 124
Salt Creek, 50, 51, 91, 111–13
Salt Creek Forest Preserve, 25, 111–13
Salt Creek Woods, 112
Sand dunes. *See* Dunes
Sand Ridge Nature Center, 119
Sand Ridge Prairie, 119
Sandbars, 12
Sandburg, Carl, 155
Sandhill crane, 9, 78, 161–62
Sandpiper, 22, 57, 103, 105
Sassafras, 25, 28, 119
Savanna, 24–25, 126, 132, 168–69
Sawmill Creek, 131
Schiller Woods North, 72, 73
Schubert's Woods, 120
Science and Industry, Museum of, 10
Shaw Woodlands and Prairies, 113–14
Shedd Aquarium, 14–15
Shoe Factory Road Preserve, 37
Shrubs. *See* Trees and shrubs
Silver Lake, 22–23
Silver Springs State Park, 114–16
Skating. *See* Ice skating
Skiing, cross-country (Chicago), 7, 10, 13, 14
Skiing, cross-country (Illinois), 23, 33, 35, 40, 41, 46, 51, 54, 55, 57, 58, 59, 63, 67, 69, 73, 75, 77, 81, 84, 86, 92, 97, 101–02, 104, 107, 111, 113, 115, 118, 120, 123, 125, 128–29, 131, 134
Skiing, cross-country (Indiana), 150, 153, 156, 157, 160, 166, 167–68, 172
Skiing, cross-country (Michigan), 179
Skiing, cross-country (Wisconsin), 140, 143
Skokie Forest Preserve Division, 116–18
Skokie River, 113, 116–17
Skunk cabbage, 98, 126
Skunk Cabbage Bottom, 44

Index · 189

Sledding, 29, 33, 51, 63, 73, 97, 101, 120, 125, 134, 167–68, 179. *See also* Tobogganing
Snow goose, 45–46, 127
Snow leopard, 11, 27
Snow tubing, 23
Snowshoeing, 140, 157, 179
Solar demonstration project, 77
Songbirds. *See* Bird-watching areas
Sphagnum moss, 85, 98, 129, 156, 171
Spring Creek, 83–84
Spring Grove Park Landing. *See* Lyle C. Thomas Park and Landing
Spring Lake Preserve, 37
Steger Woods, 120
Stoney Run County Park, 171–73
Stratton (William G.) State Park, 65, 66
Swainson's hawk, 42, 110
Swainson's warbler, 12
Swallow Cliff Winter Sports Area, 99–100, 101
Swamp rattler. *See* Massasauga rattlesnake
Swampy areas. *See* Bogs; Marshlands
Swans, 33, 46, 100
Swimming, 4, 7, 10, 13, 23, 69, 94–95, 112, 120, 140, 157, 160, 169, 178–79

Taft, Lorado, 6
Tallgrass Nature Trail, 57
Tamarack, 129, 148, 156, 171
Tampier Lake, 101
Tefft Savanna Nature Preserve, 163
Tennis, 5, 7, 8, 9, 10, 12, 13, 95, 127, 167, 169
Terns
 black, 28, 32, 93, 148
 Caspian, 105
 Forster's, 28
Teuscher, Margaret and Ruth, 141–42
Thorn Creek Forest Preserve Division, 118–21
Thorn Creek Nature Preserve, 121–23
Thornton-Lansing Road Nature Preserve, 119
Thornton Quarry, 119
Thunderbird Youth Camp, 59
Timber Ridge Forest Preserve, 123–24

Tinley Creek Forest Preserve, 124–26
Tobogganing, 29, 51, 77, 97, 101, 104, 113, 115, 129, 134, 179
Trail of the Old Oaks, 83
Trails. *See* Bicycle paths; Guided walks; Handicapped: trails for; Hiking trails; Running trails
Trailside Museum, 72
Trains. *See* Railroads
Trees and shrubs (Chicago), 8, 9, 10, 12
Trees and shrubs (Illinois), 30, 32, 34, 35, 38, 44, 46, 58, 61, 62, 63, 68, 74, 75, 78–79, 87–89, 91, 94, 98, 99, 108, 109, 110, 117, 119, 122, 124, 126
Trees and shrubs (Indiana), 149, 159
Trees and shrubs (Michigan), 177–78
Trees and shrubs (Wisconsin), 142–43
Trees and shrubs. *See also* Arboretums
Trillium, 103, 110
 large-flowered, 34, 83, 91, 170
 nodding, 91
 prairie, 170
 sessile, 83
 white, 109, 110, 116
Trout lily, 103, 109, 122
Trout Park, 126–28
Tulips, 10, 161
Turnbull Woods, 33–34, 116
Turnstone, 67

Van Patten Woods Forest Preserve, 41–42
Veery, 94, 178
Veterans Acres Park, 128–29
Viper. *See* Massasauga rattlesnake
Volleyball, 5, 7, 9, 12, 76, 167
Volo Bog State Natural Area, 129–30

Wadsworth Prairie, 42
Walnut, 58, 63, 74, 75, 110
Walton (Izaak) Preserve, 74–75
Wampum Lake, 120
Warblers, 45, 56, 62, 88, 94, 117, 165, 178
Warren, Edward K., 177
Warren Dunes State Park, 177–79
Warren Woods, 177
Water lilies, 5, 85, 93, 129

Waterfall Glen Forest Preserve, 131–32
Waterfowl, 8, 22, 28, 32, 33, 36–37, 43, 46, 56, 59, 64, 85, 88, 100, 109, 112, 115, 117, 124, 140, 148, 152, 164, 165, 178. *See also* Ducks; Geese
Waukegan juniper, 67
West Chicago Prairie, 132–33
West DuPage Woods Forest Preserve, 133–34
Wetlands. *See* Bogs; Marshlands
Whippoorwill, 25
Wildflowers (Illinois), 24, 25, 28, 33–34, 37, 39, 44, 52, 56, 59, 60, 83, 85, 89–90, 94, 98, 103–04, 107–08, 110, 114, 115, 119, 124, 128
Wildflowers (Indiana), 149, 167, 169, 170
Wildflowers (Michigan), 176
Wildflowers (Wisconsin), 141, 143
Wildflowers, prairie species. *See* Prairie plants
Wildlife rehabilitation center, 134–35
Wildlife sanctuaries, 22, 24–25, 28, 33–34, 35, 36–37, 44, 56, 61–62, 75, 78, 85, 100, 110, 112, 114, 122, 123, 152, 176. *See also* Bird-watching areas; Endangered species.
Willowbrook Wildlife Haven, 134–35
Windmill, 45
Winfield Mounds, 123
Winter sports. *See* Fishing, on ice; Ice boating; Ice skating; Skiing, cross-country; Sledding; Tobogganing
Wolf Lake, 28, 105
Womer Tract (Moraine Nature Preserve), 169–70
Woodcock, 24, 103, 162
Woodlands. *See* Trees and shrubs
Woodpeckers, 22, 65, 82, 88, 103, 109
Woodworth (James) Prairie Preserve, 136–37
Woolly mammoth, 22, 50
World's Columbian Exposition (1893), 9
Wright, Frank Lloyd, 45, 160

Yankee Woods, 124
Youth hostel, 159

Zoos, 8–9, 11–12, 25–27, 103